MEN AND WOMEN

John Nicholson lectured in psychology at the universities of Oxford (where he was educated), Reading and London, before founding the business psychology consultancy of which he is now Chairman in 1987. Since then John Nicholson Associates has helped more than eighty organizations in eleven countries make the most of their human resources. Dr Nicholson has published eleven books and several hundred articles on a wide range of psychological and business topics. Five of his books have had television series based on them. Previous books include *Habits: Why You Do What You Do* (1978), *Seven Ages: The Truth about Life Crises* (1980), *All in the Mind* (1984, jointly with Martin Lucas), *The Good Interview Guide* (1989, jointly with Susan Clemie), *How Do You Manage?* (1992) and *Men on Sex* (1992, jointly with Fiona Thompson).

D0733344

MEN AND WOMEN

HOW DIFFERENT ARE THEY?

John Nicholson

Oxford   New York

OXFORD UNIVERSITY PRESS

Oxford University Press, Walton Street, Oxford OX2 6DP

Oxford New York Toronto
Delhi Bombay Calcutta Madras Karachi
Kuala Lumpur Singapore Hong Kong Tokyo
Nairobi Dar es Salaam Cape Town
Melbourne Auckland Madrid

and associated companies in
Berlin Ibadan

Oxford is a trade mark of Oxford University Press

© John Nicholson 1984, 1993

First published 1979 as A Question of Sex by Fontana Paperbacks
Revised and expanded edition first published 1984 under title
Men and Women as an Oxford University Press paperback
Second edition 1993

All rights reserved. No part of this publication may be reproduced,
stored in a retrieval system, or transmitted, in any form or by any means,
without the prior permission in writing of Oxford University Press.
Within the UK, exceptions are allowed in respect of any fair dealing for the
purpose of research or private study, or criticism or review, as permitted
under the Copyright, Designs and Patents Act, 1988, or in the case of
reprographic reproduction in accordance with the terms of the licences
issued by the Copyright Licensing Agency. Enquiries concerning
reproduction outside these terms and in other countries should be
sent to the Rights Department, Oxford University Press,
at the address above

This book is sold subject to the condition that it shall not, by way
of trade or otherwise, be lent, re-sold, hired out or otherwise circulated
without the publisher's prior consent in any form of binding or cover
other than that in which it is published and without a similar condition
including this condition being imposed on the subsequent purchaser

British Library Cataloguing in Publication Data
Data available

Library of Congress Cataloging in Publication Data
Nicholson, John, 1945–
Men and women: how different are they? / John Nicholson.—2nd edn.
p. cm. Includes bibliographical references and index.
1. Sex differences (Psychology). 2. Sex differences. I. Title.
155.3'3—dc20 BF692.2.N53 1993 92–30066
ISBN 0–19–286157–3

3 5 7 9 10 8 6 4 2

Typeset by Best-set Typesetter Ltd., Hong Kong
Printed in Great Britain by
Biddles Ltd.
Guildford and King's Lynn

OLSON LIBRARY
NORTHERN MICHIGAN UNIVERSITY
MARQUETTE, MICHIGAN 49855

For my son Daniel, who accepts that girls too can kill dragons, and doesn't see what all the fuss is about. You will, Dan, you will ...

Acknowledgements

In 1979 Fontana published my book *A Question of Sex*. Four years later, Henry Hardy of Oxford University Press gave me the chance to modify the book, in the light of critical reaction and subsequent research developments. A revised version, based on a literature search undertaken by Kay Barltrop (now Scott), was published in 1984 under the new title, *Men and Women*.

Now Oxford University Press—in the person of Nicola Bion—has asked me to update *Men and Women*. Research evidence which has accumulated over the past decade tends to strengthen biological explanations of the differences between the two sexes in several ways. However, it has not caused me to move away from the generally interactionist position I have adopted throughout. I am grateful to Lucy Grey for carrying out a literature search; also to my colleagues John McBride and Pat Dixon, whose constant challenge of accepted wisdom leaves no room for complacency.

April 1992

Contents

Introduction

It is fatal to be a man or a woman pure and simple; one must be woman-manly or man-womanly.

Virginia Woolf

This is neither a sex manual nor a tract on sexual politics. It is a book about sex in its original sense—the difference between male and female. Neither the origin nor the purpose of this distinction is disputed. Sexual differentiation is a biological process (see Chapter 2), and it provides the basis of the mechanism by which we, and many other species, reproduce ourselves.

What follows from this? Less than you might expect. All we can say with confidence is that there are at least two respects in which males and females are clearly different when they start out. Their genital tracts are constructed quite differently, and only one sex has the potential to give birth. But even this statement has to be qualified. Genital sex can be altered by surgery (though the genetic sex of the individual concerned remains the same), and a significant number of women, either by accident or by design, pass through life without exploiting their ability to have babies. So while I have no wish to underestimate the significance of the fundamental biological difference between the sexes, I have reservations about using it as a base for sweeping generalizations about differences in the way in which men and women think, feel and act.

After all, biological sex is only *one* of the ways in which human beings differ. Why should so much attention be given to gender-related issues, rather than to whether blue-eyed and brown-eyed people—or blonds and brunettes—differ from each other in intellectual abilities and personality?

The reason the study of sex differences is so important is that your sex (unlike the colour of your eyes) dramatically affects the kind of life you lead, in many respects. In every culture people have ideas about how men and women are supposed to behave. From the very beginning, children are treated differently according to their sex, and are taught which behaviours are appropriate.

It is unclear to what extent 'feminine' and 'masculine' ways of thinking, feeling and acting are just a result of conforming to these culturally determined gender role stereotypes. We shall see that as the life-styles of men and women become more and more similar, many of the differences between them have grown smaller. This book examines which of the sex differences might completely disappear (for example, men might start to wear make-up like women) and which will not (men will never have periods).

Surveys show that most of us still believe that men and women are very different creatures. Men are thought to be physically tougher, more aggressive, more rational, better able to handle sex without love, and more likely to be successful at work by virtue of their greater will to win. Women, on the other hand, are held to be more emotional and unpredictable, interested in people rather than ideas, and too suggestible and dependent to wield authority comfortably over anyone except perhaps their own children.

The aim of this book is to identify the most influential popular beliefs about 'typically' masculine and feminine behaviour, and to see how well our intuitions stand up to objective testing. Most of the evidence I shall be considering has been obtained by researchers working in laboratories, using scientific methods. The fact that it has been gathered in this way does not give it any magical status. Nor are interpretations based on such evidence necessarily right, any more than our intuitions—that is, feelings that have not been exposed to the full rigours of scientific testing —are inevitably wrong. When the two are in conflict, my instinct as a scientist is to favour interpretations based on well-constructed experiments over those which are not, especially when the subject-matter is as emotionally involving and prejudice-ridden as human behaviour. But it is important to recognize the shortcomings as well as the advantages of so-called 'objective' evidence.

One obvious advantage of laboratory experiments is that they usually involve a group of subjects, which reduces the danger of mistaking personal idiosyncrasies for general laws of behaviour. It is also much easier to create in the laboratory an environment which is unchanging and relatively free from distractions, which brings experimenters nearer to their goal of isolating and observing a particular piece of behaviour. Finally, the ideal experiment is designed in such a way that there is only one explanation of what is observed.

Everyday, amateur psychologizing has none of these features. It tends to consist of casual reflections about our own behaviour, and that of the people around us. It is therefore based on a tiny pool of subjects who may or may not be representative of the species. Nor are individuals necessarily the most reliable observers of their own behaviour. However, everyday psychology has one enormous advantage over laboratory studies: it is based on the observation of behaviour in the real world.

The laboratory is an artificial environment, with its own rules and conventions, in which people may not behave in the same way as they do in normal life. They know they are being watched and assessed, which usually puts them on their best behaviour. Alternatively, it may make them more anxious and self-conscious. It can even make them behave worse than they would normally. For example, as we shall see in Chapter 8, the presence of a white-coated authority figure can sometimes encourage people to commit acts of aggression they would not contemplate in everyday life.

Unfortunately, it is also the case that few experiments conform to the ideals of the scientific method. Many of them have flaws in design or execution which make the value of their findings questionable. In consequence, psychological 'facts' often turn out to be short-lived, and many theories are based on results which are not supported when the experiment is repeated.

The second major source of objective evidence about sex differences is the large-scale survey. This evidence too must be treated with caution. The doorstep interview, like the laboratory experiment, is an artificial situation in which people do not always reveal their true feelings. Again, there is some strength in numbers: an opinion which has been expressed by a thousand respondents carries more weight than one which has been overheard in a single conversation in the public bar. But the results of one survey are only too often contradicted by those of the next, so it is no more prudent to rely on the findings of a single survey than it is to assume that the results of an isolated experiment will survive the test of replication.

These considerations have influenced the choice of material to be discussed in *Men and Women*. Faced with an over-researched area which is littered with contradictory findings, I have attached much greater weight to observations made by more than one investigator than to the results of one-off studies. However, I have not ignored unreplicated studies altogether, especially when their findings seem to fit into a pattern suggested by related work. But I have no doubt that parts of the case I shall be constructing will eventually turn out to have been built on sand.

I make no apology for this. Science is never more than an exercise in best-guessing, and the quality of the evidence selected is at least as important as the inspiration of the guesswork when it comes to distinguishing good science from bad. As a general rule, the more complex the matter being investigated, the less solid the evidence. And what could be more complex or variable than human behaviour?

Within the general area of human behaviour, the study of sex differences can best be described as the difficult child of thoroughly mixed-up parents. It exemplifies several of the worst faults of psychology and biology, as well as introducing some new booby-traps. For example, when a difference between men and women is identified—say, in the ability to visualize and manipulate objects in space (see Chapter 4)—it is usually small in absolute magnitude. If enough subjects are tested, however, it will become highly significant, statistically speaking. In the example I have chosen, this had led many writers to claim that men are superior to women in visual-spatial ability, and to use this assertion to explain such diverse findings as the fact that most chess grandmasters are men, and that fewer than 1 per cent of the engineers in Britain are women. But closer examination reveals that about a quarter of women are actually superior to the average man in visual-spatial ability. This is because the difference noted is an *average* difference. Although men are taller and have better spatial ability than women on average, we cannot deduce that every man is taller than his wife and beats her at chess. So the original statement, inspired though it may be by sound empirical evidence, is at best misleading, and at worst used to excuse an injustice.

This example illustrates another of the hazards associated with the study of sex differences: the uncritical acceptance of results which confirm either common-sense prejudices or more considered biases. For example, Kinsey's pioneering work on human sexuality (see Chapter 7) was marked by unusual objectivity. But even he is open to the accusation of having twisted his findings into a shape in which they seemed to support the prevailing double standard of male promiscuity and female fidelity.

At the other end of the continuum of sexual politics, the authors of the most comprehensive survey of sex differences candidly admit to a feminist bias before embarking on an analysis which several critics have considered underestimates the differences between men and women.

Finally, anyone seeking to draw practical implications from the vast research literature on sex differences has to keep in mind another source of bias, the extent of which it is impossible to assess. Only a small fraction of the research reports submitted to scientific journals actually appears in print. One of the criteria editors apply in deciding whether to publish an article—and hence allow its findings to become known—is whether or not the results support the researcher's hypothesis. Where the study of sex differences is concerned, the hypothesis almost invariably is that men and women will behave differently. If the experiment shows that they do not, it is therefore a failure in this narrow sense, even though the finding may be both interesting and surprising.

There is therefore a publication bias which operates in favour of the view that the two sexes behave differently. Five experimenters may independently fail to find a sex difference in some area of behaviour. But it is the sixth, who finds a significant difference, who is more likely to have his or her article published, even though the circumstances would strongly suggest that the positive finding is the result of some special feature of the experimental procedure, or even chance.

These then are some of the difficulties which arise in interpreting experiments which have been carried out on sex differences. Fortunately, the studies themselves are fairly straightforward. Indeed, the only sections of this book which are likely to present a problem to readers without any scientific background are the brief passages about the action of genes in Chapters 1, 2 and 4. These can be skipped without losing the thread of the argument, and in the rest of the book we shall be examining how scientists have tested ideas with which we are all familiar. After doing so, we should be in a position to answer a number of related questions, for example: Where there really is a difference between the sexes, what causes it? Is it an inevitable consequence of the fundamental biological differences between them, or merely the result of their having been brought up differently? If the latter, why do parents and teachers treat boys differently from girls? And why is it that although almost half the labour force is now female, men still get most of the best jobs?

Although the book is not a political polemic, it does seem to me that the evidence discussed in it suggests that those who attack the Women's Movement for going against nature are on very shaky ground. I must also warn you that this book is written by a convert. My interest in the psychology of sex differences dates from the late 1960s, the heyday of large-scale, biologically oriented theories of human behaviour. Writers such as Robert Ardrey and Konrad Lorenz won enormous popular acclaim by suggesting that we can explain why people in the twentieth century behave as they do by examining the way animals behave and by making guesses about how our prehistoric ancestors might have organized their lives. Psychologists were as enthusiastic as anybody about this new brand of science fiction, and it did not take them long to produce a biologico-evolutionary theory which 'explained'—and justified—the fact that we live in what is palpably a man's world. Like many others, I was seduced by the plausibility of this account of the origins of male supremacy, and if I seem unduly harsh in the treatment I give it in this book, no doubt it is because I am still annoyed that I was once taken in by it.

The biological theory of sex differences had the carpet whipped out from under it in 1974, when Eleanor Maccoby and Carol Jacklin published their book *The Psychology of Sex Differences*, an exhaustive survey of research on the subject which made it clear, to the great embarrassment of the biologists, that many of the sex differences their theory explained simply do not exist! Sex differences became a fashionable area of research after the publication of Maccoby and Jacklin's book, and there is now a wealth of evidence to support their conclusion that when we lay our preconceptions aside and examine how men and women actually think and act, the two sexes are remarkably similar. I call this remarkable because it is the *differences* between men and women that we notice. But the biological differences between the sexes are actually minute compared to the similarities, so I doubt whether we would find it surprising that men and women behave in much the same way in most circumstances if we had not been conditioned to expect otherwise.

This brings us to the heart of the controversy about sex differences, and to the two most important questions we have to answer. Is male dominance an inevitable consequence of a difference in aspirations and feelings, which makes men and women behave in different ways? And to the extent that the two sexes really do think and act differently, can this be traced back to the fact that they have different reproductive systems?

You will be able to guess my answer to these questions from what has already been said, though of course you may not draw the same conclusions from the evidence we shall be discussing.

1

MEN AND WOMEN

One is not born, but rather one becomes a woman.

Simone de Beauvoir

For most of us, the single most important influence on what we feel about another person is whether that person happens to be a man or a woman. We have fixed ideas about what men and women are like, and about what constitutes 'typical' masculine and feminine behaviour.

Given the very determined campaign which has been waged against sexism over the last twenty years, you might suppose that sex stereotypes would have gone out of fashion, or at least that people would have become reluctant to admit that they still use them. But research carried out in the early 1970s, when the influence of the Women's Movement was at its height, suggests that this is not so at all. A large sample of Americans of all ages and both sexes were asked to list the characteristics, attributes and types of behaviour in which they thought men and women differed, and their answers leave no doubt that sex stereotypes are still enormously powerful. Three-quarters of the people questioned agreed that men and women differ on more than forty aspects of behaviour, listed in Table 1. And both men and women expressed a clear preference for the behaviour they had designated masculine. The investigators were surprised to find that students were just as likely to use sex stereotypes as their elders, and there is no reason to suppose that people's views about typical masculine and feminine behaviour are more firmly entrenched in the US than they are elsewhere. Nor is it easy to get people to change their minds—researchers in both Europe and the US have found that taking a course on sex differences at university has no effect on a student's sex stereotypes. So it seems that we expect men

Table 1 *Stereotypic traits*

Feminine	Masculine
Masculine pole is more desirable	
Not at all aggressive	Very aggressive
Not at all independent	Very independent
Very emotional	Not at all emotional
Does not hide emotions at all	Almost always hides emotions
Very subjective	Very objective
Very easily influenced	Not at all easily influenced
Very submissive	Very dominant
Dislikes maths and science very much	Likes maths and science very much
Very excitable in a minor crisis	Not at all excitable in a minor crisis
Very passive	Very active
Not at all competitive	Very competitive
Very illogical	Very logical
Very home oriented	Very worldly
Not at all skilled in business	Very skilled in business
Very sneaky	Very direct
Does not know the way of the world	Knows the way of the world
Feelings easily hurt	Feelings not easily hurt
Not at all adventurous	Very adventurous
Has difficulty making decisions	Can make decisions easily
Cries very easily	Never cries
Almost never acts as a leader	Almost always acts as a leader
Not at all self-confident	Very self-confident
Very uncomfortable about being aggressive	Not at all uncomfortable about being aggressive
Not at all ambitious	Very ambitious
Unable to separate feelings from ideas	Easily able to separate feelings from ideas
Very dependent	Not at all dependent
Very conceited about appearance	Never conceited about appearance
Thinks women are always superior to men	Thinks men are always superior to women
Does not talk freely with men about sex	Talks freely with men about sex
Feminine pole is more desirable	
Doesn't use harsh language at all	Uses very harsh language
Very talkative	Not at all talkative
Very tactful	Very blunt
Very gentle	Very rough
Very aware of feelings of others	Not at all aware of feelings of others
Very religious	Not at all religious
Very interested in own appearance	Not at all interested in own appearance
Very neat in habits	Very sloppy in habits
Very quiet	Very loud
Very strong need for security	Very little need for security
Enjoys art and literature	Does not enjoy art and literature at all
Easily expresses tender feelings	Does not express tender feelings at all easily

Source: Broverman *et al.*, 1972.

and women to behave very differently, and that we value masculine behaviour more highly.

We may *think* that men and women behave differently, but do they? And if they do, why? The main purpose of this book is to try to establish which of the popular beliefs set out in Table 1 are justified—that is to say, based on real, observable differences between the sexes—and which exist only in our imagination. However, adult behaviour is the product of a lengthy process of development. We must go back to the beginning of the story to have any chance of understanding the nature and the causes of differences between the sexes.

Sexual differentiation

Before we look at what determines sex, we should ask why there are two sexes in the first place. After all, sex is not always crucial to reproduction; some organisms and plants reproduce only *asexually* (from a single organism). This is more efficient and requires less energy than sexual reproduction, but it only produces *clones*, offspring which are identical to their parents. Higher animals, however, naturally reproduce sexually, which has the great advantage of individual variation in the offspring. In sexual reproduction, the offspring is formed from a mixture of genes from two individuals, allowing genetic variation. This is advantageous to a species because it provides the raw material for natural selection and hence evolution. Offspring that show most adaptations to the environment have a competitive advantage over other members of the species and are more likely to survive and pass on their genes to the next generation. Thus sexual reproduction is necessary if a species is to adapt to a changing environment.

Now that we have a better idea of *why* we have sexual differentiation, we can look at *how* the sex of an individual is determined. In many animals (including human beings) sexual differentiation is a genetic process, determined by the presence or absence of particular chromosomes. But this is not always the case. Whether a crocodile is hatched as a male or female depends on the temperature at which the egg was kept. And in one type of coral-reef fish, *anthias squamipinnis*, sex is determined not by chromosomal differences but by differences in the environment. If there is no male in the immediate environment a female will undergo a sex change. But if there is any male around, even if he can only be seen in an adjacent fish tank, the sex change will not take place. The fact that sex is determined by environmental conditions in some species reminds us that being male or female is not always as fundamental and irreversible a defining feature as we might think.

In human beings, the female ovum and the male sperm both contain twenty-three chromosomes. These are tiny thread-like bodies which are found in every one of the billions of cells of which we are composed, and they contain the genetic instructions which make a major contribution to the development of every single characteristic of our bodies—from the colour of our eyes to the length of our toes.

If you start with the belief that men and women are very different, you might expect there to be two quite different sets of genetic instructions governing male and female development. There would be a male blueprint which caused the formation of male genitals, large muscles and extensive bodily and facial hair, and a female pattern which would result in the development of the characteristic female shape and appearance. In fact, this is not at all how things are. Both sexes actually receive very similar genetic instructions, not only for characteristics like eye colour and hair texture which do not distinguish between them, but even for the features we use to tell them apart. For example, the shape and size of a woman's breasts are very different from those of a man, but we all have the same raw material to develop breast tissue. What happens is that both sexes receive sets of instructions dealing with breast development, but in only one sex are the instructions acted upon. The same applies for all the other physical characteristics which obviously distinguish men from women: genitals, shape, muscle growth, voice-box development, body hair and so on.

But it is not simply a matter of luck whether a newly created embryo becomes male or female, though chance is of course involved. So far as genetic sex is concerned, an irrevocable decision to develop consistently along either male or female lines is made the moment the sperm and ovum unite, and it is made on the basis of the composition of the twenty-third pair of chromosomes, the sex chromosomes. Every pair of chromosomes is made up of one from each of our parents, and in all but the sex chromosomes the two are roughly the same in size and structure. But the two sex chromosomes can either be similar or very different. When they are similar, this means that the ovum and the sperm have both contributed what is known as an X chromosome (so called not because of its shape—all chromosomes are X-shaped—but because scientists discovered it after the other twenty-two pairs, and named it X for extra), and the resulting embryo is genetically female. One X chromosome comes from the sperm, and one from the ovum. But an ovum can contribute only an X chromosome to the newly formed egg, since the woman from whom the ovum came has no other sex chromosome. A pair of X chromosomes is the hallmark of femaleness, but in a male the sex chromosome pair consists of one X chromosome plus a different, much smaller chromosome called the Y chromosome, which always comes from the sperm. There is a fifty-fifty chance of the sperm contributing a Y chromosome. Whenever this happens, the resulting embryo will have the XY combination on its sex chromosome, and it will be genetically male. This is how sex is determined genetically, and there is an interesting point to note: the sex of a child is determined solely by its father. If he contributes an X chromosome, the child will have two Xs and will be female; if he contributes a Y, the child will have an X and a Y and will be male.

Occasionally, however, something goes wrong and one of the sex chromosomes is damaged around the time that the egg is fertilized. If the remaining undamaged chromosome is X, the egg may survive; but if it is Y, it cannot do so. Between 1 and 2 per cent of all embryos conceived are thought to have only one sex chromosome, but most perish *in utero*, and only one in every 3,000 babies is born with what is known as Turner's syndrome. These babies, with one X chromosome only, are infertile, and they may have a number of other physical peculiarities, but their internal and external genitals are clearly female. The fact that life is possible without a Y chromosome but impossible without an X raises the interesting possibility that human embryos may be basically feminine. Perhaps Eve was the first to arrive in the Garden of Eden. Even more startling is the theoretical possibility that women could reproduce without men, although scientists have not yet been able to produce an embryo by combining two eggs in a test tube. But other instances of chromosomal abnormality where the egg contains a Y and two or even three X chromosomes convey a rather different message. On these occasions, the result is always maleness, which suggests that even if the Y chromosome is the junior of the two types of sex chromosome, it is sufficiently powerful to triumph over several of its rivals.

Although the composition of the sex chromosomes is determined at conception, a month and a half passes before there is any visible sign as to which of the two sets of genetic instructions is going to be followed. Embyros of both sexes contain tissue which will eventually develop into either male gonads (testes) or female gonads (ovaries). They also have a genital tubercle which will become either a penis and scrotum or a clitoris and labia, and two sets of ducts, one of which will turn into whichever internal reproductive structures are appropriate to the sex of the particular embryo. About six weeks after conception, the genetically male embryo will begin to develop testes. In the female embryo, nothing happens for several more weeks, and then the ovaries start to be formed. Once formed, the gonads begin to secrete the sex hormones. In males, these organize the development of the appropriate reproductive structures and later the external genitals. In females, though this is the time when hormones start being produced, they are not responsible in the same way for the development of the genitals.

The dominant sex hormones in males are androgens, the most powerful of which is called testosterone. The major female sex hormones are oestrogen and progesterone. Calling these 'male' and 'female' hormones is actually misleading, because both sexes produce both hormones, and the only difference lies in the balance between them. At birth, for example, boys have a greater concentration of testosterone in their bloodstream than girls do, but there is no consistent difference between the sexes in the level of 'female' hormones, and the two sorts of hormone are very similar chemically.

At every stage in the process of human sexual differentiation, changes in the male direction occur before changes towards femaleness. There is no neuter sex, and nature's plan seems to be that the embyro will become female unless it has a Y chromosome which leads to the formation of testes which produce testosterone. This is not the case with all species. In birds, for example, the basic blueprint is male, and females are the departure from the norm. The old-fashioned belief about hens turning into cocks is actually entirely plausible, since if a hen's supply of female hormones dries up for any reason, the basic male pattern of development can reassert itself. Returning to humans, we have already seen that if the Y chromosome is destroyed the child will be born female with Turner's syndrome.

There is only one conclusion to be drawn from this account of the clearly distinct developmental sequences followed by unborn males and females: your sex is decided long before the time when you officially enter the world, and the decision is made and implemented by biological forces. Nor does the influence of biology stop at birth. At birth, the physical differences between boys and girls are actually very small (except of course for their genitals), but shortly before puberty there is a massive increase in sex-hormone production which leads to the physical divergence between the sexes that we shall discuss in the next chapter. Notice, however, that we have so far established only that there are fundamental biological differences between males and females. It is quite possible that the only significance of these differences is that they equip men and women for their different reproductive roles. As yet we have no evidence that they cause men and women to behave differently in any other respect.

Before leaving the process of sexual differentiation as it operates in more than ninety-nine cases out of a hundred, we must also look at the exceptions, because they raise the possibility that although sex is normally just a matter of straightforward biological development, it is not necessarily always so.

Even if the foetus is clearly male or female genetically, the development of the appropriate sexual apparatus is importantly influenced by the presence or absence of male hormones. If for any reason the testes of an XY embryo fail to produce testosterone then the baby will be born looking like a normal female (though genetically male). On the other hand, an XX foetus exposed to male hormones will result in a baby looking like a normal female. Very occasionally, as a result of an inherited gland malfunction, a female foetus produces too much of the male sex hormone. This error occurs after the internal reproductive structures have developed, but early enough to affect the appearance of the external genitals. When these children are born, they may either have an ambiguous protrusion which could be either an unusually large clitoris or a tiny penis, or there may even be a contradiction between internal and external genitals, that is, the combination of ovaries and a penis. This condition has also been induced artificially. Some years ago, a number of pregnant women were given the synthetic hormone progestin to avert miscarriage, before it was known that the testosterone derivatives contained in it could have a masculinizing effect on female foetuses.

Happily, this is a rare condition, but the experience of those who suffer from it provides fascinating evidence of how good we are at improvising successfully when the normal course of development is disrupted. In the most severe cases, children who are genetically female (and have female internal genitals) have a phallus with a penile urethra opening at its tip, and they are almost always raised as boys. At puberty, if they are given extra male hormones, they develop male characteristics like a deep voice and facial and bodily hair. When they become adults, they can enjoy a successful sex life, even to the point of orgasm. However, most children born with this condition receive corrective surgery to provide them with conventional female external genitals, and they are raised as girls. They show no signs of lesbianism, but they are described by their parents as unusually tomboyish and uninterested in such traditional feminine pursuits as looking after small children. Some researchers have suggested that the large doses of androgens they received before birth somehow masculinized their brains. But the fact that they can, with the help of appropriate surgical adjustment, be raised successfully and happily as either boys or girls is a salutary reminder that although sex may usually be determined biologically, we are not—as some writers have suggested—helpless slaves to our biology.

You might argue that children born with abnormal genitals are too unusual to tell us anything about the normal course of sexual development. But these examples show us that we base our judgement of whether a person is male or female on their appearance and behaviour, not on their sex chromosomes. We have seen that foetuses with the XY combination deprived of male hormones (perhaps due to androgen-insensitivity syndrome) are born and grow up looking female. Such children behave and are treated as women, and they have no athletic advantage. However, women athletes competing in the 1992 Winter Olympics were still tested for the presence of a Y chromosome, and disqualified if the test was positive. This was opposed by twenty-two French biologists and geneticists, including two Nobel prize winners, who thought it discriminatory to women. The group claims that femininity cannot be determined by a genetic test—and after all, when we talk about 'men' and 'women' we are referring to *gender* (whether a person looks and acts in a masculine or feminine way) rather than to biological sex.

The rare conditions in sexual development discussed above highlight the fact that a person's gender is not always determined by his or her biological sex. Most young people with these unusual conditions have an unequivocal sense of themselves as male or female in accordance with their sex of rearing. In fact, the way a child is brought up seems to be the most important single influence determining his or her subsequent gender.

There is at least one case in which the way a child was raised successfully counteracted its genetic sex and the action of its prenatal hormones. Some years ago, an American boy who had been born without any abnormality suffered an accident while he was being circumcised at the age of seven months which left him virtually without a penis. His parents were advised by doctors that surgery would not allow him to lead a normal life as a male, so they authorized his transformation into a girl. When he was about one and a half, surgeons began to reconstruct his genitals and his parents made great efforts to encourage him to develop as a girl, both in appearance and in interests. The boy was one of a pair of identical twins, so it is possible to see just how flexible development can be by comparing the newly created girl's behaviour with that of 'her' brother. In fact, 'she' acquired all the tastes and behaviour patterns of a stereotypical little girl. Although she was a bit of a tomboy, she liked frilly dresses and bows in her hair, and even went through a phase of flirting and being coy with her father.

Beware biologists

The interplay of biology and culture, and how far each is responsible for sex differences, will be one of the central themes of this book. I do not want to play down the importance of biology, tempting though it is to try to counteract the biological determinism of writers such as Desmond Morris and Konrad Lorenz. But before turning to the influence of culture on children's ideas of masculinity and femininity, I would like to point to the folly of two assumptions made by those who detect the influence of biology in everything we do. The first assumption is that the study of animal behaviour can explain human behaviour, and that what goes for rats probably goes for man too. The second is that behaviour which made good sense for Stone Age man is 'natural', and we abandon or seek to change it at our peril, however different our life-style is from that of our ancestors.

So far as the first assumption is concerned, we need look no further than the sex hormones we have been talking about to see the pitfalls. If a group of rats is castrated, they lose their sex drive. Inject them with sex hormones and they will show normal sexual behaviour. So sex hormones govern sexual behaviour. But do the same thing with a group of monkeys and the results are not nearly so predictable. A group of female talapoin monkeys may be treated in such a way that each has exactly the same level of circulating hormones. But only one of them—the dominant female—will make any attempt to interest a male, and her attentions will be directed exclusively at the dominant male (and his attentions only at her). The explanation of this is that the effect of sex hormones is drastically reduced in species which have any form of social organization. Sex hormones may have an effect on what a monkey is ready to do, but what it actually does depends entirely on the situation. Since human social and cultural organization is still more complex, we are unlikely to learn much about human sexuality from experimenting with rats, and it is for this reason that I don't have much to say about their behaviour in this book.

As for attempts to explain behaviour in terms of the pressures which operated on primitive man, it strikes me as ironic that those who are most ready to point to the biological importance of particular customs seem to ignore the fact that evolution has not stopped. The most successful species are those which modify themselves to accommodate changes in the environment—the race is won by the swiftest to adapt. When trying to explain the differences between men and women, some writers make a lot of the advantages that a clear delineation of separate tasks and status along sex lines had for primitive hunter-gatherer societies. But external circumstances have changed so dramatically since then that changes in the way we behave may not only be possible, but very likely desirable. Attempts to conserve hunter-gatherer behaviour in modern society—as some biologists recommend—may actually be dangerous.

In fact, we know that the evolutionary trend is for men and women to become more similar. If you look at the skulls of one of our earliest collateral ancestors, *Australopithecus robustus*, you will see that the female skull is generally smaller than the male's. His skull also has a bony ridge along the top which hers lacks, because he needed the extra bone to support the muscles of his much larger jaws. The difference in size between Australopithecan males and females was probably about the same as the difference between male and female gorillas today. But a look at the skulls of our more recent ancestors shows that the nearer we get to the present, the more similar male and female skulls become.

This is not at all surprising. Men and women live in the same environment. Since there is a particular size and shape best suited to every environment, we might expect the sexes to be similar in all but their reproductive organs. The advantages of sexual reproduction were discussed earlier, but it is not immediately obvious why the requirement of a basic sex difference should result in the many anatomical, physiological and behavioural differences between a male and a female of the same species. Why do peacocks but not peahens have brightly coloured tails? Why do male deer have antlers? Why do male canaries sing, but not female ones? Why do men have beards and women breasts? The question we ought to be asking is why men and women ever became so different in their physique. Opinions differ about this, but the best guess is that it was our male ancestors who branched off on a separate course of development, and that they did so because they were polygamous. In any species where the male is not prepared to settle for a single sexual partner, he must expect to find himself fighting other males in order to satisfy his appetite for variety. In these circumstances the biggest and strongest males are obviously most likely to win the fights, and since they are going to get the lion's share of the sexual action, it is their characteristics which are most likely to be passed on to the next generation of males. Virtually all the features of male animals which distinguish them from females—their size, bright colouring, large horns and teeth—are probably the result of many thousands of years of this kind of competition.

But at some point in our history things changed. Perhaps the men decided that women weren't worth spilling blood over and found subtler ways of settling disputes, or they came to the conclusion that their children were more likely to survive if they stuck to one woman at a time and thereby doubled the number of adults with a stake in the protection and rearing of a child. Whatever the reason for the change, polygamy is no longer the norm for human sexual behaviour. Monogamy or serial monogamy is favoured in most industrialized societies, and even in those societies where polygamy is practised, it is unusual for males to have to rely on their physical prowess to gain access to the females of their choice.

Gender roles and culture

So far we have been talking mainly about sex—maleness or femaleness—which tells us a lot about how men and women come to be different physically. But when we think about what is meant by being a man or a woman, we are usually less interested in biological sex than in gender, the concept which covers masculinity and femininity, so we must now try to establish how a child comes to think of himself or herself as a boy or a girl, and how children develop the idea that it is masculine to behave in one way and feminine to behave in another.

Babies appear to have very little sense of self-awareness, so presumably they start life oblivious of what sex they are. However, two British psychologists have suggested that we discriminate gender from a very early age. Babies between ten and eighteen months old spend more time looking at pictures of babies of the same sex than of babies of the other sex. From this they conclude that babies can discriminate gender even before they learn to talk. The sex of a baby is important to parents even earlier, and their attitude clearly cannot be disregarded since they play a crucial role in the child's development. We know that parents are concerned about the sex of a child even before it is born. In 1954, a group of young American adults were asked whether they cared about the sex of their first child. Two-thirds of them replied that they did, and more than 90 per cent of these expressed a preference for a boy. You might expect that attitudes would have changed since then, but when the study was rerun in America in the early 1970s, almost identical results were obtained. The desire to have a boy is greater in fathers than in mothers, and it presumably explains the fact that parents who have two daughters are more likely to expand their family than those who already have a son.

The feeling in favour of boys as first children may not be universal, however. In 1976, I put the same question to readers of the British edition of *Cosmopolitan* magazine, as part of a wider investigation of their attitudes towards the role of women, and found that only a quarter of the women and a third of the men wanted their first child to be a boy. The vast majority of readers of both sexes said they didn't care one way or the other.

But *Cosmopolitan* readers can hardly be regarded as representative of the general population, and it seems possible that for many parents the feeling of joy at the safe delivery of a child may still be tinged by disappointment when that child is a girl rather than a boy. This suggestion was confirmed by the results of a study carried out recently in a London hospital, which showed that first-time mothers who had had a boy baby felt a greater sense of achievement than those who had given birth to a girl.

When it comes to what babies do, there is little difference between the sexes. Not all babies behave in exactly the same way; on the contrary, signs of a distinct individual personality can be seen in the way a child behaves from the very beginning. But an infant's sex is not a particularly strong predictor of how it is likely to behave. There is far more variety of behaviour amongst babies of the same sex than there is between a 'typical' boy and a 'typical' girl—an observation which applies to virtually every sex 'difference' between adult men and women.

This is not to deny that there are any sex differences in babies' behaviour. Several researchers have found that boy babies are slightly more restless and cry more. One team of British scientists who failed to observe these differences suggested that they might appear only when the baby boys in the studies had recently been circumcised. More recently, however, researchers have found small but significant sex differences between babies even when none of the boys had been circumcised. For example, a Swedish psychologist observed that by the fourth day after birth, boys were adopting more of a 'little and often' approach to breast-feeding, while girls showed a more regular feeding pattern. Other researchers have found that baby girls smile more often, and they may differ in the way they respond to being held or spoken to. Boys react in the same way to both, whereas girls react more to being spoken to than to being held. Girls show a greater interest in communicating, spending on average twice as long as boys maintaining eye contact with a silent adult. So it is perhaps as a result of the baby's behaviour that, within forty-eight hours of birth, mothers tend to talk to and smile at their babies more often if they are female, and pick them up and play more boisterously if they are boys.

Despite such findings, the most striking thing is how similarly babies of the two sexes behave. In fact, trained observers consider that it is impossible to guess the sex of a new-born baby simply from watching its behaviour.

However, the way things are is not always the way people think they are, and there is a great deal of evidence which suggests that most people firmly believe that little girls and little boys are—or ought to be—very different creatures. In the study of first-time mothers referred to earlier, more than half of them said during pregnancy that they believed the behaviour of boy and girl babies was different. After giving birth, 38 per cent said they felt their relationship with the baby was affected by its sex. Nor is it just mothers who think that boy and girl babies are different. You can discover this yourself by carrying out the following simple experiment.

Take a baby out into the street, stop the first twenty people you meet and tell them you are conducting an experiment to find out how people react to babies, and then ask them to hold 'Mark' and tell you what sort of baby they think he is. Repeat the procedure with twenty more people, only this time ask them what they think of 'Mary'. The baby will be the same in both cases (you can add an extra frill to the experiment by covering 'Mark' with a blue blanket and 'Mary' with a pink one), but the responses you get from the two sets of people will be quite different.

Whatever the baby's real sex, 'Mark' will be described as bouncing, cheeky, mischievous and strong, while 'Mary' will be seen as lovely, sweet, gorgeous and cute. Of course these are the reactions of strangers to a baby they are meeting for the first time, so the experiment does not tell us anything about what parents think of their own children. But it has been carried out a number of times, usually with the results I have described. As you might expect, the effect is strongest amongst adults with traditional attitudes, and it depends to some extent on the degree to which 'Mark/Mary's' behaviour conforms to the popular stereotypes of how little boys and girls should behave. But it is a powerful effect which leaves no doubt that such stereotypes exist, and that they influence the way we perceive boy and girl babies.

Does the fact that our spontaneous reactions to baby boys and girls are so different mean that we actually treat them differently? To answer this question, researchers at Sussex University invited thirty-two mothers into their laboratory, invited them to play with a baby they had never seen before, and filmed the results. As in the previous experiment, the same baby was presented to different women as either a girl or a boy, and once again this had a marked effect on how 'he' or 'she' was treated. As you might expect, the women's first choice of toys was governed by what sex they thought the baby was: a toy hammer for the 'boy', for the 'girl' the inevitable doll. But even more striking was the fact that they interpreted exactly the same behaviour by the child in a different way when they thought 'he' was a boy than when they thought 'she' was a girl. When 'he' became restless and started to wriggle, they took this as a sign that he wanted to play and went along with what they took to be his wishes. But when 'she' made the same movements, she was assumed to be upset and in need of soothing.

If this is typical of the way mothers respond to babies, it seems likely that boys and girls, from an early age, will form very different views about their ability to influence other people and to dictate the course of events. We can assume that if boys are allowed to call the tune in this way, they will be encouraged to behave independently and to expect that if they make their wishes known, they will get what they want. But the only lesson girls can learn from their treatment is that they are expected to lie quietly, passively waiting for things to happen before reacting.

Of course, this experiment—like the previous one—only tells us how mothers react to other people's children. Researchers have found it much more difficult to show that mothers treat their own boy and girl babies differently. This is not because mothers treat all their own children in exactly the same way, but because mothers treat each child according to his or her individual personality, regardless of whether it is a girl or a boy. She may believe in sexual stereotypes, but these seem to be much more influential when she is confronted by an unknown child. However, there *are* differences in the way mothers treat their own boy and girl babies, and one of these ties in with the results of the experiment we have been discussing.

Studies show that mothers spend more time holding and soothing their baby daughters than they do their sons, despite the fact that boys actually cry more and sleep less than their sisters.

Both parents make a greater investment in encouraging their daughters to be sociable: they smile and talk to them more, encouraging them to smile and gurgle back, and they tend to be more verbally affectionate towards girls, using terms like 'honey', 'precious' and 'angel'. With boys, less time is spent on these embryonic conversations and more on stimulating them to be active and outgoing.

These different ways of treating boys and girls may be a response to the infant's behaviour: parents may spend more time talking to girls because girls respond more to this sort of stimulation, whereas boys respond more to physical activity. So an infant's behaviour might encourage us to treat it in a particular way, and this in turn will have a profound effect on the child's development.

Fathers may be particularly important here. There is some evidence that a small child would rather play with its father than with its mother. Part of the explanation for this must be his greater rarity value. But fathers also tend to be more physical and imaginative playmates than mothers, particularly when playing with boys. When children find a task difficult, fathers are more likely to give them practical assistance, while mothers tend just to offer general encouragement. The role of fathers in bringing up children is something researchers are only now beginning to investigate, but it looks as though they are more influenced than their wives by the sex of a child. Fathers touch new-born sons more than daughters, and are especially attentive to first-born boys. Later, it is they rather than their wives who are more concerned that their daughters should be 'feminine' and their sons unmistakably 'masculine', and they have more rigid ideas about the different sorts of games it is appropriate for boys and girls to play. In fact, there are big sex differences in the way three- and four-year-olds play. Boys of this age play more rough-and-tumble games than girls in every society (the sex difference is slightly smaller among Kung bush people in the Kalahari because girls there do more of it than girls in London, for example). Toddlers also want to play with different toys, boys choosing to play with boys' toys, whereas girls select girls' toys both in action and pretend-play.

Because of these different preferences, children tend to play with other children of the same sex, creating two different cultural worlds. Boys tend to play in large groups with the emphasis on physically based status, and they fight a lot. Girls' friendships are more exclusive. They prefer to play intensively with one or two 'best friends'; they co-operate and take turns.

Although boys and girls don't usually play together, it is interesting to see what happens when a child does cross the gender boundary. Girls who are tomboys seem to gain in status, and are perceived as doing fun masculine things like climbing trees. But boys who don't conform to the gender role become objects of ridicule—they are teased for being sissy and girly, and are thought to play with dolls and cry a lot. It is as if masculinity is a club, to which you have to gain entry by being tough and daring.

How do children become aware of their gender and start thinking in terms of masculinity and femininity? The obvious assumption is that their parents tell them about it or else allow them to deduce the importance of gender from the fact that boys and girls are treated very differently. But it is not as simple as this. Parents do not actively instruct children in gender roles by saying this is how boys/girls behave; you are a boy/girl, so this is how you should behave. Nor is there much evidence to suggest that parents shape boys and girls into behaving in the ways we think of as masculine and feminine by rewarding different behaviour in the two sexes.

It does not seem to be the case that boys are more aggressive than girls because parents tolerate or even encourage aggression in boys but not in girls. In fact, research shows that it is equally discouraged in children of both sexes, and that boys are actually more often punished for displaying it than girls are (boys generally receive more punishment than girls). But parents do of course draw children's attention to gender by dressing boys and girls differently after the first year or so, and they encourage them to develop different interests and perhaps different behaviour by providing them with different sorts of toys. Even the harmless old tradition of blue for boys, pink for girls reflects a bias in favour of boys, because it used to be popularly believed that blue wards off evil spirits!

Of course parents aren't the only source of information young children are exposed to on the subject of the significance of gender. Other children are an important influence, especially older brothers and sisters: young children of both sexes become more masculine if they have an older brother and more feminine

OLSON LIBRARY
NORTHERN MICHIGAN UNIVERSITY
MARQUETTE, MICHIGAN 49855

if they have an older sister. Nor should the influence of the media be underestimated. According to one American calculation, the typical four-year-old has already watched some 3,000 hours of television (the figure must be smaller in countries without all-day TV broadcasting). Analysis of the contents of TV programmes—and most children's books, for that matter—leaves no doubt about the message the media convey.

As a general trend, heroes outnumber heroines by something like three to one. More specifically, a study carried out in the US confirmed that the old stereotypes are very much alive in the minds of those who make television programmes. Men are still portrayed at work more often than women, while women tend to be shown at home and, more often than not, in emotional distress. Men on TV are more likely to solve their own problems, while women, though proficient at dealing with other people's troubles, usually require assistance to handle their own.

Several British studies have found that the picture was no different during the commercial breaks. Analyses of hundreds of British TV advertisements shown in the 1970s and 1980s produced predictable results. Whereas men were typically portrayed as authoritative, autonomous and knowledgeable, presenting arguments in favour of a product, women were shown as silent and ignorant consumers of domestic goods. Interestingly, there was a tendency for such stereotyping to be more pronounced in the evening (perhaps pandering to the prejudices of the traditional man as he comes home from work to his wife). As an indication of the bias in TV advertisements, one of the studies pointed out that although more than 40 per cent of adult women in the UK were in paid employment at the time they carried out the research, they represented only 13 per cent of the central roles of the commercials being studied. Even where a woman did have the central role, she tended to be presented as an ignorant, impulsive buyer, more concerned with the social desirability of a product than with whether it is practical or represents good value.

The role which television plays in inculcating sexual stereotypes in children is hard to assess. Expert opinion seems to have swung quite sharply away from the once popular view that children are not much affected by what they see on the screen. On the other hand, there do seem to be some grounds for cautious optimism about the willingness of at least some TV directors to present a less biased view of the adult world. For example, another survey of American TV commercials carried out at the end of the 1970s found that women were more often shown working in traditionally masculine jobs than in earlier studies. However, men were never shown in traditionally feminine occupations outside the home, and although they were sometimes seen to be cooking and cleaning, this was invariably being done under the supervision of their wife, usually to make a humorous point.

Where children's books are concerned, we might expect the media to exert a more liberal influence. But this does not seem to be the case, at least where the USA is concerned. Researchers who investigated how men and women were depicted in nineteen prize-winning children's picture books published between 1972 and 1979 detected few signs of the considerable changes which had taken place in sex roles in the real world. Comparing these books with prize-winners from the period 1967–71, they found that although the ratio of male to female pictures had changed dramatically (from 11:1 to 1.8:1, for human characters), the authors, regardless of their own sex, still seemed to be locked into traditional sex-typing when it came to what the characters did. Almost without exception, the female characters were presented as warm, caring and affectionate, but dependent and incidental to the plot. The male characters, on the other hand, were tough, self-sufficient and aggressive, and it was around them that the stories revolved.

How much children are actually affected by what they see and have read to them is still a vexed question. But we know that they are not indifferent to the message of the media, and the only lesson they can learn about sex roles is that men and women are very different and unequal beings. Surprisingly, there is considerable controversy about the extent to which parents or other adults are instrumental in instilling sexual stereotypes. It has long been assumed that young children imitate the behaviour of their same-sexed parent. But this has not proved easy to demonstrate convincingly in the laboratory. Recently, however, Australian psychologists have provided clear evidence that by the time they are eight or nine, children of both sexes can be swayed in their preferences by observing the choice made by young adults of their own sex.

Even more alarming is that sex stereotypes can affect performance and success, not just preference. Some British psychologists used a simple experiment to demonstrate a powerful stereotyping effect. They used the 'wiggly-wire task', a game where you have to move a ring along the length of the 'wiggly wire' without touching it. If the ring touches the wire, a bell sounds, and this counts as an error. The researchers found that the number of errors made by children aged eleven, thirteen and sixteen varied dramatically according to what skills they thought the task was testing. Half the children were told that it was a test to see how good they would be at mechanics or at operating machinery, so they saw the task as 'masculine'. The others were told it was a test to see how good they would be at needlework, showing the task to be a feminine one. Children of both sexes made significantly fewer errors when the task was seen as appropriate to their gender. This is a fascinating demonstration that children do better on tasks which are seen as appropriate for their sex, and it has important educational implications. Girls may be worse at mathematics than boys simply because it is seen as a boys' subject, rather than because of unmodifiable psychological characteristics.

Although children are clearly influenced by gender, it is not clear how this happens. Researchers have been surprised by how little overt sex-typing children experience from their parents. They are very rarely told to behave in a way appropriate to their sex, though they may be actively discouraged from engaging in behaviour thought to be appropriate only for the opposite sex. This is particularly so for boys. Little girls are allowed to get away with quite a lot in the way of masculine behaviour—no one minds a tomboy although parents are less concerned about boys getting their clothes dirty than girls—but parents, especially fathers, are swift to stamp out signs of effeminacy in their sons.

This is perhaps the main difference in the way sons and daughters are brought up, and there are a number of possible explanations for it. We could go back to the suggestion made earlier in the chapter that femaleness is the natural state and maleness a more recent development. If this is the case, you might expect femininity to be something a child slips easily into while masculinity needs to be learned. Alternatively, parents may be worried about the prospect of their children becoming homosexual. There are assumed to be more male than female homosexuals, so parents are more likely to be on the look-out for incipient signs of homosexuality in boys than in girls.

But perhaps the most likely reason why parents are more concerned about their son's masculinity than their daughter's femininity is that he is more important to them, because boys are more highly valued than girls. If you find this hard to swallow, remember that people would much rather their first child were a boy. Remember too the evidence produced at the beginning of this chapter which showed that men and women alike value most masculine characteristics more highly than most feminine ones.

Since children are surrounded by adults with preconceptions about masculine and feminine behaviour, it is tempting to assume that they first become aware of gender as something adults seem to think is important. But some theorists have suggested that children would take on a gender role without any outside assistance, as an inevitable consequence of the biological differences between the sexes, specifically in their genitals. Psychoanalysts claim that there is a connection between people's genitals and their personality. The fact that the penis is an organ which intrudes into the world is said to lead to men being out-going, adventurous and aggressive, while the internal reproductive system of a woman is alleged to make her passive, receptive and peaceful. When parents talk to their children about the difference between their genitals, they sometimes give the impression that girls are people who lack penises. According to Freud, this leads to the condition of penis envy, which he claimed is one of the most powerful influences on the developing female personality, and at the root of women's feeling that they are inferior to men. But while it is true that children are keenly interested in their genitals and anxious to understand why there are two different models available, we shall soon see that the psychoanalytic explanation of the development of gender roles cannot account for all the facts.

An alternative explanation is that masculinity and femininity develop in the same way as the physical differences between the sexes we shall be discussing in the next chapter, as a result of the action of the sex hormones which circulate in our bodies. The problem with this explanation is that children start responding to gender at a time when the overall production of sex hormones is at a low ebb, and when there is very little difference between the sexes in hormonal activity.

In fact, when children of different ages are asked questions to discover what they think about masculinity and femininity, it transpires that the concept of gender is not something which just becomes clearer and clearer as the child grows up. On the contrary, the willingness of children to accept gender roles seems to wax and wane as their thought processes change, and no single principle—whether of biology or learning—can explain what actually happens. Instead we are confronted with a complicated mixture of biological change, the influence of parents' and teachers' views about boys and girls, and a child's own determination to make sense of the world and of other people's attitudes and behaviour.

Children and gender

By the time a child first becomes aware of itself as an individual— at about eighteen months—it will already have been influenced by its parents' reactions and expectations, and we have seen that these are very different for boys and girls. During the next three or four years, gender is only one of the many concepts a child is trying to work out. Before they go to school, children are not dominated by sexual stereotypes. They are not unduly bothered if Mummy is taller than Daddy, or if he does the cooking and she mends the fuses. But by the age of five or six the situation has changed: most children conform to the accepted stereotypes of masculinity and femininity and they are ready with an explanation for the differences between men and women. They point to bodily appearance—size, strength, length of hair and so on—and will assure you that men are more competent and powerful than women because they are born that way. Mummies *have* to stay at home and look after the house while Daddies must go to work, and a six-year-old may be quite upset if his parents fail to conform to this pattern. In short, he or she is a hard-line biological determinist when it comes to sex differences.

A couple of years later, however, the child's position has become more liberal. He or she can now recognize that people are masculine and feminine regardless of what they look like, and is prepared to accept that masculine and feminine traits can stem from habit or training rather than from biological necessity. The eight-year-old is aware of the importance of an individual's personality. If his or her mother chooses to wear a mannish suit and cut her hair short, she is doing her own thing rather than threatening one of nature's laws. The greater tolerance of the eight-year-old can be seen in the reply of one little girl when asked what she thought of a woman with big muscles: 'Well, it is all right. Some people say it is not feminine. I think it is all right. What is the matter with having big muscles? I am always lifting things for my mother and father and my mother always says, "You should not do that". Well, there is nothing the matter with it.'

By the age of ten, however, there is another change, and children have developed what I can only call a realistic pessimism on the subject of sex differences. After two more years of exposure to the attitudes of parents and teachers, the ten-year-old has once again come to see the different roles of men and women as fixed and unchangeable, not because of their biology but because of the workings of a social system which the child is now beginning to grasp. At this age, children will explain the fact that boys and girls behave differently not just by pointing to differences in biology or in the way they have been brought up, but by referring to the very different roles they are going to play in the future. Here is the reply of one ten-year-old boy to the question, Who do you think is more intelligent, men or women, and why? 'Men are smarter because they have to do a lot of things like thinking. They have to work at their jobs.'

Whereas the eight-year-old thought that any behaviour could be tolerated because it was biologically possible, ten-year-olds are worried about what their friends or parents might think if they started to behave in the 'wrong' way. They admit that they could act differently, but know what is expected of them, and it does not occur to them to ask whether the status quo ought to be changed. Two years later, however, their thinking has developed a stage further. Now they can recognize that masculine and feminine traits are neither biologically or socially necessary, but simply the product of arbitrary historical forces. When asked the question about how intelligent men and women are, a twelve-year-old boy replied: 'You can't tell . . . it is not whether you are a man or a woman. It's whether you are smart.'

Like the eight-year-old—but not the six- or ten-year-old—twelve-year-olds recognize that masculine and feminine stereotypes exist, but they think gender is less important than an individual's personality. They want people to be able to act according to their own convictions and self-interest instead of always having to conform to gender stereotypes.

Before the age of eight, children's views about gender were

almost entirely focused on biological differences between the sexes. Then their attention shifted to the constraints society imposes. Perhaps the most important feature of adolescence is that it is the time when you start trying to establish your personal identity—what sort of person you are. Because it is a period of emotional upheaval and uncertainty, it is not surprising to find that fourteen- to sixteen-year-olds tend to accept and conform to gender stereotypes. As part of their search for an identity, young adolescents are keen to establish their status as masculine or feminine, and they define 'being yourself' as being able to conform to traditional gender roles. Adolescents of both sexes may admit that these rules are arbitrary and even unfair, but they are not prepared to allow such considerations to threaten their precarious sense of identity or to jeopardize their first heterosexual relationships. A fourteen-year-old girl who said she was a feminist was asked how she would react to a man who wore a midi coat and high heels (the height of feminine fashion at the time this study was done). Her reply illustrates the young adolescent's intolerance of behaviour which challenges gender stereotypes: 'I wouldn't go near him, ugh! . . . They must have something wrong with them, maybe they were brought up that way, because they shouldn't act feminine; that is our identity, that is our position, not theirs. They should be masculine.'

By the end of adolescence, however, many of our problems about who we are have been resolved, and we are once again prepared to be more flexible about masculinity and femininity. A lot of us arrive at a curiously inconsistent position. We have definite views about 'typical' masculine and feminine behaviour even though we accept that our attitude not only discriminates unfairly against women but also perpetuates an injustice because our feelings affect the way we bring up our own children. An eighteen-year-old American man who took part in the study of attitudes towards gender from which I have been quoting throughout this section expressed what many people feel: 'I say stereotypes should be abolished, but I can't help what has been put into me during the years.'

The question is often asked, is it biology or culture which makes men and women what they are? We have yet to tackle the job of deciding what men and women in fact are, but I hope that my description of how we come to think of ourselves as men and women will have convinced you that the question is based on a false distinction. The process of becoming a man or woman begins at conception and never really stops. We can no more escape from our biology than we can avoid being influenced by the norms of the society into which we are born, though we know that the message carried by a person's genes about his or her sex can sometimes be modified. We also know that the relative weight an individual attaches to the biological or sociological aspects of masculinity and femininity depends on the way he or she interprets them, and that this varies predictably, according to what stage of development he or she happens to have reached.

We have seen that we need a male/female distinction for sexual reproduction, and that we are aware of and influenced by this distinction from a very early age. Social and cultural forces act to exaggerate and extend these basic biological differences: clothing and make-up are obvious ways of highlighting the differences between men and women. It is not always so obvious that distinctive ways of acting and thinking may also be culturally, rather than biologically, determined exaggerations of the differences. Such man-made and woman-made gender differences may enhance the individual's attractiveness to the opposite sex.

Finally, notice that we have not so far come across any evidence which forces us to accept that men and women must *behave* differently because they are different biologically.

2

PHYSICAL DIFFERENCES

Nature has built man as a four-litre, and woman as a three-litre car.

An exercise physiologist

In Chapter 1 we saw that men and women are different in their chromosomes and in the balance of their sex hormones. These are aspects of the body's internal chemistry which we are rarely aware of, but which make an important contribution to one of the most obvious and incontrovertible differences between the sexes—Mr Average is bigger and stronger than Mrs Average, and he is also a different shape. In this chapter we are going to see exactly how men and women differ physically, when and why these differences appear, what effect they have on what the two sexes are capable of doing, and whether there is any sign that men and women are becoming less different physically.

Size and growth

So far as height is concerned, the average British adult male is five foot nine while the average female is five foot four. In other parts of the world, the difference in average height between the two sexes varies according to the average height of the whole population. For example, fewer inches separate the average pygmy and his wife than divide the average adult male and female Nuer (the Nuers, who live in the Sudan, are one of the world's tallest people). But relatively speaking, the picture is the same everywhere: men are about 7 per cent taller than women.

So much for height. Measuring strength is a more complicated business, but it is probably true to say that the average untrained British adult male is 30 per cent stronger than his female counterpart. It is generally assumed that he can also run faster and has more stamina (that is to say, he can keep going at some strenuous physical activity over a longer period of time), though we shall see that this is a matter of dispute. Of course, as with height, we are again talking about averages. There are very few men who can match the performance of outstanding women sprinters or shot-putters. So far as shape is concerned, women typically have smaller shoulders, larger hips, more fat and a smaller limb to body-length ratio than men. This summarizes the visible differences in physique as well as the differences in physical accomplishment between adult males and females and it applies universally. We must now see what causes the differences and when they appear.

I said in the last chapter that new-born boys and girls are very similar. However, the average girl is actually slightly shorter at birth than the average boy, and she remains so until puberty. At birth, boys also have significantly longer forearms relative to the length of their bodies, and there is a mysterious tendency for the index finger to be longer than the finger next to the little finger in girls more often than in boys. Much later, Miss Average may briefly enjoy a height advantage over Master Average, because she reaches puberty up to two years before him and her adolescent growth spurt begins first.

The growth spurt is set in motion by a sudden upsurge in production of either male or female sex hormones (androgens and oestrogens), which causes the internal environments of the two sexes to diverge sharply and leads eventually to the distinctive masculine and feminine shapes, as well as to reproductive maturity. The process starts first in girls. But the age at which the growth spurt (and puberty generally) begins varies enormously amongst perfectly normal children of both sexes. In boys, for example, it may begin as early as ten and a half or as late as sixteen, so that one boy may have almost completed his physical development before another has even begun the growth spurt.

For the average girl, the growth spurt begins shortly after her eleventh birthday and ceases when she is about fifteen and a half. For boys the whole process occurs later, though neither sex stops growing altogether at the end of the growth spurt. The physical growth spurt in a girl tends to coincide with the earliest of the changes in her reproductive system which occur at puberty, while in boys it rarely begins until the period of genital growth is almost completed, and it is never the first sign of puberty.

Despite the large difference between the sexes in the timing of their adolescent growth spurt, only nine months separate the first appearance of pubic hair in boys and girls. This is usually the earliest sign a child receives of impending puberty, though it may be the appearance of breast buds in girls or a marked acceleration in the speed with which the penis is growing for boys. This occurs at about twelve and a half in the average British boy, though it may come as early as ten and a half or as late as fourteen and a half. Although the average British girl will first notice that her breasts are beginning to swell at eleven, it can happen as early as nine or not until she is thirteen. Puberty finishes for the average boy at fourteen and a half, within the range of twelve and a half to sixteen and a half, while girls have their first period relatively late in puberty.

This has a number of consequences. It means that late-maturing boys can be reassured that they will become taller if their genital development is still at an early stage, while girls who are worried about becoming too tall can relax in the knowledge that they will soon stop growing upwards once they have their first menstrual period. Ovulation is more affected by body fat than by overall size, because the process whereby androgens are transformed into oestrogens takes place in the cells which surround the fat cells. This means that a small fat girl will begin to ovulate before a larger thin one. It also explains why young female athletes are often slow to begin their periods: even swimmers, who are often quite heavy, may be late in starting to menstruate because their extra weight consists of muscle rather than fat. For all this variation, however, girls do not reach the stage of sexual development at which they become able to conceive a child before they are physically big enough to produce one.

Moreover, a sexually precocious boy is not likely to have the physical strength to impose his will on a girl of his own age. Girls stop gaining height at about the age of fifteen and a half, while boys continue to grow for two more years, but the period when the average girl is taller than her male counterpart comes to an end when they are both fourteen.

As for weight, girls tend to be slightly lighter than boys when they are born, equal to them by the age of eight, and heavier by

nine or ten. The average girl continues to be heavier until the end
of her growth spurt, at about fourteen and a half. This sequence
can be explained by differences in the growth of fat and muscles
in the two sexes, as well as differences in the rate at which they
grow. Girls are born with slightly more fat than boys, a difference
which continues throughout childhood. During the adolescent
growth spurt, the rate at which boys gain body fat slows down
(they may actually lose fat on their limbs), while girls continue to
accumulate fat steadily, especially on their trunk.

At birth, boys grow faster than girls, but this difference is
reversed between the ages of about seven months and four years.
After this, there is little difference until puberty, when the girls
shoot ahead. But throughout her development, the average girl is
always nearer than the average boy of the same age to her final
mature stature. For example, at birth she is four to six weeks
ahead of him in skeletal development, and she reaches half her
adult height by the time she is twenty-one months old, three
months before he reaches the same landmark. But it would be
rash to conclude from this, as some writers have done, that little
girls are ahead of little boys in every aspect of development. An
alternative way of assessing a baby's developmental progress is to
see how much time it spends awake and how much sleeping
(babies tend to sleep less as they get older). On this measure, there
seems to be virtually no difference between the sexes or even a
slight indication that boys are ahead of girls.

Although there are physical differences between males and
females throughout childhood, some of which are already present
at birth, it is not until puberty that the two sexes really begin to
diverge physically, a process which produces the distinct physical
characteristics of adult men and women. In the year immediately
before he reaches puberty, the typical boy gains 5 centimetres in
height; in the next three years, he grows by 7, 9 and 7 centimetres
respectively. Girls have a slightly lower rate of growth: they grow
by 6, 8 and 6 centimetres during their height spurt, which you
will remember occurs earlier than that of boys. In both sexes,
there are large individual differences in timing and although early
developers tend to reach a higher peak during their growth spurt,
they do not end up taller.

There is usually nothing abnormal about being an early or a
late developer, but the age at which an individual reaches physical
and sexual maturity can have an effect on his or her life not

only at the time but later. Boys and girls who are early physical maturers tend to have slightly higher than average IQ scores both as adolescents and as adults. But it is not the case that early maturity actually *causes* greater intelligence, since the small but reliable advantage enjoyed by early maturers is present long before puberty begins. The tendency is for cleverer children to reach maturity earlier, rather than for early maturers to become cleverer.

The position is further complicated by the fact that early maturers also tend to come from smaller families, so it would be a mistake to exaggerate the connection between age of reaching maturity and intelligence at the expense of all the other factors which may be at work. Remember too that the difference in IQ scores between early and late maturers is small, and applies only to the average score obtained by large numbers of children reaching puberty relatively early or late. The variation within the two groups is incomparably greater than the difference between them, so many late-maturing children will be much brighter than those whose physical development is ahead of theirs. However, research confirms that there is a link between physical and mental development. For example, girls who have reached the menarche (onset of first menstruation) perform better on IQ tests than those of the same age who have not, and one researcher has gone so far as to claim that during the growth spurt each extra inch of height gives the early developer an advantage of one and a half IQ points over a late developer. There is no difference in height between early and late developers when both have finished growing, but even among adults there is a small but significant correlation between height and IQ score.

The fact that taller people tend to be slightly more intelligent may simply reflect the fact that they tend to come from the higher social classes, but it could also be a hangover from adolescent experience. Children who reach maturity earlier gain kudos with their peers, and are more likely to be accepted as leaders. Early maturers may gain confidence and a chance to expand their social skills, which could explain why early developers tend to become less neurotic and more sociable adults than late developers. Teachers too may unintentionally favour the early developer. Perhaps ideas put forward in a mature baritone are taken more seriously than those presented in a shrill treble, while female teachers may feel a closer bond with girls with whom they know they share the most noticeable mark of womanhood.

We may not be able to say that early maturity causes children to be cleverer, but early maturers gain certain advantages they never lose, especially if they are boys. The effect is less marked in girls, perhaps because of the greater ambiguity about the role which girls and women are expected to play. And there is some consolation for late developers. Early maturers may do slightly better on IQ tests but, as we shall see in Chapter 4, there is at least one important aspect of intellectual ability where it seems to be an advantage to be a late developer.

Returning to adolescence, the results of the height spurt are seen more on the trunk than on the legs, which explains why boys stop growing out of their trousers before they stop growing out of their jackets. The fact that boys end up with legs that are longer relative to their total height than girls do is due largely to their delayed growth spurt. Immediately before puberty, legs are growing faster than the trunk, and although boys have the more dramatic growth spurt, when it is the trunk which is growing most, this is not enough to cancel out the effect of the period just before puberty.

At puberty, the head also gets bigger (physically, that is), though probably not the brain, and there may be changes in the shape of the face, especially in males. The forehead becomes more prominent and both jaws grow forward (this change is less marked in girls).

But the most striking way in which boys and girls diverge at adolescence—genitals and breasts apart—concerns their hips and shoulders. Here we can detect the influence of the different sex hormones. In both sexes the first event of puberty is an upsurge in production of sex hormones, and we now know that cartilage joints in the hip are sensitized to respond to oestrogen, while those in the shoulder respond to androgens, especially testosterone. Whereas before adolescence boys and girls have roughly similar shaped hips and shoulders, this rapidly ceases to be the case once the growth spurt begins.

There is one difference between boys and girls which is apparent long before puberty, and that is the shape of the pelvis and the angle at which it is tilted. At birth, girls have a wider opening at the bottom of the pelvis, this being the narrowest part of the passage which babies have to traverse on their way into the outside world. Much of the rapid build-up of fat on the adolescent girl accumulates around her hips, breasts, upper arms and legs.

This increase of fat is another consequence of the flood of oestrogen which is released into her bloodstream at the beginning of puberty, and it leads to one of the most important physical differences between adult men and women: 25 per cent of the typical adult female's body consists of fat, compared with only 12 per cent of the typical adult male. We shall see later that this enormous difference can account for male superiority in most forms of athletic endeavour, though it can also sometimes be turned to a woman's advantage.

As an adolescent girl's hips broaden, so do a boy's shoulders. At the same time boys become generally bigger and heavier because testosterone (unlike oestrogen) stimulates bones as well as muscles to grow. The greater overall strength of the adult male can also be traced back to puberty because the more pronounced muscular development of the adolescent boy stems from structural and biochemical changes in his muscle cells which once again may stem from the action of the male sex hormone. Before puberty there is not much to choose between male and female muscular development, except in the hands and forearms, where boys have the advantage. Because girls begin their growth spurt earlier, there is a short period when they are not only bigger but also stronger than their male counterparts. But things change as soon as boys reach their growth spurt, and by the time they are adults, men have bigger muscles (the muscles of the average adult man are about 15 per cent longer and up to 30 or 40 per cent thicker than a woman's), and some scientists believe that men's muscles are also chemically different from women's. During puberty, the strength of the arms, for example, increases two and a half times in boys, but only one and a half times in girls.

Strength

There are two different kinds of muscle fibre: red fibre and white fibre, familiar to poultry fans as dark meat and white meat. The first of these are slow-twitch fibres, fuelled by fatty acids, which enable us to perform feats of endurance such as long-distance running or mountain-climbing. White fibres (fast twitch) are higher powered, fuelled by glucose or glycogen, and are involved in sudden bursts of physical exertion like sprinting or weight-lifting. The balance between the two types of fibres is genetically determined, and how much of either fibre an individual has determines how good he or she is at the two sorts of activity. Most people have an equal balance between the two and so excel at neither activity. However, some of us have an excess of one or other type of muscle fibre. Studies have shown that the muscles of long-distance runners and swimmers average about 80 per cent slow-twitch fibres, whereas sprinters tend to have about 75 per cent fast-twitch fibres.

Some scientists think that an imbalance between the two fibres occurs much more often amongst men than amongst women. However, this may simply reflect the fact that men are more likely to exercise than women. Training can effectively alter the balance by causing fast-twitch fibres to behave more like slow-twitch fibres (although the reverse is not true). This may be able to explain why men sprint much faster than women but only just keep ahead in marathons. A woman who trains will be able to increase the number of muscle fibres involved in endurance activities, making up for the lack of muscle bulk (relative to men) by increasing the proportion of slow-twitch fibres. On the other hand she cannot increase the number of fast-twitch fibres in this way, and because she has less muscle bulk than men, she will be at a disadvantage. Men are also better able to fuel the fast-twitch muscles, developing larger heart and lungs, higher blood pressure, a lower resting heart-rate, and a greater capacity for transporting oxygen through the bloodstream coupled with greater ability to get rid of the chemical products of physical exercise. Men and women differ even in the composition of their blood, because at adolescence boys acquire more red blood cells and haemoglobin (the pigment which carries oxygen from the lungs to the muscles) whereas girls do not. Not only are the lungs of the average man larger than those of the average woman, but they can also take in one and a half times as much oxygen as hers. All these differences have an effect on our powers of endurance, since we can only go on being active as long as our muscles get the oxygen they use as fuel. If men have larger lungs which can take in more oxygen, more powerful hearts to pump that oxygen round and more haemoglobin to carry it to the muscles, it is hardly surprising that the average adult male has more stamina than the average woman.

However, there are ways in which women's muscles give them a strength which men do not have. Because of her menstrual cycle, a woman must have muscles which are equipped to survive in a constantly changing chemical environment in which hormone levels rise and fall and the amount of water retained varies according to the time of the month. Male muscles exist in a comparatively (though not entirely) stable environment, and as a result seem less able to cope when the body's chemical balance is unexpectedly disturbed, for example by illness. This may be one reason why men feel shaky and are more likely to complain of aches and pains when they get flu.

Exercise and athleticism

We have seen that some of these physical differences between males and females exist at birth, which suggests that they are a consequence of the distinctive chromosomal make-up of the two sexes, but that most of them become pronounced only at puberty, at the prompting of the sex hormones. However, biological factors do not tell the whole story. Muscles, lung capacity and size of heart can all be increased by exercise, and many experts believe that the difference in physique between men and women is exaggerated by the fact that they lead different sorts of lives and have different attitudes towards taking physical exercise. Women in many countries routinely do work that would be beyond the capacity of most British or American women—indeed it would tax most British or American men—and their greater strength is almost certainly due to the fact that they took more exercise as children. Exercise in childhood, particularly just before puberty, can boost muscle size, lung capacity and so on far more dramatically than exercise taken later in life when the relevant hormones have declined. Moreover, the fitness built up in this fashion during childhood lingers on into adulthood, long after a person has stopped taking exercise. And it is not just organized sport which boosts strength and endurance. Researchers in Hong Kong found that children living in flats with lifts and leading comparatively inactive lives had 8 per cent less lung capacity than children of hillside squatters who led a very active outdoor life. So it seems that children's strength is determined not just by what sex they happen to be but by how physically active they are. If this is so, the fact that teenage boys in Britain and America are three times more likely than girls to take part in extra-curricular athletic activities presumably means that the gap in muscle power between the sexes in these countries might be much smaller if adolescent girls were prepared to take more exercise.

The reason they are reluctant to do so is not hard to discover. When they are asked, many adolescent girls say they are worried about getting hot and sweaty because they are afraid this would make them unfeminine. So it may be their concern with gender identity—which, as we saw in the last chapter, is acute at the beginning of adolescence—that prevents girls from developing to their full physical potential. This ensures that at least one aspect of traditional gender stereotypes—that men are strong and women weak—remains true, a nice example of a self-fulfilling prophecy. If further proof were needed that both sexes believe strength to be a masculine attribute, studies show that women consistently underestimate what they are capable of when they are asked to rate their own strength, while men do exactly the opposite. Where less importance is attached to notions of masculinity and femininity, things can be different. Although information about Eastern European athletes has to be taken with a pinch of salt, it is true that women in these countries received much more encouragement to take part in athletics, which may account for the fact that measurements of muscle power and lung capacity for the average man and woman were much closer there than in the West, before the Iron Curtain came down.

Talk of athletics leads us to another question. We know that ordinary, untrained men and women have very different physical capabilities, and we have a pretty good idea why they are different. But what about trained athletes, who regularly drive themselves to the limit of their physical capacity and so presumably realize their full physical potential? If you look at the record books and see what progress the fastest men and women in the world have made over the last forty years or so, you can get a clear indication of the extent to which women's physical inferiority stems from cultural expectations rather than from biology. Take the 800 metre track race, for example. The first time women competed in this event at the Olympic Games was in 1928, when many of the competitors were overcome by exhaustion. The event therefore disappeared from the Olympic programme until 1960, on the grounds that it was clearly dangerous for women to run so far. The graphs in Figure 1 show the mean speeds for the world records at Olympic running events throughout this century. You can see that the male advantage has been eroded right across the board. While both men's and women's records have been increasing steadily, the *rates* of improvement are strikingly dif-

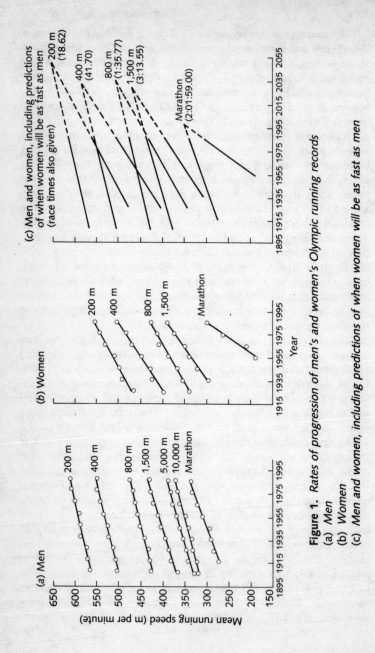

Figure 1. Rates of progression of men's and women's Olympic running records

(a) Men
(b) Women
(c) Men and women, including predictions of when women will be as fast as men

ferent, with women getting faster much more quickly than men. In fact, two American scientists have pointed out that if the current progression rates of men's and women's records remain unchanged, there will be no difference in the times of men's and women's world records within the first half of the twenty-first century. After that, current progression rates suggest superior performance by women.

It is hard to imagine that women might soon compete against men in the Olympics and win, since at the moment women lag some sixty years behind over the shorter distances: current women's world record times for five of the nine comparable track events—100 metres, 200 metres, 400 metres, 400 metres hurdles and 1,500 metres—would have taken the men's gold medal in the Amsterdam Games of 1928. Ingrid Kristiansen of Norway, who holds the current marathon record of 2:21.6, would have won the men's Olympic gold medal in 1956 and the silver medal as recently as 1968. It is not clear why marathon speeds are converging so much faster than speeds for other events, although it may be that the physiological limiting factors are different from those of other races, as suggested in the above discussion of muscle fibres. In any case, from the current rates of progression we may predict that the women's world record will match the men's in 1998. Time will tell whether these rates of progression will be maintained and the startling predictions realized.

The statistics for swimming events show a similar pattern, and it is salutary to note that the woman who held the world record for the 400 metre free-style in 1982 would have beaten Mark Spitz in the 1972 Olympics! When it comes to long-distance swimming—crossing the English Channel, for example—women are actually faster than men, which makes it somewhat ironic that the organizers of international swimming meetings rarely include 800 or 1,500 metre races for women. No doubt they are still haunted by the fifty-year-old memory of elegantly clad ladies collapsing in the half-mile track event.

There are two other aspects of a woman's biology which might be expected to have deleterious effect on her performance as an athlete—the menstrual cycle and pregnancy. However, these seem to be less of a handicap than might be supposed, if the results of the Olympic Games are anything to go by. At the 1976 Olympics, an American swimmer won three gold medals and broke a world record while at the height of her period. And so far as pregnancy is concerned, the Russians revealed after the 1964 Games that no fewer than ten of their twenty-six female champions were pregnant when they earned their medals!

Feminists may find all this very encouraging, but there is a snag. Women can certainly narrow the gap in physical perform-ance between themselves and men, but they do so by making themselves more like men. Successful female athletes reach a state of physiological fitness in which they bear a closer re-semblance to male athletes than to non-athletic members of their own sex. As a result of training, women athletes can reduce the proportion of their body which is fat to less than 10 per cent, compared with 25 per cent for the average unfit woman and 12 per cent for the average unfit man, and they are also able to tip the balance between the red and white fibres in their muscles in favour of the endurance, but not the sprinting, fibres.

However, other anatomical and physiological factors make it very unlikely that women will ever become men's equals in sprinting. The size and shape of their pelvis and hips and their less favourable leg to body-length ratio are problems that no amount of training can overcome (successful female athletes tend to be born and to remain a rather 'masculine' shape), while the greater ability of a man's muscles to break down lactic acid and so avoid cramp is another factor which must always handicap women over a short sprint.

There can be little doubt that women will come nearer to matching men's athletic performance, as long as attitudes con-tinue to change, more women are attracted to the sport, and the necessary additional facilities are made available to them. Regulations like that restricting women under twenty-one to races of 4 miles or less might also be reconsidered in the light of what we now know about women's physical capabilities. It is ironic that some of the most determined opposition to the cause of female athleticism still comes from athletics officials. A spokesman for the International Olympic Committee, the most prestigious body in athletics, gave a fair indication of their thinking on the subject when explaining why the IOC were re-jecting a suggestion that the 1980 Olympic programme should include a women's 3,000 metre event: it was, he asserted, 'a little too strenuous for them'. At the time that he was speaking, the percentage difference between the men's and women's world records for the marathon stood at 12.8; two years later, a woman ran the marathon in a time which would have won her a gold medal in every Olympic men's marathon up to 1948; and forty-five years *earlier*, a young South African schoolmistress, the legendary Miss Geraldine Watson, had finished sixth in an otherwise all-male field competing in the Durban 100 mile race!

But it is not just the athletics authorities who continue to have reservations about woman as athletes. According to the results of a survey carried out among Scottish schoolchildren in 1977, even apparently neutral sports like swimming are still perceived as essentially masculine activities by both boys and girls. The Amazon image of the sportswoman may be on the decline, however, thanks in part to the increased coverage of athletics on television, which has dispelled the myth that athleticism in women is incompatible with physical attractiveness. The idea that sport is defeminizing now also has to contend with much greater public concern about personal health, and a new awareness of the benefits of keeping fit.

The awareness may be there, but it is only slowly being translated into action. In Britain, for example, women still participate in sports far less than men. The results of the 1980 General Household Survey revealed that whereas 45 per cent of adult men interviewed had taken part in some outdoor sport in the previous month, only 31 per cent of women had done so. (If these figures sound high, bear in mind that the definition of outdoor sport includes taking a walk of more than two miles.) However, the difference between the sexes was smaller than it had been in earlier surveys, and the fact that it was much greater for indoor sports, which tend to be much less physically demanding, supports the idea that the masculine bias which sport still undoubtedly has is based on cultural rather than biological factors. It is not, after all, a woman's lack of physical prowess which makes her an unfamiliar sight at the dartboard or the snooker-table. Moreover, the 1987 General Household Survey showed that the only sports in which more women than men participated were clearly 'feminine' ones: netball, horse-riding, keep-fit, yoga, aerobics and dance exercise.

Other writers who have reached this conclusion have gone on to claim that as the cultural barriers come down, the differences in athletic performance between men and women will eventually disappear. Trends like those shown in Figure 1 (a) and (b) have led to some more bold and startlingly specific predictions: for example, that female track stars will be competing on equal terms with men by the year 2077, top swimmers by 2056 and the best women cyclists by 2011.

Such claims seem to me to be based on bad biology as well as doubtful mathematics. I say this because when you look at the differences between trained men and women, they often turn out to be *greater* than those between untrained, unfit Mr and Mrs Average. For example, if you take the average untrained couple out jogging, the man will pump 100 millilitres of oxygenated blood with every heartbeat, compared to the woman's 75 millilitres. After training, however, he will be pumping 160 millilitres to her 110, so that the difference between them has actually doubled. The same thing applies to the efficiency with which the lungs extract oxygen from the blood. Before training, the average man's muscles can extract 50 millilitres for every kilogram he weighs, while a woman's take 40. But when they are both fit, he will be able to extract 84 to her 70. The performance of her muscles has actually improved by a slightly greater percentage than his, but this cannot compensate for the fact that the absolute gap between them has widened.

These are the sorts of observation which gave rise to the remark of the exercise physiologist quoted at the beginning of the chapter: nature has built man as a four-litre, and woman as a three-litre car. A three-litre car can be tuned up to run better than a four-litre when the larger vehicle is not firing properly, but it cannot keep up when both are operating at maximum efficiency. This is a crude analogy, and there is every reason why women should make the most of their physical potential (it is estimated that the average unfit adult woman could become 10 to 20 per cent stronger in a month if she did proper exercises, and up to 40 per cent fitter if she kept on with them subsequently). However, it illustrates why I for one am sceptical about the more extreme claims we have been discussing.

Why the difference?

The *purpose* of the difference in physique between men and women was discussed in Chapter 1. I suggested there that it is a legacy from the days when men had to fight amongst themselves to get access to women, and this idea can be supported by looking at differences in size between the sexes (sexual *dimorphism*) in other species. Male baboons, for example, are almost twice the size of females, whereas there is almost no difference between the two in gibbons. The explanation for this probably lies in the different life-styles of the species. Baboons mate only at one particular time of the year, when there is a mad scramble amongst the males to get at as many females as possible, and only the biggest and strongest males are successful. So only they produce offspring, who inherit their physique, and in this way the size of the male baboon has increased over the generations. The male gibbon is a creature of very different habits. Unlike the baboon, he is territorial and he is obliged to be monogamous because he cannot defend enough territory to provide food for more than one mother and her children. He therefore selects a mate and stays with her for life. Since there are enough females to go round, large and small male gibbons both get a chance to pass on their genes, so no difference in size has evolved between the two sexes. Human beings seem to come somewhere between baboons and gibbons: men are on average 7 per cent taller and 20 per cent heavier than women, compared with 22 and 80 per cent for baboons, and virtually no difference for gibbons.

There are two points to notice about physical dimorphism between the sexes. First, it is not a universal rule. In a number of species—bats, rabbits, hares and hyenas, for example—females tend to be larger than males. The blue whale is another case in point, and since this is the largest species on the planet, the biggest animals in the world are actually female. The second thing to notice is that the reason given for the difference in size between men and women ceased to be relevant thousands of years ago, when we abandoned polygamy. So why do men continue to be bigger and stronger than women?

People who ask this question have often misunderstood an important aspect of the process of evolution: once a particular feature has developed and become a characteristic of the species, it will not just disappear again if it ceases to be useful. Men became bigger than women in the first place because smaller men either did not survive or were denied the opportunity of passing on their genes (including those which determine size) by being prevented from breeding. If the difference in height and size is to disappear, it will have to be bred out in the same way. The biggest men would have to die without breeding, which seems very unlikely because the historical bias in favour of taller men is reinforced by the fact that women generally select as mates men who are taller than themselves. (There are, of course, well-publicized exceptions to this rule.) In order to even out the size differences between the sexes, women everywhere would have to refuse to have children by anyone taller than them, and only after they had done so for some 250 years would the size difference begin to disappear. Remember, though, that sexual dimorphism is less marked in human beings than in most other species (perhaps we were never all that polygamous), and that the fossil evidence discussed in the last chapter suggests that men and women have in fact become more similar over the years. I do not, however, think that we can expect the difference in physique between them to disappear, since in our society large and small individuals have more or less the same chance of reproducing themselves.

But does it matter? Before we had machines to help us, physical strength was obviously very useful, and in the days when disputes between factions or tribes were often settled by individual combat between their two leaders, it made sense for the rulers to be chosen on the basis of the strength of their right arm. Present circumstances are very different. Outside the sports arena, few matters are now settled by physical prowess, and the Equal Opportunities Commission believes that, in this country at least, there are no longer any jobs from which women are barred by their physique. Even in primitive societies where the division of labour is determined strictly according to gender, the tasks which fall to women do so not because they have an inferior physique but because their mobility is reduced by having to care for children. In the animal kingdom, size is certainly significant because it is associated with dominance—stature helps to gain status. An animal preparing for a fight (or perhaps hoping to gain a walk-over by convincing its prospective opponent that the result is a foregone conclusion) puffs itself up to look as large as possible, and part of its ritual for conceding defeat is to curl up and try to look smaller. Ethologists suggest that we behave in much the same way when we find ourselves in a similar situation. But adult humans so rarely fight that it may be more fruitful to see whether size affects our everyday dealings with other people.

We might deduce that height is important from the fact that Jimmy Carter is the only man in this century to have beaten a taller opponent in the race to the White House! Several laboratory studies confirm that we still associate size with power and status. In one experiment, researchers described two men who they said had applied for a prestigious job, and asked people which of the two they would select if the choice were theirs. According to the descriptions, the applicants had very similar qualifications for the job, but the researchers let slip the information that one of them was five foot five and the other six foot one. This was enough to convince most of the people taking part in the experiment that the taller candidate was the right man for the job. In another study, a man was brought into different classes of students, and introduced variously as a fellow student, a research demonstrator, a senior lecturer and a visiting professor. After they had seen him, the students were asked to estimate his height, and it was found that the more distinguished they thought his rank, the greater their estimate of his height. Those who thought him a professor judged him to be a good two and a half inches taller than those who thought him a mere student! Nor is this effect confined to men. When female student nurses took part in a similar experiment and were asked to guess the height of four women, two of them students and two members of faculty, they tended to underestimate the students' height and to overestimate that of the staff.

What these experiments show is that the more successful we believe someone to be, the taller we think them. But are taller people *really* more successful? The *Wall Street Journal* tried to answer this question by investigating the income of all the graduates of a particular American university and relating this to their height. Their findings? Men over six foot two were earning 12 per cent more than those who were under six foot. But we must be careful how we interpret this finding because we have already seen that height is related to social class. It might be that the taller men were earning more not because of their height, but because they tended to come from a more privileged background which helped them to get more highly paid jobs after they left college.

It seems then that our size certainly has an effect on what other people think of us, and it may influence what sort of people we are and how successful we become, though we still do not understand this connection properly. As far as sex differences are concerned, men seem to be cashing in on an attribute which has lost most of its original practical value, while the average woman's feeling about her own importance is probably influenced by the fact that she is condemned to spend her life looking up to—in a literal sense—the average man.

Health, sickness and death

As I have described them so far, the physical differences between men and women all seem to operate to the man's advantage. But like all good stories, this tale has a sting in it. Men may be better at lifting dumb-bells or running races, but when it comes to sheer ability to survive, women have a definite edge on them. Perhaps it is no more than elementary justice that the very features which put women at a disadvantage in feats of strength work in their favour when the going gets really rough. If food is scarce, the larger stores of fat which hold a woman back as an athlete now provide her with more to live on, and her small frame ensures that she loses less heat than the bulkier man when the climate becomes very cold. Similarly, the fact that women burn up food and oxygen more slowly means that they require less of both to keep going. It seemed reasonable to describe the less dynamic metabolism of a woman as inefficient when we were talking about athletic performance, but things look very different when the prize is survival rather than a new world record.

Of course, survival is rarely a pressing concern to those of us who live in the Affluent Society, so you may think that the fact that women are better equipped for it than men is a matter of purely academic interest. Nothing could be further from the truth. There is abundant evidence that even in societies like ours, where starvation is virtually unknown and people very rarely freeze to death, men are physically much more vulnerable than women from the moment they are conceived until they die.

Consider the following statistics. For every 100 females conceived, there are estimated to be between 107 and 124 males. But the male embryo is more likely to abort spontaneously, perhaps by a factor of 135 to 100. As a result, only 106 boys are actually born for every 100 girls. This figure varies slightly from year to year, place to place, season to season and even according to time of day: more boys are born in the periods before sunrise and sunset, more girls around midnight and noon. The parents' age and the size of the existing family are also significant factors: the older a woman, and the more children she has already, the less likely it is that she will give birth to a boy. Fascinating though these findings are, the mechanism behind them remains a mystery. However, the fact that boy babies are also more likely to succumb to perinatal complications such as lack of oxygen may explain why they originally became more highly valued than girls, while the fact that girls were more often the victims of infanticide in societies which used this form of birth control was perhaps the price they paid for being easier to replace.

Of course, most boys survive birth, but their problems are only just beginning. A new-born boy is more likely than a girl to die before he is one year old, is more susceptible to infection, and has a greater chance of being born with some congenital illness or of suffering from the kinds of brain disorder which lead to epilepsy, cerebral palsy or febrile convulsions. In our society, those who live through the first year have an excellent chance of reaching the age of thirty-five. But the majority of those who fail to make it are men. During these years men are more likely to die in accidents—particularly on the road—and they continue to be more susceptible to fatal infectious diseases. They are also more prone to heart attacks and ulcers. And despite the fact that more young women try to commit suicide, more young men succeed in doing so. As a result, by the age of thirty-five there are roughly the same number of men and women left alive.

It is after the age of forty that fatal diseases really begin to take their toll. Women are more likely than men to suffer from cancer of the reproductive organs and from various diseases related to the hormones, like diabetes and thyroid disorders, but men are far more susceptible to most other forms of serious illness. For example, they are four times more likely to get lung cancer, three times more likely to contract heart disease, and they are also significantly more prone to suffer strokes and disorders of the respiratory system like bronchitis and emphysema. In consequence, the numerical balance between the sexes, which was originally weighted so heavily in favour of the male, now tips the other way, and by the time we get to seventy, there are two women for every surviving man. At the time of writing, the average British woman can expect to live until she is seventy-eight, six years longer than the average man. Amongst the 4,000 centenarians alive in Britain today, women outnumber men by four to one.

What is it about men that makes them superior in trials of

strength but worse at the ultimate test of staying alive? Social factors are clearly important. In some less developed countries the life expectancy of women is lower than that of men, and women are more likely to be malnourished and have less access to health care. So the excess of male mortality in the Western world is likely to be related to their different living patterns, and it may merely be that men's lives are more dangerous. Perhaps the fact that more men die in car crashes just means that they spend more time on the road (it may also have something to do with the difference between men's and women's driving styles). When trying to explain why men suffer more from coronary heart disease, lung cancer and other diseases of the respiratory system, we obviously cannot ignore the fact that more men than women smoke. Men also drink more alcohol than women, and more men than women drink to excess, making them more vulnerable to diseases like cirrhosis of the liver. We hear a lot about work-related stress these days, and it is generally assumed that men are more likely than women to have jobs which either involve physical danger (being a deep-sea diver, for example) or are so demanding in terms of mental energy, heavy responsibility and long hours that they endanger a person's health.

Some psychologists have suggested a gender role theory to explain sex differences in health and life expectancy. They argue that it is not a man's biological sex which is hazardous to his health, but specific behaviours and ways of thinking associated with his gender role. Conforming to this role makes men prone to more high-risk behaviour than women. These include smoking, alcohol abuse and engaging in violent or dangerous activities.

These differences first appear in the playground: boys play in a more adventurous and dangerous way, and get injured more often. The masculine role encourages aggressive behaviour, which might help to explain why more men than women are murdered and commit suicide. Masculine competitive and aggressive characteristics might also predispose men to certain stress-related health problems. For example, researchers have found that there are certain personality traits associated with an increased risk of coronary heart disease mortality in both men and women. These are the stereotypically male characteristics of competitive achievement, striving, excessive concern about time, and the potential for hostility. An unrelenting reliance on masculine coping behaviours to solve problems is therefore likely to lead to stress—

particularly in men, who have a higher blood pressure at rest than women, and greater physiological responses during acute behavioural stress. Despite this, men less often seek professional help for personal problems, perhaps because it's not manly to admit to vulnerabilities and ask for emotional support. They are more likely to turn to alcohol: heavy drinking can serve as a manifestation of masculine toughness and a way of reducing stress without violating gender norms.

But masculine ways of coping are not always bad. They can be very useful for both men and women. In fact, we will see later that the female gender role may be just as dangerous to a woman's *mental* health as the male gender role is to a man's *physical* health. The healthiest people seem to be those who have a balance of masculine and feminine characteristics.

There is a popular stereotype of the woman as physically weaker, and unreasonably fussy about her physical condition. But as we've seen, the opposite could just as well be true. Women are more sensitive to and commonsensical about matters of health and sickness, and there are social pressures on men which lead them to take risks with their health. This points to an unfortunate consequence of the convergence in life-styles of men and women: as women smoke and drink more, there is a corresponding convergence between the sexes in mortality. Recent figures show that the percentage of fifteen- to twenty-four-year-old women in the European Community who smoke cigarettes is 34 per cent—nearly as high as men (39 per cent). In several countries, more teenage girls smoke than teenage boys, so this gap may soon disappear. Similarly, the general trend is for men to drink less and women more, which is worrying because women are far more vulnerable to the physiological ill-effects of alcohol than men.

But differences in life-style may not tell the whole story of women's superior survival ability. Any lingering doubts about this are dispelled by the findings of a team of researchers who had the inspired idea of investigating the actuarial prospects of 40,000 monks and nuns. These were all white, unmarried, native-born Americans, doing the same job—teaching. None of them smoked or drank alcohol; all had the same diet and were equally free from the stresses of family or business life. But in spite of their similar life-styles, by the age of forty-five the nuns could expect to live an average of five and a half years longer than the monks. In fact, the difference in life-expectancy between the sexes in this group, who did not indulge in any of the excesses of modern living, was actually greater than in the general American population at the time. This may seem very unfair to non-smoking teetotallers who thought they might be notching up some extra years by their abstemiousness—especially strong-minded husbands who were hoping to steal a march on wives who smoke and drink. It means that we must once again turn to the biological differences between the sexes for an explanation of why men and women differ in their susceptibility to disease and in their ability to survive.

Various theories have been put forward and, as you might expect, it looks as though chromosomes and sex hormones are involved. So far as inherited diseases and childhood infections are concerned, the answer appears to lie in the twenty-third pair of chromosomes, where the presence or absence of a Y chromosome determines a person's sex. Unlike the Y chromosome, which carries little if any genetic information and whose only positive effect is to lead to maleness, the larger X chromosome contains a lot of information about how we develop. For example, its instructions can affect the colour of the eyes, composition of the blood and skin texture. Occasionally, the X chromosome is flawed: it may contain too little information for a certain part of the body to develop properly, or perhaps the message is jumbled up. When this happens, all is lost for the male. He has only one X, and to the extent that it is at fault, some aspect of his development must necessarily be faulty. His body has no choice but to obey the faulty instructions on his single X chromosome, and as a result he is born with an abnormality. But females have a second X, carrying duplicate information, and so long as this is not damaged in the same way, it will be able to supply the relevant information in the correct form, and thus cancel out the effects of the defective chromosome. A female only suffers if both her X chromosomes have identical faults. Since they come from two different donors (her two parents), the odds against this happening are obviously much greater than the chances of the male's single X being flawed. There are a number of what are known as X-linked diseases, including colour-blindness, haemophilia, rickets, diabetes, immunoglobin deficiency and hyperthyroidism, all of which are more common amongst boys than amongst girls. Colour-blindness, for example, affects more than one man in twelve but less than one woman in a hundred. However, when a man is colour-blind, it is always as a result of receiving a faulty X chromosome from his mother. A woman who is a carrier has an even chance of passing it on to her child who, if male, will inevitably be colour-blind.

The X chromosome may also be responsible for regulating the antibodies which fight off infection. Infections rarely prove fatal now that antibiotics are available. But when deaths do occur it is usually in the first year of life, when boys are more likely to die than girls. Some scientists have suggested that the extra genes provided by a second X chromosome give women a chemical back-up system which men lack. This may help to keep women's bodies on an even keel chemically, and hence make them less vulnerable than men to all kinds of biochemical disturbance. The reason for thinking that sex chromosomes can affect the balance of the whole body is that when there is something wrong with a baby's sex chromosomes, not only its sexual development but also its intelligence and general health tend to be affected.

This line of reasoning is pleasantly straightforward, but unfortunately it is incompatible with a second, equally compelling hypothesis which has been put forward to answer another of the questions raised by the genetic differences between males and females: given that women have two X chromosomes, and men have only one, why aren't the two sexes more different? Many biologists believe that the best way to explain this is to make the assumption that a woman's second X chromosome is inactive, in the sense that the information it contains is not acted upon. But the theory we have been discussing assumes that it *is* active. Both theories cannot be right: at present, however, we simply don't know which needs to be replaced.

As for sex hormones, if they are involved in the differences between the reactions of the two sexes to disease, it is not at all certain what the connection is. Doctors now agree that there is something about the female sex hormone *oestrogen* which gives women extra protection against some of the diseases that seem to favour men as their victims. This is why the incidence of heart disease in women suddenly rockets after the menopause, when production of the sex hormones drops. Oestrogens also seem to protect against psychosis: schizophrenic symptoms are exacerbated in premenstrual women (when there are low levels of oestrogen), and women become more vulnerable to schizophrenia after the menopause. But during pregnancy, when oestrogen levels are high, there is relative freedom from relapse.

While women are protected by their sex hormones, it looks as if men may be killed off by theirs. In support of this suggestion, there is some evidence that men who are given extra male hormones are more likely to die from an early heart attack. This ties in with the results of rather a bizarre piece of research, which relates to the days when being a patient in a mental hospital was a more hazardous business than it is today. Examination of the medical records of one such hospital in the US shows that male patients who had been castrated tended to live an average of thirteen years longer than those who had not. It is difficult to know how much weight we should attach to this evidence, since all the patients, whether their genitals were intact or not, tended to die much younger than people in the general population and from atypical causes. But it is at least suggestive that men deprived of their main source of sex hormones may live longer than those who are not.

The reason why

It seems clear that the physical differences between men and women go far beyond what is necessary for sexual reproduction. Not only do men have distinctive genitals, they are also designed for a shorter though perhaps more physically active life than women. At first sight, this doesn't seem to be an ideal arrangement for either sex. Men often drop dead while still in their physical prime, whereas women are not only undervalued on account of their 'inferior' physique, but are also condemned to spend their final years without the comfort of a familiar partner. It also looks as though a basic biological principle is being infringed: since men and women share the same environment, they ought to be physically similar. So what is Dame Nature up to? The most plausible answer to this question is that she is arranging things in accordance with the most important of all biological principles, the survival of the species.

Two conditions have to be met if the species is going to survive. A sufficient number of people must produce babies, and these babies must survive long enough and in good enough health to reproduce themselves when their turn comes. The first of these conditions needs the co-operation of both sexes, which is why both men and women have a sex drive and—according to some but not all experts—an innate desire to have children. Until quite recently, the second condition could be met only if women were prepared to supply their milk to sustain babies in the first months of life. But once a child has been conceived, it can reach maturity without any further male assistance. So only women are essential at this stage.

Nature may forcibly coerce women into co-operating in this matter via the influence of her sex hormones (we shall look at the evidence for the existence of a mothering-instinct in Chapter 6). But whether or not this is the case, the invention of powdered milk for babies has not altered the fact that the task of bringing up and caring for children still almost invariably falls to women, with occasional assistance from men. Since most women have children by men roughly the same age as themselves and a woman's child-bearing days generally come to an end by her early fifties, this means that most men have completed their contribution to the continuation to the species in their mid or late fifties. After this, nature has no particular interest in a man's survival. Indeed, she may think him a positive liability, because the food he eats might otherwise go to someone still involved in the process of reproduction or child-rearing.

A woman's position is very different. Her role as child-rearer makes her a vital link in the chain which ensures that the species will not die out until her last child has reached the age when it can fend for itself. She must therefore be kept alive that much longer.

This has been used to explain the last of the physical differences between men and women. Like so many other biological explanations, it now sounds out of date. No doubt it made very good sense for primitive societies whose daily concerns were getting sufficient food and staying alive, but surely we could (and often do) organize things differently now. For example, many people now believe that children do not have to be brought up by their mothers or even by other women. We shall see in Chapter 6 that alternative arrangements can work satisfactorily. Advances in medical science may also go some way towards narrowing the gap between the sexes in their susceptibility to illness and in life-expectancy. And as more women enter the 'man's world' and the difference in life-styles diminishes, we can expect the female mortality rate to approach that of men. But biology is a power-ful force for conservatism, and I have the feeling that these differences—though they may be reduced—are no more likely to disappear altogether than any of the other physical differences between men and women.

3

CREATURES OF
EMOTION

Women—the plural of whim.

Anonymous

When the song-writer Frank Loesser described women as perpetual emotion machines, he was expressing one of the most
powerful of all the popular beliefs about femininity. If you turn
back to Table 1 on page 10, you will see that we also believe that
women cry very easily and are incapable of hiding their emotions;
that they are subjective rather than objective, illogical and unable
to separate feelings from ideas; and that they are very excitable in
a minor crisis and have feelings which are very easily hurt. The
portrait of a typical woman which this list paints is not a flattering one, and remember that this is how both men and women see
her.

In this chapter, we are going to examine how accurate the
picture is. Are women really at the mercy of the feelings of their
hearts, while men follow the reasons provided by their heads? If
so, is there something about female biology which makes women
like this, or do they just learn that this is how they are expected
to behave? And if men do show fewer signs of emotion, is it
because a man actually feels less than a woman or because he has
been taught that it is unmanly (or just bad tactics) to allow his
upper lip to unstiffen?

First, we have to decide what being emotional means. According to the dictionary, emotions are strong feelings. So to be
emotional is simply to have strong feelings. But we have to find
some way of measuring how emotional a person is before we can
say that he or she is more emotional than someone else, and this
is much more difficult. The problem is that although we all know

how *we* feel when we are angry or afraid, happy or jealous, we can never know directly what someone else is feeling. Since we cannot get inside another person's skin to feel what they are feeling, we can never be sure that two people who say they are angry are actually feeling the same, which makes it difficult to say that one person is more or less emotional than another. This is the main difficulty about studying emotion, and no amount of experimental ingenuity can really solve it. So in trying to decide whether women really are more emotional than men, most of the time we shall have to rely on indirect and often rather ambiguous evidence.

Measuring emotion

Scientists have three ways of measuring emotion. The first is simply to observe what people do over a period of time, making a note whenever they show what looks like emotional behaviour and labelling it as one emotion or another. This method has been used most often with children, whose tears, temper tantrums, joy and elation are usually quite easy to recognize. But it is not a truly objective procedure, because observers have to decide on the meaning of what a child is doing, and their interpretation may be influenced by their own prejudices. Suppose, for example, they believe that boys are more aggressive than girls. If a child is seen to beat its hands together, this may be recorded as a sign of repressed aggression in a boy but as an expression of pleasure in a girl. Good observers are alert to this danger and make every effort to be as objective as possible. But observing others is not the ideal way to study something so private as emotional feelings, especially when dealing with adults who have learned to hide what they are feeling.

Another way of setting about it is to ask people to record their own emotions, by getting them to rate how they feel at a given moment. They are given a list of adjectives describing various emotional states (angry, sad, happy and so on), and asked to tick the point on a seven-point scale ranging between 'very' and 'not at all' which best describes how each adjective applies to them at that moment. These *adjective check-lists* are quite an effective means of seeing how a person's feelings change from one day to the next, or of establishing the effect of some experimental task on their mood. But they are not much help in deciding whether one person is more or less emotional than another, because we can never be sure that feeling 'very sad' means the same thing to different people. A very reserved person may have suffered the most appalling tragedy. But you would never guess it from their response to an adjective check-list, even though you might think you could prove that they were deluding themselves, if there were some more reliable way to measure emotion.

In fact, there *is* a more objective way of measuring emotion. When we experience an emotion such as fear or anger, the feeling is accompanied by certain physiological changes—including changes in the balance of our hormones, the body's unconscious control system—which can be measured in samples of urine or blood. We can't tell what particular emotion a person is feeling by measuring their hormone balance, but it does give us objective and unbiased proof that they have experienced *some* emotion. It is therefore an improvement on both the other methods, and it also provides a basis for saying that one person is more emotional than another. Measuring hormonal change is as close as we are likely to come to getting inside someone else's skin, and we shall see later that it tells us something rather unexpected about the different ways in which men and women react to danger and uncertainty.

Although any strong feeling counts as an emotion, when people call women emotional they usually have in mind only the negative aspects of emotion. They mean that women cry more, and that they are more anxious and easily upset. But is this true? So far as crying goes, if you select a group of men and women at random and ask them how often they have wept in the last month, you will almost certainly find that the women have cried more often than the men. But if you were to observe babies or children at a nursery school, you would find something very different—there would probably be no difference between the sexes, but if either cried more, it would be the boys. So the reason why adult women cry more than men must lie somewhere between infancy and adulthood, or in adulthood itself.

Of course, it is partly a question of how children are brought up. Boys and girls are both told that crying is babyish, but boys are also taught that it is unmanly. Girls, on the other hand, may learn that crying can help them get their own way, and that tears are an acceptable part of the feminine, but not the masculine, armoury. As one (no doubt male) wit put it: if at first you don't succeed, cry, cry and cry again. The fact that adult women cry more often than men may also have something to do with their biology—some women are more prone to tears when their hormone levels fall at the end of the menstrual cycle than at other times of the month—and it may be a reflection of the different lives they lead: perhaps women have more to cry about than men. We shall come back to both these suggestions.

Two other pieces of evidence are often put forward to support the idea that women are more emotional than men. When adults are asked to describe themselves by using adjective check-lists or by filling in personality questionnaires, women generally emerge as more anxious, moody and emotional than men. The same applies to children, and when teachers are consulted, they say that the girls in their classes are more timid and anxious than the boys. But the odd thing is that although children and teachers are agreed on this, they may well be wrong. When researchers observe children they find no difference in timidity between the sexes. For example, girls starting at nursery school show no more distress when their mother leaves, and they are no less courageous than boys when confronted with a frightening new experience like having to walk along a narrow plank. So although girls are expected—and expect themselves—to be more easily frightened than boys, they don't actually seem to behave more fearfully. Why is this? The most obvious explanation is that by the time she is old enough to answer a personality questionnaire, a girl has been taught that to be feminine is to be fearful. A boy may be just as easily frightened—as observational studies have shown—but he has already learned that it would be unmanly to own up to his fears. This suggests that boys are less truthful when answering personal questions about themselves, and at least one researcher has found that boys are more often caught out by trick questions designed to see if the questionnaire is being answered honestly.

In the same way, adult men may be more reluctant than women to admit to fears which they think are 'neurotic', and this perhaps explains why they get lower anxiety scores on self-rating tests. But this is not the only reason to be suspicious about the evidence of personality questionnaires, especially when we are trying to decide whether boys are less anxious than girls. Among the questions used to measure anxiety are: 'Do you get scared when you have to walk home alone at night?' and 'When you are home alone and someone knocks at the door, do you get worried feelings?' Since little girls will have been warned on many occasions of the danger of being molested, these questions are almost guaranteed to elicit an anxious response from them. Many of the items in children's personality questionnaires fall into this category, while few relate to boys' special fears—for example, seeming cowardly to his peers, or being humiliated in public. So it may well be that the tests are constructed so as to make girls appear more anxious and fearful than boys. Adult questionnaires have the same fault: most of the items contributing to the anxiety score concern situations which women have good reason to find more frightening than men do, and very few questions relate to situations which involve particularly masculine fears. All in all, the fact that women get higher anxiety scores on personality tests is a flimsy basis for claiming that they are more emotional than men.

But there is another piece of evidence which many people think clinches the argument. People suffering from neurosis have intense and irrational feelings, and it is generally accepted that women are more susceptible than men to psychosomatic illness and other forms of neurotic disorder. But it is not neurotic to be emotional, nor is it necessarily irrational. On the contrary, negative emotions like fear are essential to our well-being since they stop us doing things we might afterwards regret, and force us to acknowledge the existence of problems we need to solve, while positive emotions like happiness are what make life worth living. But excessive emotionality is a sign that all is not well—for example, fears which get out of hand become phobias, and wild swings between elation and depression are a symptom of mania.

So the argument runs as follows: too much emotion means neurosis, women are more likely to be diagnosed as neurotic than men, therefore women must be more emotional than men. It sounds convincing, but there are complications. The first stems from a recent study which showed that doctors, like the rest of us, have different expectations about the two sexes, and that this affects their diagnosis. The investigators found that, confronted with exactly the same set of ambiguous symptoms in two patients, doctors were more likely to label them psychosomatic in a woman and physical in a man. So we obviously have to be cautious about clinical diagnosis as a measure of the incidence of psychosomatic disorders in men and women. Further evidence of medical thinking on this subject comes from the results of a survey of American doctors which found that their idea of a 'normal' woman coincided to a large extent with their description of someone suffering from clinical depression!

A diagnosis of a 'mental' illness such as depression carries with it a much greater load of messages and judgements than something like tonsillitis. It is therefore revealing to look at what counts as mental illness. Alcoholism, and the personality disorders more often displayed by men, do not. By contrast, doctors seem more willing to describe common female conditions as mental illness. In 1987, the American Psychiatric Association approved the inclusion of premenstrual syndrome in its official diagnostic manual, which would result in it being classified as a mental illness. If a woman is more likely to be labelled and treated as mentally ill, then the idea of women as more physically and emotionally vulnerable is reinforced.

Pessimism about women is not a new phenomenon in the medical profession. In 1900, the President of the American Gynaecological Society became positively poetic when asked to summarize the 'scientific' evidence on the subject of feminine weakness. A young woman's life, he suggested,

is battered and forever crippled in the breakers of puberty; if it crosses those unharmed and is not dashed to pieces on the rock of childbirth, it may still ground on the ever-recurring shallows of menstruation, and lastly, upon the final bar of the menopause ere protection is found in the unruffled waters of the harbour beyond the reach of sexual storms.

Around this time there was a great increase in the number of female nervous complaints diagnosed. Doctors suggested that this was due to the increased mental activity of women, which was assumed to put an additional strain on their already delicate nervous systems! So much for the calm objectivity of the voice of medical science!

Nevertheless, if you look at studies which compare the mental health of married men and married women, you will find that almost twice as many women as men have neurotic symptoms. Part of the difference may be explained by doctors' prejudices, and the fact that women are more prepared to admit to problems. But there does seem to be a genuine difference between the sexes in their response to stress, and it is women who are more likely to become neurotic and very emotional. And it is not just that women are more prone to the emotional, effective symptoms of mental illness. A recent Australian study shows that the sex difference is no less marked for somatic (physical) symptoms. However, this does not necessarily mean that women are more susceptible to stress than men. Equally debilitating conditions like alcoholism are much more common amongst men, and who is to say whether a neurotic woman or an alcoholic man is the more emotional? It may just be that the two sexes have different escape routes when life becomes too much for them.

However, there is some evidence that the difference is diminishing. An upsurge in alcohol consumption amongst women has been one of the most striking social trends of recent years. In Britain, for example, criminal offences related to drunkenness committed by women doubled between 1967 and 1976, while the number of women admitted to mental hospitals for treatment for alcoholism tripled between 1964 and 1975. And although it is often assumed that men and women differ not only in their proneness to mental disorder but also in the causes which trigger it, a recent Canadian study found a remarkable similarity in the pattern of events in their lives (for example, the loss of a parent before reaching maturity, and marital problems) which makes both sexes more vulnerable to clinical depression.

Many people have offered explanations for the fact that twice as many women as men in Western industrialized countries suffer from neuroses like depression. A popular theory is that there are some aspects of a woman's biology which make her more vulnerable to these forms of mental illness. A woman seems to be more at risk from depression during particular times of life when hormonal changes are taking place, like the days and weeks following childbirth or the menopause. Depression and irritability are common premenstrual symptoms, and oral contraceptives are said to precipitate depression in some women. All this lends support to the idea that women are vulnerable to disturbances of mood triggered by chemical cycles over which they have no control.

However, we must not overlook the fact that hormonal changes in women happen at times of life when other important changes are taking place. Becoming a mother, for instance, brings with it a heavy burden of responsibility and often demands dramatic alterations in life-style. It could be these sorts of disruptions which contribute to depression, rather than hormonal changes. Similarly, it is unlikely that menopausal depression is hormonally caused, since hormone replacement therapy has little or no effect on mid-life depression in women.

In fact, there is one striking feature about women's susceptibility to neurotic illness: it mainly affects married women aged between twenty and forty, who are at home caring for young children. Contrary to what many people believe, up to this age single women are very much less likely to become severely neurotic not only than married women, but also than men, married and single. This is part of an intriguing but little-discussed difference between the sexes. Whereas married men tend to be healthier and to have better jobs than single men at all ages, the opposite is true for women—perhaps there is more truth in the feminist axiom that a woman without a man is like a fish without a bicycle than in the traditional view that women need men in the same way that men need jobs! Certainly, the fact that it is only married women who are particularly prone to neurosis seems to suggest that being a mother and housewife rather than being a woman is what leads to the situation which has prompted one cynical observer to describe a woman's life as not so much a bed of roses, more a bed of neuroses.

What is not clear is whether it is being unmarried that protects young women from mental illness, or that unmarried women of this age are more likely to have a job than those who are married. It is certain that a woman's role and social position generally change more on marriage than her husband's, which may be why being married does not in itself offer a psychological advantage to women as it apparently does to men. According to the results of a recent British study, women who are both married and in employment are particularly well protected against symptoms of depression. It may also be that the protection marriage offers men operates only when their wives are not working: what keeps them out of hospital may simply be that, compared with single men, they are better looked after at home!

The reason more women than men become depressed may simply be that they are more ruminative, tending to analyse their emotions and problems and their causes. Things go wrong for everybody, but how people deal with problems determines whether they become clinically depressed. The female style of brooding on misfortunes may amplify depression, making it harder to snap out of a low mood. On the other hand, men tend not to sit around talking about their problems, but are more likely to take some exercise or go to the pub. By distracting themselves, they avoid amplifying and prolonging the depressive episode. The active response to a low mood may be more adaptive on average than a less active, ruminative response.

There are other aspects of the different ways that men and women think which make women more vulnerable to depression. During their lives, women receive more 'helplessness training' than men, being taught to think that they have no control over what happens to them. Girls are encouraged to develop this attitude by their treatment both at home and at school. Parents tend to praise or criticize boys and ignore girls, and teachers pay more attention to boys' academic work and respond more to their misbehaviour. As a result, boys are trained to be self-reliant and active, girls to be dependent on others. Girls are more likely to attribute success to luck, and failure to lack of ability. If they think like this, it is not surprising that they are less likely to snap out of depression.

If the imbalance in the rate of neurotic disorders is the result of socialization factors like these, then we can expect it to decrease as women become more assertive and achieve a degree of control over their lives comparable to that of men. Even now there are certain groups of people where the numbers of men and women becoming depressed are equal. This tends to be in sections of society where gender differences do not necessarily mean role differences—for example, amongst students, or in higher-status career groups where women are behaving like men and not trying to balance domestic responsibilities with work.

Social influences also play a causal role in eating disorders like anorexia nervosa and bulimia nervosa. These show the greatest sex difference of all psychological disorders, with ten to twenty times as many women affected as men. People with eating disorders are abnormally preoccupied with their body shape and weight, which they try to correct by dieting, taking energetic exercise, vomiting after eating or taking laxatives. If this gets out of hand, the dieter can become dangerously thin.

If eating disorders are initiated by feeling too fat, and many more women than men have eating disorders, then presumably women are more likely to think that they are too fat. Why should this be? We saw in Chapter 1 that the media place women firmly in a decorative role, indicating that their central asset is beauty. Being thin is a central feature of the contemporary ideal of female attractiveness, and women are generally more dissatisfied with their body weight and shape than men. Pressures to be thin are present in early adolescence, and some girls start to diet when they are extremely young. But people have not always thought that slim women are the most attractive, as we can see from Romantic paintings of voluptuous Venuses.

It is a disturbing fact that over the last twenty years the average body size of Miss America contestants and of *Playboy* centrefolds has gone down, while the average weight for women under the age of thirty has increased. So while young women have become heavier, the beauty ideal for the same age group has become lighter. This means that women who have internalized society's message that they should care a great deal about how they look are more likely to regard themselves as overweight. As one psychologist put it, 'Being a woman today means feeling too fat.' These factors are so important that some psychologists argue that the increased incidence of mental disorders in women is all to do with the cultural pressure to be thin: women either succeed at losing weight and become anorexic, or fail to lose weight and become depressed!

In conflict with the social demands which make it more important for women than for men to be thin, there are biological factors which make this goal harder for women to attain. Men generally have a higher metabolic rate and so waste more food as heat rather than storing it as fat. This allows them naturally to assume a body that corresponds with society's ideal male figure. But women store a much higher proportion of fat, and this difference increases during their lifetime. An increase in female hormones seems to encourage the laying down of fat, perhaps because it provides a store of energy which can be called upon during childbirth or child-rearing.

Regardless of cultural or social factors, then, women are fatter than men, and not many women 'naturally' match the extremely thin ideal. Social pressures encourage women to diet, but this in turn makes the body more efficient, so it becomes easier to gain weight and harder to lose it. Because losing weight is such a challenge, a very strict diet commands respect, as well as having effects which are visible and highly valued. The pursuit of thinness thus has several rewards and offers a form of power and control. It may be for this important sense of power that an anorexic continues to diet and take energetic exercise despite having attained a dangerously low weight.

We have seen that although many more women than men suffer from psychological illnesses, this seems to be largely due to the conflicting demands placed on them by society, rather than because they are inherently more emotional. But the belief persists: in American TV programmes, woman characters are four times more likely to display emotional behaviour than their male counterparts. But so far as empirical evidence is concerned, there is surprisingly little support for the belief that women are the more emotional sex. According to the results of a large Californian survey, they are more prone to shyness, a condition which is usually assumed to spring from a variety of emotional causes ranging from fear of being rejected to a narcissistic preoccupation with oneself. But since the same investigation confirmed that shyness is a much less socially desirable quality amongst men than amongst women, it would be reasonable to assume that this finding reflects a weakness in questionnaires of the sort discussed earlier. Similar doubts must affect our interpretation of studies of anxiety amongst teenagers, including the recent survey of British secondary school pupils which found that adolescent girls are more often and more deeply troubled by social and family problems than boys are. Interestingly, this study found no sex difference in worries about personal adequacy, health or money.

When sex differences relating to the emotions do emerge in the laboratory, they tend to be associated with the more acceptable face of emotionality. For example, it has been found that women are significantly more affected by other people's emotions, a difference which seems to go back to the cradle, since baby girls are more often moved to tears than baby boys by the sound of another infant crying. Similarly, women have been found to be more sensitive at interpreting pictures of faces displaying basic emotions, and more facially expressive when asked to imagine themselves in situations associated with different emotions.

But this is not what most people have in mind when they say that women are the more emotional sex. They are thinking of the negative aspects of emotionality; and when asked why women should be more emotional than men, the usual reply is that it is inevitable—women are the victims of their monthly cycle. This is a claim we have to examine very closely, not only because it is so widely believed but also because, if it is true, it would seem to settle once and for all the question of whether or not women are more emotional than men.

The belief that there are days in the month when a woman

simply cannot be expected to cope is immensely attractive, not least because its applications are almost limitless. I have recently noticed it being used to justify such diverse measures as refusing promotion to an American woman police officer, continuing to deny women entry into the priesthood, and even—in an English court of law—as a successful defence against a charge of manslaughter. The implication of this legal decision is simple: premenstrual tension makes women mad. Or, as the widow of the victim in the case put it, 'Women can now use it as an excuse for anything.'

Not surprisingly, it is now regularly produced as a trump card by anyone who wants to justify the practice of paying women less than men for doing the same job. For some reason, the fact that men are more prone to virtually every type of incapacitating illness is rarely mentioned in this context. (Interestingly, British official statistics show that there is no difference between the sexes in absenteeism from work due to sickness.) It is also cited, along with the fact that women have babies, as sufficient justification for discriminating against women who try to enter certain of the professions. In fairness to men, it has to be admitted that it is not only wicked male employers who find the menstrual cycle a convenient excuse. Every woman knows that nothing silences male protests faster than a shy reference to 'that time of the month', and many women use this aspect of being female to get out of doing something they do not want to do.

Mood and the menstrual cycle

How important an influence is a woman's menstrual cycle on how she feels and what she can do? We shall wait until Chapter 4 to explore the effects of fluctuating hormones on intellectual ability. But even with simpler functions, there is an enormous gap between myth and reality. According to folklore, women should not go swimming during their period, and yet, as we saw in Chapter 2, an Olympic swimmer won three gold medals while in the middle of her period! Other myths affect us all: for example, investigators have discovered that half the men and women in a representative sample of people living in the San Francisco Bay area never have intercourse during a woman's period, though there is no medical reason for this abstinence. A host of similar myths surround the flow of menstrual blood in most societies, and even the word 'menstruation' seems too strong to be used in polite conversation. Instead, a variety of euphemisms are used, ranging from 'riding a white horse' to 'falling off the roof'. Some of these are not, strictly speaking, euphemisms at all, bearing in mind that a euphemism is a polite way of referring to something we find distasteful. Many English women talk about 'the curse', while French women are even ruder—they say, 'The English have arrived'!

The belief that women are at the mercy of their cycle is not just a popular belief. Many experts agree. According to one, the hormonal changes which occur during the week before she gets her period are responsible in women for such disasters as failing exams, battering babies, having motor accidents, committing suicide and even falling off tightropes. The same expert advises women not to plan dinner parties, go for interviews, sit exams or make hairdressers' appointments on these crucial days. Her advice is to spend as much of the time as possible in bed. In other words, she is telling women that for a quarter of their reproductive lives they are likely to be an emotional danger to themselves and to others. If she is right, we can hardly blame employers who refuse to treat women as men's equals.

But before trying to decide whether hormonal changes can really be blamed for all these misfortunes, we must establish what actually happens to a woman's hormones during her monthly cycle. A woman's reproductive cycle is a constantly changing cocktail of hormones. Four different hormones are involved in the process of developing a mature egg, releasing it from the ovary, preparing for its fertilization and then discarding it if it is not fertilized. But for the purpose of seeing how hormones influence a woman's behaviour and how she feels at different times of the month, we can simplify things by concentrating on just two of them—oestrogen and progesterone. Changes in the levels of these two hormones are shown in Figure 2.

At the beginning of each monthly cycle, the pituitary gland sends a chemical message to the ovaries to step up the production of oestrogen. This hormone is responsible for a rapid growth of cells in the lining of the uterus, and it also acts as a signal to the pituitary to release a different hormone which causes one of the follicles in the ovary to break and release an egg (ovulation). By the time ovulation occurs, in the middle of the cycle, the level of the oestrogen is falling, but the follicle that released the egg turns

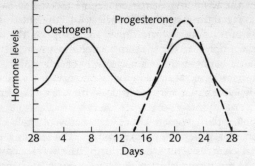

Figure 2. *Female hormone levels during the menstrual cycle (after Dalton, 1978)*

into a temporary gland and secretes progesterone. This is some-times called the pregnancy hormone, and it helps to prepare the lining of the uterus to receive the egg, in the event of the latter being fertilized. The production of oestrogen rises again to assist in this process, and both hormones are at a peak between the twenty-first and twenty-fourth days of the cycle, as the uterus waits expectantly for the fertilized egg. But if conception does not occur and the egg remains unfertilized, oestrogen and progesterone levels decline again, and a week later the egg and the now un-necessary extra lining of the womb are expelled from the body in the menstrual flow.

The idea that these changes inevitably make women behave more emotionally than men is an ancient one, but it was first aired in a medical journal in 1939, when two doctors published a report based on conversations with fifteen of their female patients. They suggested that women are at their happiest and most self-confident in mid-cycle, at the time of ovulation, but that they become tense, unstable and depressed in the week before and during menstruation, when hormone levels are declin-ing to their lowest point. This article gave folk wisdom scientific respectability, and it also sent medical researchers scurrying off to establish the symptomatology of a new syndrome which became known as premenstrual tension (PMT). Fifty years later, PMT is still shrouded in mystery. Almost all doctors accept that a sig-nificant number of women suffer regularly from a variety of physical ailments and feel low towards the end of their cycle, but there is very little else they agree about, and most of the important questions still have no answers. For example, the cause of PMT is disputed. If it stems from the drop in hormone levels, is it because this leads to a drop in the blood sugar level or is it due to a change in levels of the enzyme monoamine oxidase, which is known to affect the nervous system and to be linked with depression? Why are some women more affected by PMT than others, and what proportion of women suffer at all? Estimates vary enormously from 15 to 95 per cent.

Much of the uncertainty comes from the fact that doctors cannot reach agreement on the symptoms of PMT. Some think the syndrome should be confined to emotional symptoms such as irritability, depression, anxiety and hostility, while others have no hesitation about including physical complaints like headaches and backache, as well as unusually painful menstruation. According to a pamphlet published by Women's Health Concern, PMT has six major physical symptoms and ten psychological ones. But the pamphlet acknowledges that most sufferers will experience no more than three of them (depression, irritability and bloatedness).

So the answer to the question 'How many women suffer from PMT?' obviously depends on how you define the symptoms. It also depends on how you investigate the condition. Some researchers have given women a list of the symptoms believed to be part of the syndrome and asked them how many they themselves have experienced, while others have asked women to keep a daily diary describing how they felt, without specifying that they were interested in the menstrual cycle. Not surprisingly, these two approaches have produced very different results. Another source of confusion is the fact that some of the best-known studies of PMT were carried out on women receiving psychotherapy, whose emotional experience and fluctuations of mood are unlikely to be typical of women in general. These tend to be the studies which paint the blackest picture. At the other extreme, there are many studies which find little change in mood over the menstrual cycle.

One thing is absolutely certain. By no means all women suffer from PMT, which suggests that it may not after all be caused by hormonal changes. If it is not, the most likely cause is anxiety about the event of menstruation.

Whatever the immediate cause of menstrual anxiety, none of the symptoms of PMT is unique to the syndrome. They are all symptoms of stress, which has led some doctors to dismiss PMT as a convenient label which neurotic women have been encouraged to apply to a ragbag of aches, pains and misery which at any other time they would put down either to having had a difficult day at the office or to their rather neurotic temperament. I think this view is misguided, and that those who put it forward are displaying as great an ignorance of the facts about PMT as those who have gone overboard in the opposite direction.

For a start, it is by no means certain that women who suffer from severe PMT are generally more neurotic than those who do not. According to the results of a study carried out at one of the London teaching hospitals, women who become very anxious premenstrually show levels of anxiety indistinguishable from non-sufferers at other times of the month. The same study found a high correlation in almost half the cases investigated between how anxious a woman felt on Day 22 of her cycle and the level of progesterone in her blood: the more progesterone production had fallen, the more acute her anxiety. Other researchers have come up with completely contradictory results. They claim to have found a clear connection between general neuroticism and susceptibility to PMT, but no sign of any link between severity of symptoms and hormonal levels. The picture is further confused by a dispute about the effectiveness of hormone replacement therapy for PMT. If the cause of the syndrome is a drop in hormone levels, we might expect it to be alleviated by artificially boosting the hormones. And so it is—but not for all sufferers.

Where neuroticism is concerned, we have to be very careful about drawing causal inferences even from those studies in which it has been found that PMT sufferers are generally more neurotic than non-sufferers. It might be that a neurotic disposition makes women more prone to PMT, but it is no less likely that suffering from PMT causes them to become more neurotic. More important than any of these disputes between researchers is the fact that pain is equally distressing whether its origins are physical, psychological or a mixture of the two.

But it is clearly wrong to suggest that all women should expect to be incapacitated during the last week of their cycle, and that those who do not experience any of the symptoms of PMT are unfeminine freaks. As a matter of fact, there is some evidence that successful career women have fewer menstrual problems than those who play the traditional wife-and-mother role. But we also know that women in some primitive tribes have no menstrual problems at all. Indeed, they sometimes have no idea what visiting anthropologists are talking about when they ask about this. There is an instance where the women of a tribe experienced no problems until the arrival of Western female missionaries, when suddenly they started to report the familiar symptoms. This is a fascinating finding, because it supports the idea that the effects of menstruation vary not only according to what sort of person you are, but according to what you expect to happen. In other words, a woman's experience of menstruation— and whether or not she experiences PMT—is not just a matter of her hormones, or of the interaction between her hormones and her personality. It may also be greatly influenced by what she hears and reads about how it affects other people. Although the menstrual cycle is a biological phenomenon, the effect it has on an individual woman is at least partly decided by social factors.

Much of what I said earlier supports this view. We also know that the cycles of women who share flats or work closely together often become synchronized, which confirms that hormones are open to environmental influence and are not rigidly fixed by biology. This puts experts who write about PMT in a difficult position, because although their articles may ease the burden of women who already suffer from it, they may also increase the incidence of the condition if they give other women—and especially girls who are just reaching puberty—the impression that PMT is the norm. Similarly, mothers whose own experience of menstruation has been unpleasant may unintentionally make it more likely that their daughters will suffer as they do, if they allow their experience to affect what they tell their daughters about menstruation. And it is obviously essential that young girls should have this aspect of their biology explained to them sympathetically and in unfrightening terms, instead of being scared out of their wits by the inaccurate and exaggerated stories they hear from older girls in school cloakrooms. If a girl is told that menstruation is dirty, painful and debilitating, there is a good chance that this is how she will experience it. But if she has what is going on inside her body explained to her, and knows that having a period need not stop her dancing, making love or breaking Olympic records, she may never experience the misery of PMT or understand why 'the curse' got its name.

But what about those women who do suffer from PMT? Are they really destined to go through their reproductive lives failing exams, falling off tightropes and battering babies if they are rash enough to leave their beds during the week leading up to menstruation? Two different claims have been made about the effect which PMT has on the way a woman behaves. The first is that her work inevitably suffers, because she is too depressed and anxious to concentrate properly. A study carried out in the late 1950s claimed that more than a quarter of a group of English schoolgirls did less well in tests of academic work just before menstruation than in mid-cycle. However, most of the girls did equally well, and 17 per cent of them actually performed better in the premenstrual period. Moreover, later investigators have failed to find any evidence that women do worse in examinations at one time of the month than another. They may feel worse, but most researchers find that this does not actually affect their performance. For example, researchers at the University of California have monitored the examination performance of nearly 250 female medical and paramedical students throughout the course of a year. They found no sign of any link between a woman's performance and the stage of the menstrual cycle she had reached.

The second claim is that women become more dangerous—to themselves and to other people—in the week before menstruation. The evidence for this is more impressive. If menstruation had no effect on a woman's behaviour, we should expect about a third of the misfortunes she suffers to occur during menstruation and the premenstrual period. In fact, half of the women who commit crimes, have serious road accidents, require a home visit from their GP, commit suicide and are admitted to hospital suffering from psychiatric disorders are in this phase of their cycle (with schizophrenia the figure is nearer two-thirds).

So for some women there is certainly a connection between time of the month and danger. However, we cannot make the inference that the events happen *because* of the time of the month. They may do, but the connection could be the other way round: after all, it is well established that a woman's period may be delayed by the tension that builds up with the anticipation of a stressful event. And even if we were certain that PMT was the cause of these misfortunes and misdemeanours, it has to be remembered that most women do not suffer from debilitating PMT. Moreover, a variety of treatments are available which can alleviate, or even eliminate, its effects in almost three-quarters of those who do suffer. Most of the treatments are based on hormone or vitamin replacement therapy, with counselling and psycho-therapy playing a useful supporting role, and two-thirds of the women who go for treatment have no serious symptoms six months later.

Finally, since our main interest is in the difference between men and women, it is also important to remember, when think-ing about the connection between hormonal fluctuations and the tendency to commit crimes or even suicide, that women commit far fewer crimes and are less likely to kill themselves than men, who have no hormone cycle to blame.

Or have they? I have written at some length about the menstrual cycle, partly because no book about the differences between men and women can ignore an event which every month reminds us that the two sexes are not the same biologically, and also because it is so often put forward as an explanation for the fact that women are more emotional than men. I hope that the evidence discussed so far will at least have planted a seed of doubt in your mind, both about the claim that women actually are more emotional than men, and about the suggestion that it is the hormonal fluctuations of the menstrual cycle that make them so. I do not share Frank Loesser's view of women as perpetual emotion machines, and I am not at all certain that they are even cyclic emotion machines. Until now, my attack has been based on the observation that many women patently are not at the mercy of their hormones. Neither their behaviour nor their feelings are subject to fluctuations which affect their ability to work and function satisfactorily at all times of the month, and it may well be that women whose emotions go up and down with their hormones are the victims of social and cultural expectations as much as of female biology. But this is only half of the argument against the view that women must be more emotional than men because only they have fluctuating hormones.

Men and their hormones

We have known for many years that the amount of testosterone in a man's blood varies from day to day. But it has only recently occurred to anyone that these ups and downs might not be haphazard, but instead form a regular cycle, analogous to the female menstrual cycle. This possibility was first investigated by scientists at Stanford University in America, who took blood samples from a group of young men every other day for two months, and asked them to keep a diary of how they felt and what they did each day. Hormone levels were measured from the blood samples, and it turned out that 60 per cent of the men did indeed have a regular testosterone cycle, though the length of the cycle varied between one man and another, from eight to thirty days.

The researchers also found a striking link between how much testosterone a man had in his blood and the way he felt. In the group as a whole, a high level of testosterone tended to be accompanied by a feeling of depression. But there was a lot of individual variation. Although most of the men were more depressed when testosterone production was at its peak, some were more aggressive, and others felt more sexy. However, amongst the men who had a regular hormone cycle, there was a consistent link between testosterone level and some specific emotional feeling.

Other researchers have found the same thing, and it now seems that at least some men have a hormonal cycle no less regular—if less noticeable—than women's. Indeed, the testosterone cycles of some men have been found to coincide exactly with the menstrual cycle of the women they are living with. Men's other hormones also fluctuate quite regularly, and their muscles, too, go through a cycle of decline and rebuilding. Even their ability to appreciate musical pitch and tone declines and improves cyclically (as does a woman's), so it seems clear that men, like women, have their bodily ups and downs. And this is not all. When husbands and wives were asked in two recent studies to rate how they felt every day for a month, it turned out that the men's moods varied just as much as their wives', as can be seen from Figure 3.

Research on the male hormone cycle is still at the pioneering stage, and many questions remain unanswered. Why, for example, do only some men have a regular cycle, and what distinguishes those who do from those who do not? When the moods, and even the hormone levels, of a couple fluctuate in synchrony, who is in the driving seat and who the helpless passenger? Or is it just that both of them are responding to the same external stresses and strains? Finally, does the male hormone cycle serve any useful

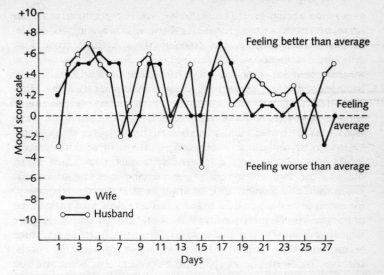

Figure 3. *Variation of mood of husband and wife over a month*

purpose? It certainly appears to be a much less powerful biological phenomenon than its female counterpart, but that it exists at all, albeit only in some men, is further proof that men and women are less different than we thought. From the point of view of trying to understand the emotional experience of the two sexes, perhaps the most interesting finding about the male cycle is that the same hormone—testosterone—is linked with different feelings in different men. When large amounts of testosterone are present, one man is depressed, another angry and a third feels the sap rising.

This may seem puzzling, but it is actually not at all inconsistent with what we know about the way in which what we feel is influenced by the state of our hormones. Unlike women, men rarely think about their hormones. As boys, they were not taken aside by their fathers and warned about the miseries of the testosterone cycle, and the chances are that they are quite unaware that there is such a thing, or that it might affect how they feel. When men *are* affected by their hormone cycle, the effect it is most likely to have on a man ignorant of its existence is simply to boost either the most important aspect of his personality or what-

ever mood he happens to be in. So we would expect it to make an
aggressive man more aggressive, and one who is being harassed by
overwork even more so. Of course, things might become very
different if someone were to invent a do-it-yourself testosterone
measurement kit, especially if at the same time articles started
to appear in men's magazines about something called the High
Testosterone Depression syndrome. Who knows? HTD might
become as feared as PMT, with men taking to their beds every
few weeks for fear of being a menace to themselves and to others!

On a more serious note, other experiments in which hormone
levels have been measured reveal a very important difference in
the way the two sexes react to emotionally arousing situations.
When men and women are placed under stress in the laboratory,
for example by being asked to carry out a complicated task under
noisy conditions, men are found to show a much greater physiological response—their blood sugar level and heart-rate change
much more than women's. But when we study adjective check-
lists which describe how people feel before and after being stressed
in this way, it looks as though the women have been more affected
consciously by the experience. So it seems that men and women
respond to emotion in different ways, women verbally and men
physiologically. And this difference is not just confined to the
laboratory. Stressful situations in real life, such as taking an
exam, competing at sport or driving a car also produce a greater
physiological response in men, though you would get the opposite
impression from hearing the two sexes talking about it. Perhaps
this is why it is so difficult to answer the question, Are women
more emotional than men? The truth of the matter is that emotion
affects men and women differently, and it is impossible to say
which sex is affected more.

Nor is it easy to decide which reaction to emotion is preferable.
The tendency of women to put their emotion into words may
have earned them an unenviable—and perhaps unjustified—
reputation as the more emotional sex, but it may have brought
them benefit in another way. By responding to stress and emotion
physiologically rather than verbally, men can disguise their
feelings, but only at a cost. The physiological response to stress
takes a toll on the body's resources if it occurs too often or for too
long, so the masculine way of dealing with emotion may contribute to the fact that men are more prone to disease and tend to
die younger than women. A man's upper lip may be stiff, but so

is the price he pays to keep it that way. Because he is used to bottling up his feelings and unaccustomed to talking about emotional matters, a man who is under severe pressure may be unwilling to seek professional help until it is too late, which may contribute to the fact that more men than women often become alcoholic and commit suicide. But all is not lost for them. They could take a leaf out of the feminine book, and learn to become more emotionally expressive. There is some evidence that a man who does so can hope to reduce his physiological response to emotion, to the benefit of his health.

The dangers associated with the feminine way of handling emotion are rather different. A woman who needs an audience to listen to her analysing her emotions runs the risk of becoming over-dependent on other people, and becoming depressed as she realizes the extent to which she relies on them. Some doctors believe that one of the reasons why women are more than twice as likely to become clinically depressed as men is that they tend to live their lives too much through other people.

Women may now be faced with a new danger. As increasing numbers of them make successful careers in jobs which were once thought to be suitable only for men, there are signs that women are starting to react to stress and emotion in the masculine way, with the potentially harmful physiological stress response. For example, evidence from the American National Institute of the Heart, Lungs and Blood indicates that working women with two or more children now have the same incidence of stress-related heart disease as their male counterparts. And, as confirmation of what has just been suggested, the women at risk were found to be less likely to display overt anger than either non-working wives or men.

The extent to which individual men and women show the extreme masculine and feminine patterns of emotional reaction may well be a function of the extent to which they accept—and try to live according to—the traditional sex-role stereotypes. It may also be the case that conforming too rigidly to these stereotypes restricts our ability to cope with certain important areas of life, and so makes us more vulnerable to breakdowns of different kinds. In some situations we need to be sympathetic and comforting, but on other occasions we have to be assertive and independent. It is therefore an advantage for both men and women not to be tied too rigidly to the traditional stereotypes,

Table 2 *How androgynous are you?*

On a scale of 1 to 7 indicate how well each of the following characteristics describes you: 1 means the item is never or almost never true, and 7 means that it is always or almost always true.

1. self-reliant
2. yielding
3. helpful
4. defends own beliefs
5. cheerful
6. moody
7. independent
8. shy
9. conscientious
10. athletic
11. affectionate
12. theatrical
13. assertive
14. flatterable
15. happy
16. strong personality
17. loyal
18. unpredictable
19. forceful
20. feminine
21. reliable
22. analytical
23. sympathetic
24. jealous
25. has leadership abilities
26. sensitive to the needs of others
27. truthful
28. willing to take risks
29. understanding
30. secretive
31. makes decisions easily
32. compassionate
33. sincere
34. self-sufficient
35. eager to soothe hurt feelings
36. conceited
37. dominant
38. soft spoken
39. likeable
40. masculine
41. warm
42. solemn
43. willing to take a stand
44. tender
45. friendly
46. aggressive
47. gullible
48. inefficient
49. acts as a leader
50. childlike
51. adaptable
52. individualistic
53. does not use harsh language
54. unsystematic
55. competitive
56. loves children
57. tactful
58. ambitious
59. gentle
60. conventional

Scoring

(a) Add up your ratings for items 2, 5, 8, 11, 14, 17, 20, 23, 26, 29, 32, 35, 38, 41, 44, 47, 50, 53, 56 and 59, and divide the sum by twenty. This is your Femininity Score.

(b) Add up your ratings for items 1, 4, 7, 10, 13, 16, 19, 22, 25, 28, 31, 34, 37, 40, 43, 46, 49, 52, 55 and 58, and divide the sum by twenty. This is your Masculinity Score.

(c) Subtract your Masculinity Score from your Femininity Score, and multiply the result by 2.322 (this approximates the score derived by more complicated statistical procedures). If the result is greater than 2.025, you are sex-typed in the feminine direction. If it is smaller than −2.025, you are sex-typed in the masculine direction. A score between 1 and 2.025 is considered 'near feminine' and a score between −2.025 and −1 to be 'near masculine'. A score between −1 and 1 means you are not sex-typed in either direction: you are androgynous.

Source: after Bem, 1974.

and to be able to respond with the characteristics usually associated with the opposite sex when the occasion demands it. Researchers studying Californian students found that about half of them showed a predominance of the characteristics popularly associated with their own sex, 15 per cent showed more of the traits associated with the opposite sex, and about 35 per cent scored equally highly on both masculine and feminine traits, which is known as being *androgynous*. It has been reported that androgynous people are less likely to become mentally ill and better able to handle marital problems than those who conform rigidly to the stereotypes, though these findings have been disputed. You can see how androgynous you are by taking the test in Table 2. You may be interested to know that highly sex-typed people also tend to be less intelligent and creative.

Perhaps the most important message which comes out of the research into sex differences in emotion is that men and women have something to learn from each other when it comes to dealing with emotion. But it is vital that we should not just pick up each other's worst habits. I am not suggesting that women should try to become more aggressive or that men should suppress any feelings of competitiveness, but rather that it is undesirable that either should find themselves in a situation where they cannot do what they know is right for fear of being thought unmasculine or unfeminine.

4

BRAIN AND INTELLECT

A great mind must be androgynous, having the characteristics
of both sexes.

Samuel Taylor Coleridge

Are men more intelligent than women? For thousands of years,
the answer to this question seemed so obvious that no one
bothered to discuss it, let alone ask why it might be so. Of course,
men were more intelligent, just as of course the earth was flat. It
is only in the present century, however, that any attempt has
been made to check whether men actually are the more intelligent sex. A hundred years ago, it hardly seemed necessary,
since women made very little contribution to intellectual life and
virtually all jobs which called for thought were carried out by
men. Besides, there was no scientific way of measuring intelligence. So nineteenth-century scientists concentrated instead on
finding an explanation for the 'fact' that men were cleverer, and
the obvious place to look was the brain.

The brain

The first idea put forward was that men were cleverer because
they had bigger brains. It is true that the average new-born boy
has a greater brain weight and head circumference than the average
new-born girl. But this is only to be expected because he is generally bigger and heavier than she is. Anyway, brain size cannot tell
us much about intelligence: Anatole France's brain weighed only
35 ounces, at a time when the weight of the average European
man's brain was 59 ounces, but this did not stop him becoming
one of Europe's leading writers.

But men's brains are not just bigger than women's; they are proportionally heavier, even when the overall difference in body weight has been accounted for. This relative difference in boys' and girls' brain weights appears when they are about two years old, and gradually increases. By the time they are adults, men's brains are on average 15 per cent larger then women's—about twice the difference in average body size between the two sexes. But even the ratio of brain to body size tells us little about intelligence—if it did, we would have to expect not only dolphins, but also marmosets and even some strains of mice, to outshine us intellectually, since these species all have a more impressive brain to body-weight ratio than we have.

So this idea was quietly buried, only to be replaced by the suggestion that men are more highly developed in those parts of the brain specifically concerned with intellectual activity. In the 1870s, scientists believed that intellect was housed in the frontal lobes. Several neuro-anatomists claimed to have found that this area of the brain was bigger in men, and that women had larger parietal lobes. By the end of the century, they had changed their minds: they now thought that it was the parietal rather than the frontal lobes which were the seat of intellectual activity, and, as if by magic, neuro-anatomists suddenly began to find that the parietal lobes were larger in men. This about-turn is not much of an advertisement for the objectivity of scientists, and it probably came about as a result of those involved knowing the sex of the person whose brain they were dissecting and simply finding what they expected (and perhaps hoped) to find.

We saw in Chapter 1 that the default sex in mammals is female, and this is as true for the brain as for the rest of the body. Male hormones must be present very early in life to masculinize the brain as well as the genitalia. And when the brain is masculinized, so too is the behaviour. If scientists inject female monkey pups with male hormone, this alters the structure of the brain and induces specific masculine behaviours, like indulging in more rough-and-tumble play as infants, or more male-type sexual behaviour (mounting) when they become adults. In contrast, if a male monkey pup is deprived of male hormones his brain will not become masculinized. He will spend more time playing in a maternal way as an infant, and engage in female sexual behaviour when he grows up.

Researchers have investigated other examples of behaviours

where the males and females of a species differ, and tried to relate this to differences in the brain. For instance, in some types of songbird only the male sings, and brain areas mediating singing are larger in the male than in the female. Again, these areas, and the corresponding behaviours, can be manipulated by hormones. If female chaffinches or canaries are given testosterone, there is an alteration in the brain structure, and they can be made to sing. This is another example of the clear evidence of sex differences in the brain, which are influenced by hormones, and provide a biological basis for the different behaviours of the male and female.

But human beings are much more complex, and it is very difficult to find evidence of behavioural differences between men and women where the underlying brain mechanism and hormonal influences are clear. This is because both the behavioural and neurobiological levels at which these differences are studied in humans are too coarse. Complex cognitive processes will be determined by a network of neural structures. And even if we knew which neurobiological level to look at, the structures are hard to see clearly in tissue slices.

Scientists have therefore tried to start with something simpler than neural evidence of functional sex differences in cognition. The most successful investigations linking gender differences in behaviour to differences in the brain will be where the behaviour is simple, carefully defined and consistent from animal to animal. An obvious example is sexual behaviour. Many studies have together established that reproductive functions are influenced by a small area of the brain called the hypothalamus, so this would be a good place to start looking for differences in the brains of men and women.

Several investigations have reported sex differences in two of the four cell groups in a particular area of the hypothalamus. These nuclei are found to be over twice as large in men as in women. This area of the brain is known to influence maternal and sexual behaviour in several species of mammal, and is dependent on testosterone levels before and immediately after birth. It is not really surprising to find that we probably have a similar biological substrate for sexual drive as other mammals.

More interestingly, this may help in our understanding of sexuality. An American scientist has recently provided some fascinating new evidence in a study of the brains of homosexual men who have died of AIDS. He found that one of these nuclei in the hypothalamus in homosexuals has the anatomical form usually found in women. Perhaps this is why homosexuals, however frowned upon, are to be found in every human society—as a result of natural variations in brain structure and other biological factors which determine sexual preference. To find out more about how the structure of the brain might influence sexual preference, it would be interesting to study the brains of lesbians. But these are more difficult to obtain for research, since sexual orientation is rarely recorded in deaths from causes other than AIDS.

We have evidence of differences in the areas of the brains of men and women which are known to be related to sexual behaviour. It is much harder to find evidence of brain differences related to intelligence, which is difficult to define and measure. But lack of evidence has not prevented people in the past from having strong ideas about the difference in intellectual abilities between men and women. In the late nineteenth century, it was suggested that women's intellectual activity needed to be limited, because they required all their energy to develop their reproductive functions. Too much thinking, it was argued, could make women infertile, and thus endanger the future of the species! Such claims appeared even in reputable medical journals such as the *Lancet*, and they were seized on by those who wanted to deny further education to women. The spirit of the times can be gauged from the following observation made by Herbert Spencer: 'Most of the flat-chested girls who survive their high-pressure education are incompetent to bear a well-developed infant and to supply that infant with natural food.'

Only in the present century has it become possible to measure how intelligent a person is with any reliability and objectivity. Belatedly, educationalists began to suspect that many children from poor homes were being prevented from fulfilling their intellectual potential because their parents could not afford to keep them at school. So the search began for some means of assessing native brightness, in order that children most likely to benefit from extended formal schooling could be selected for education at the state's expense. Thus was born the IQ test, a far from perfect instrument for assessing a person's intellectual capacity, but the best we have, and still our major source of information about the intelligence of individual children and adults. Although it was initially greeted with some scepticism, IQ testing offered far too many exciting possibilities for it to be confined for long to the purpose for which it was designed. The Army, for example, were quick to spot that IQ tests for adults could help them recognize potential officer material, and it was not long before such a test was developed and in use.

There are now a number of tests designed to measure adult intelligence, so it ought to be fairly easy to decide whether men are really more intelligent than women. There is one problem, however. During the first part of this century, when most of the major IQ tests were being constructed, the attitude of scientists towards sex differences in intelligence was no more open-minded than that of their predecessors, the only difference being that they were now convinced that no such differences existed! So whenever the early IQ testers found that one sex did consistently better than the other on an IQ test item, they simply discarded that item, on the grounds that there must be something wrong with it. Fortunately, not all IQ tests have this flaw, and we now know the answers to many of the questions about the intellectual abilities of the two sexes.

Equal but different

The most important fact is that men are not more intelligent than women. The average man's overall IQ score is indistinguishable from that of the average woman. The same holds for children, except that there may be a small difference between the sexes under the age of seven, when girls get slightly higher scores than boys. However, some of the studies in which this has been found have been carried out on children of less than one year, when all that can be measured is perceptual and motor ability, which may not tell us anything about a child's later intellectual ability. Assessing infants' intelligence is an unrewarding task, because it is not easy to engage their attention (in one study, the investigators rated babies as alert on only 77 out of the 5,400 observations they made!). This means, of course, that the babies who do co-operate may not be typical, so studies of babies' 'intelligence' are of doubtful value. Moreover, when a sex difference is found, it may be due to the fact that girls are relatively more mature physically. Generally, baby boys and girls are very similar in what they can learn, remember and perceive. There are sex differences in the various sensory modalities: girls are slightly more sensitive to smells and to touch, as well as to auditory stimulation, and more girls than boys can sing in tune. Men on the other hand, have a greater average visual acuity. However, it is safe to say that the two sexes are born roughly similar in general intelligence, and remain so throughout their lives.

Although the average IQ scores of the two sexes are not different, many textbooks claim that there is a significant difference in the *range* and amount of variety in their scores. According to the provocatively entitled Mediocrity of Women hypothesis, the cleverest and most stupid people tend to be men, while women's IQ scores all fall in the middle range. If this is true, it means that most geniuses will be men, and so will most idiots. A number of ingenious explanations have been put forward to account for the mediocrity of women, including the suggestion that the Y chromosome makes men more variable in intelligence as well as in other respects. But the ingenuity would have been better spent thinking of ways to test the truth of the original observation. Although boys and men do seem to be over-represented at the bottom of the IQ ladder (more males are classified as educationally and severely subnormal), the two highest scores ever obtained at the major IQ testing centre in the US were both obtained by girls, who scored 200 and 201 respectively. At present, the Mediocrity of Women is no more than a hypothesis.

Nevertheless, there may be a difference in type of intelligence between the sexes. Many investigators have reported that women tend to get slightly higher scores than men on those sections of IQ tests consisting of verbal items, while the reverse holds for visual-spatial items. According to these researchers, that the two sexes end up with very similar overall IQ scores simply reflects the fact that most tests have a roughly equal number of the two sorts of questions. (Remember that IQ tests were designed so that no overall difference was shown between men and women.)

Items in IQ tests which measure verbal ability cover many different aspects of language. A child might be asked to name an object or be tested for the size of his vocabulary, while adults are assessed on such skills as the ability to understand a complicated passage of prose or to solve a logical conundrum. The ability to visualize and manipulate objects in space is measured by tests like the one in Figure 4, in which you are shown a picture of an object (the one on the left of the row) and have to say which of a

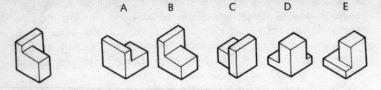

Figure 4. *Item from test for visual-spatial skill*

group of similar objects is the same as the original one, seen from a different angle (the answer is given at the end of this chapter).

Even if there is a sex difference in these two aspects of intelligence, we must be very careful what practical conclusions we draw from it. For example, although the average man may have a more highly developed visual-spatial sense than the average woman, this is absolutely irrelevant when it comes to making decisions about individual men and women, because the scores of the great majority of both men and women fall within the same range. Confronted by this situation, which is constantly cropping up in the study of sex differences, the correct strategy to follow is that adopted by Dr Johnson. The great lexicographer may have been a misogynist, but when asked whether he thought men were more intelligent than women, he had the good sense to reply: 'Which man? Which woman?' (When asked by a woman what difference there was between the sexes, he is alleged to have replied: 'I can't conceive, Madam; can you?')

In fact, something like a quarter of adult women do better than the average man on the visual-spatial questions of an IQ test. This means that we cannot predict anything about the ability of a particular man or woman simply on the basis of his or her sex. It would, for example, be totally wrong to give preference to a male candidate when choosing students for a course in architecture or engineering, on the grounds that success in these professions demands good visual-spatial ability, since you could never be sure that the individual in question would obtain a visual-spatial score which placed him in the ability range where men are more heavily represented than women.

What might make men superior at visual-spatial and women at verbal tasks? Before trying to answer this, we need to see when the difference first appears. As babies, girls show a greater interest in communicating, and most researchers agree that they learn to speak earlier than boys. By the age of three, 99 per cent of girls' speech is comprehensible, but it usually takes boys about a year longer. The age at which you learn to speak does not, it seems, predict intelligence—Einstein did not speak until he was five! Boys are more likely than girls to have reading problems—for some reason, the difference is much more marked in the US than Britain—but this may be primarily due to a difference in motivation. When they are interested in what they have to read, boys are found to perform much better, whereas girls seem to do equally well, irrespective of whether they find what they have to read interesting.

If there really is a sex difference in reading ability between young boys and girls, it may just reflect the developmental lag that was discussed in Chapter 2. Alternatively, it may be a side-effect of a sex difference in personality. Poor reading is associated with being impulsive, and there is evidence that boys are more impulsive, and girls more reflective, from a fairly early age.

It is tempting to see the sex difference in reading ability as part of something larger. Not only are young boys more affected by reading difficulties, but adult males are up to eight times more likely to suffer from stammering than females. Some writers have put these two findings together and presented them as evidence in favour of the view that males are relatively deficient at all aspects of language.

But although the research literature is very confused on the subject, the results of one of the largest and most recent studies on the subject suggest that girls may not be better at all aspects of verbal ability. While girls are better readers than boys, verbal analogy tests reveal male superiority.

The confusion here is due to a major problem in this area of research. This is simply that the measures used are often too crude to pick up subtle male/female differences which change with age and ability level. Observers make generalizations about 'verbal ability' without recognizing that this covers a variety of skills including reading and speaking fluency, analogies, spelling, writing and comprehension. Similarly, the typical male advantage in visual-spatial ability varies widely depending on who is tested (the middle-range ability level shows a smaller gender gap) and the subskill being tapped (for some reason, the largest differences are found where reaction time is a dependent measure). If we look at samples of the general population, girls at elementary and middle schools perform slightly better than boys at computational tasks. We can be confident of this result, which is based on the testing of millions of subjects, and so we might be tempted to say that girls are better at maths. But differences favouring boys in problem-solving emerge in high school and college. These gender differences grow larger with increasingly selective samples and samples of the highly precocious. This is partly due to greater male variability—there are always more males at the extreme ends of a distribution. So we have to modify sweeping statements about male or female superiority by referring to the population and the type of subtest used.

Some psychologists have used similar reasoning to argue that the female superiority in verbal ability is underestimated. They say that the data do not include students with very poor verbal skills, who are much more likely to be male, and would therefore drag down the average male score. Boys are over-represented at the very low end of the verbal ability distribution, having more learning disabilities (such as dyslexia) than girls. There are ten times more boys than girls with severe dyslexia, and because these students are unlikely to take written exams, they are not counted in much of the data examining verbal skills. But if the very low end of the verbal ability distribution (heavily weighted with boys) were included, the male verbal average would be lower, and a clear female advantage would be seen.

Studies have also cast doubt on the truth of two other claims sometimes made by teachers: first, that girls at primary school learn more easily by rote while boys respond better if they understand what it is they are supposed to be learning, and secondly that girls—but not boys—find it easier to absorb new information when it is presented in a way which involves people. In fact, before they reach secondary school there seems to be no difference between boys and girls in how much or what sort of information they can take in.

But perhaps the most important finding to emerge from recent research in this area is that the gap between the sexes in all aspects of verbal and mathematical ability seems to be narrowing. Some of the more socially oriented researchers use this evidence to question the value of research which looks at brain differences to explain cognitive differences. The fact that the gender gap is waning threatens the existence of the phenomenon biological theories were supposed to explain. Both in the US and in Britain, reports coming out of the major intelligence-testing centres indicate that the difference between the sexes in verbal and mathematical ability is significantly smaller now than it was twenty-five years ago. No one knows why this has happened. New IQ tests have been developed in this period, but many of the old tests are still frequently used. New reading primers have been introduced, and it may be that they are sufficiently interesting to persuade boys that it is now worth making the effort to learn to read them. But we should also bear in mind that the great majority of primary school teachers in most industrialized countries are women, many of whom must be aware of the demand made by the Women's Movement that boys and girls should receive similar treatment at school. I have no hard evidence that teachers are treating boys and girls less differently in recent years than in the past, but we cannot rule this out as a possible explanation of the fact that what was once a clear-cut difference between the sexes now seems to be disappearing. Perhaps fewer little boys now believe that reading is cissy.

In the same way, if the gender gap in mathematical performance is diminishing, this may reflect girls' changing attitude to maths. As they see more female role models and receive more encouragement, their confidence and expectations will increase.

But although it seems to be politically correct to support the view that cognitive gender differences are disappearing, the facts are not at all clear. Most of the evidence that the gender gap is narrowing comes from meta-analyses, which crunch data independently gathered by different psychologists all over the world into a coherent set of results. There is a problem with this method: pooling the data from many different experiments might blur rather than clarify the differences, masking the overall complexity of the pattern.

Anyway, gender differences do not seem to be vanishing in all areas. For instance, in the long-running American Study of Mathematically Precocious Youth, the superiority of boys over girls has remained constant over the past four decades. Now, it is always difficult to know what part is played by social and environmental factors: brainy boys may well be more highly selected and receive more encouragement from their parents and teachers. But together with the uncertainty about whether gender differences are really narrowing, this finding suggests that there may be an intrinsic masculine advantage in mathematical ability, possibly with a biological basis.

Another area where male superiority is still apparent from puberty onwards is in tests of visual-spatial ability. Since this difference between the sexes is often given as the reason why men tend to dominate such diverse human activities and professions as science, engineering, architecture, surgery, watchmaking, playing chess, playing cricket or baseball, painting and even composing music, we obviously have to take it very seriously. The ability to manipulate objects in space may sound like a pretty specialized and esoteric skill. But to the extent that women are at a disadvantage in this respect, they are handicapped in several very important ways. For example, throughout adolescence American boys consistently get better marks on physics tests, but only on those items which call for visual-spatial skills. On verbal questions, girls do as well if not better, so the fact that most of the questions in physics tests have a visual-spatial slant may make girls appear to be worse at the subject than they really are. From about the age of eleven onwards, boys are also better than girls at maths. We shall look into the reasons for this later in the chapter. But at least part of the explanation may lie in the fact that maths—and especially geometry—has such an important spatial content.

From adolescence onwards, men also do better than women at visual-spatial tests where the task is to identify a simple shape which is hidden in a more complex one. In the embedded-figures test shown in Figure 5, you have to concentrate on a figure—in this case, the shape on the left—when it appears in a more complicated setting—somewhere in the right-hand picture. To solve the problem, you need to suppress your response to the right-hand drawing as a whole, and reconstruct one part of it—the lines which form the figure on the left. How easy you find this party game may be more important than you imagine, because some psychologists think that it is a good measure of your ability to think analytically.

The same is said about the rod-and-frame test, which is shown in Figure 6. For this test, you sit in a darkened room in which all you can see is a luminous rectangular frame tilted at an angle, with a rod suspended inside it. You have a lever which allows you to move the rod by remote control, and what you have to do is to get the rod into a vertical position. The tilted frame is there to

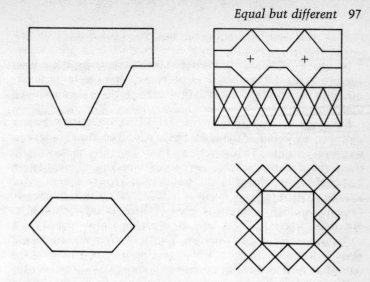

Figure 5. *Examples of drawings used in the embedded-figures test*

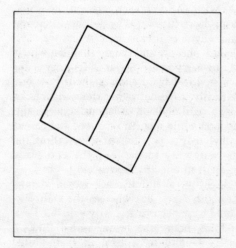

Wrong

Correct

Figure 6. *The rod-and-frame test*

distract you, and once again the task is to concentrate on one aspect of what you can see in front of you, while ignoring everything else. Because men are better at both these tasks, it has been suggested that the two sexes might have different styles of thinking, with men being more analytical and flexible in their thinking than women.

But it would be a mistake to draw this conclusion from the fact that men are better at the tasks I have described. Another way to test people's ability to restructure a figure is to give them a figure made out of matchsticks, and ask them to make a different figure by removing or changing the position of a certain number of matches. When the task involves touching rather than looking at a figure, women are just as good as men at restructuring it. Similarly, when you test how good people are at separating a particular aspect of the situation from its background by asking them to listen to one voice while ignoring another, women again do just as well as men. In other words, these tasks are easier for men only when they have a visual-spatial component, and they do not show that men and women have different styles of thinking.

Why are men better at visual-spatial tasks and—perhaps— women at verbal tasks? As with all differences between the sexes, this question needs breaking down further: Why did the difference arise in the first place, and why does it exist now? What we have to establish is its evolutionary purpose and the mechanism which brought it into being and now supports it. So far as its origins are concerned, we are again forced to hazard guesses about how our ancestors lived and, specifically, to assume that their chances of survival were improved by a rigid division of labour between the sexes—men produced the food while women produced and reared the children. These are obviously very different jobs, calling for different skills, and it is quite easy to see why the two sexes might have developed different intellectual aptitudes.

The argument is that high overall intelligence would always have been an advantage to both sexes. But whereas the ability to aim a spear accurately would have been particularly valuable for a man in helping him to bring home the bison, verbal fluency would have been especially helpful to women in their child-rearing duties. Of course, these considerations would have become relevant only after the invention of weapons suitable for throwing, and the evolution of language. Because the two sexes found different abilities useful, men with superior visual-spatial ability and women who were good with words would have been most likely to survive and pass on their genes, thus causing men and women to develop different intellectual strengths.

Perhaps this is *why* the difference developed, but *how* did it happen, and what keeps it going? The obvious explanation is that genes were—and still are—involved. The most plausible genetic theory says nothing about verbal ability, but it offers an account of men's superiority in visual-spatial ability which seems quite convincing when you first look at it. The theory is that superior visual-spatial ability is passed on from one generation to the next on a recessive gene carried on the X chromosome. This would make it rather like colour-blindness or haemophilia, the transmission of which was discussed in Chapter 2. In simple terms, this means that if a boy inherits a recessive gene on the X chromosome he receives from his mother, the message it contains (in this case, to excel at visual-spatial tasks) will be acted upon, because he has no second X chromosome to contradict the instructions. But when a girl inherits exactly the same recessive gene on the X chromosome she inherits from her mother, the message will be obeyed only if the gene is also present in its recessive form on her second X chromosome, which she inherits from her father. Unfortunately for her, there is a fifty-fifty chance that this second X chromosome will contain the gene in its dominant rather than its recessive form, in which case the message carried on her maternal X chromosome will not be acted upon, thus destroying her chances of developing superior spatial ability.

The theory sounds quite plausible, but is there any evidence to support it? In fact, only one of the predictions it makes seems to be accurate. Studies of visual-spatial ability show that twice as many men as women have superior visual-spatial ability, and this supports the theory, since only half of the girls who have a 'good' visual-spatial gene on their maternal X chromosome will have a matching gene on their paternal X chromosome, while all boys who have the 'good' gene will show superior visual-spatial ability. But in the other main area in which the theory has been tested, the results have been less impressive. The theory predicts that the visual-spatial ability of a particular boy ought to resemble that of his mother, while girls should be more like their fathers in this respect. This is because, according to the theory, all the genetic information a boy receives about visual-spatial ability comes from his mother, and none from his father—how could it, when the information is carried on the X chromosome, which, being a boy, he cannot have received from his father?

A girl, on the other hand, receives genetic information about visual-spatial ability from both her parents, since both give her an X chromosome. But while she can receive the 'good' gene only from her father if he himself has good visual-spatial ability (remember that he, being a man, has only the single X chromosome), she can be given it by her mother, even though her mother does not herself have good visual-spatial ability. This is because there is a fifty-fifty chance that the dominant ('poor') gene on the second X in her mother cancelled out the message contained on the recessive ('good') gene, in which case her mother would not have been good at visual-spatial tasks. But she carried the gene and has now passed it on to her daughter, where it may be luckier. If it is, her daughter will develop superior visual-spatial ability, but will not resemble her mother in this respect. So the genetic theory predicts that there should be a correlation between the visual-spatial abilities of children and those of their opposite-sexed parents.

This is where the theory seems to come unstuck, because although some researchers have found the relationships between children and their parents to be as the theory predicts, just as many have not. As a result, the genetic explanation of the sex difference in visual-spatial skill remains a subject of great controversy. But it is certainly not established that the ability is inherited via our sex chromosomes, so it seems prudent to explore alternative explanations for the fact that men and women excel at different sorts of intellectual activity.

As always, we come back to the problem of deciding whether we are looking at a biologically based phenomenon, or a product of some difference (or differences) in the way boys and girls are brought up. One reason for supposing that there may be a biological basis is that it is not confined to human beings. Male rats, for example, are better than females at learning the quickest way through a maze to reach food, though there is no difference between the sexes when the task to be learned does not have a visual-spatial component. So maybe there is a single explanation for the fact that men are better than women at reading maps just as male rats are better at getting through a maze. However, studies carried out in different cultures make it clear that it is not just a matter of biology. The difference between the sexes in visual-spatial ability is particularly marked in countries where women play a very submissive role (parts of India, for example), whereas it is non-existent in other parts of the world, for example amongst Eskimos. That Eskimo men are no better than women at visual-spatial tasks may mean that natural selection has taken account of the fact that the ability is indispensable in the largely featureless environment of the Arctic. But it may also be significant that Eskimo women are not at all submissive to men; in fact they are as different in this respect as it is possible to be from the women in India who are so much worse than men in visual-spatial ability. So although there may be a biological basis to the sex difference in this ability, how good you are at visual-spatial tasks also seems to be strongly influenced by environmental factors.

Even more important is the fact that you can improve your ability with the right sort of training. Students at Reading University who were tested for visual-spatial ability before and after the first year of an engineering course showed a significant improvement, while children who were given just three weeks of coaching on visual-spatial tasks like the one in Figure 4 (page 92) showed a greater improvement in their marks on geometry tests than other children who had studied Euclid during the three weeks. This is an important finding, because it suggests that even if there is a biological basis for the sex difference in visual-spatial ability, we can narrow the gap, by offering girls remedial classes in visual-spatial skills, just as boys have remedial reading classes.

It also shows that gender differences in behaviour can exaggerate what may be just a very small biological advantage. Boys more naturally involve themselves in experiences which sharpen their spatial skills, because of the sorts of games and toys they enjoy. At the same time, girls tend to develop their interpersonal skills, being more interested in communicating with others from birth. These different behaviour patterns might be influenced by biological as well as sociocultural factors, and can affect the developing pattern of cognitive skills.

But is there a biological basis for the suggestion that men and women have different intellectual specializations? The notion of *specialization* is crucial here, because it leads us into a theory very dear to the hearts of those who believe that there are large, biologically based, differences between the ways in which men and women behave.

Lateralization, or taking sides

The top part of the human brain—the *cerebral cortex*—is divided into two hemispheres. If an adult's cortex is damaged, their intellectual performance is likely to suffer, from which we deduce that the cortex is involved in intellectual activity. But which particular abilities are affected varies according to which side of the brain has been damaged, and this implies that the two hemispheres specialize in different intellectual functions. In about 95 per cent of the population, the division of labour is as follows. The left hemisphere is primarily responsible for verbal skills, such as learning and remembering verbal material, understanding what other people say and reasoning verbally. These are the skills which suffer when the left hemisphere is damaged. But if the right hemisphere is injured, the victim's verbal ability may not be affected at all. Instead, it is the visual-spatial skills which are likely to suffer. They may lose their sense of direction, become unable to locate objects in space, and may even lose the knack of putting on their clothes in the morning. So the two halves of an adult's cortex specialize in carrying out different jobs, and the two main categories of intellectual activity—verbal and visual-spatial—are most efficiently performed by the left and right sides of the brain respectively.

Although this 'sidedness' or *lateralization* exists from birth, there is a degree of flexibility in the infant brain, before it is fully developed. Unlike adults, young children who suffer brain damage can sometimes make a complete recovery, which is based on the ability of the undamaged parts of their brain to take over whatever intellectual functions would normally have been performed by the damaged areas. As we get older, we lose this flexibility, and different regions of the brain take on specific intellectual functions. This specialization is a mixed blessing. As long as nothing untoward happens, the fact that your brain is divided into little pockets of expertise makes you more effective as a thinking machine. But it also means that if you receive an injury to part of your brain which specializes in some vital function, the effect will be much more drastic than it would have been had your brain remained more adaptable.

Neurological evidence shows that the intellectual impairment in brain-damaged patients is affected not just by which bit of the brain is damaged, but also by the sex of the patient. After a left-hemisphere stroke, men are more likely to have a pervasive and lasting language disorder, whereas women often recover. From this it seems that men and women are not lateralized in exactly the same way. A popular theory is that men are more strongly lateralized for verbal and spatial abilities than women, who are more likely to use both hemispheres for these functions. Women will be less likely to suffer language problems after a stroke because they have language areas in the non-damaged hemisphere which they can use. Men are more likely to have the language areas of the brain located in the left hemisphere only, and if this gets damaged, they have no back-up system.

The suggestion that cognitive functions are represented more bilaterally in women was supported by the finding of some scientists that the *corpus callosum*—the bundle of fibres which connects the two halves of the brain—is larger relative to brain size in women. This provided evidence for a theory which explained female intuition, and the fact that women are better able to express their feelings. The idea is that a woman's right brain, which is where emotional functions are located, is better connected to her left brain (for verbal expression). So she is more in touch with her emotions than men, who do not tend to use different areas of their brain together as much.

Unfortunately for this theory, three recent studies using the sophisticated technique of *magnetic resonance imaging* failed to find sex differences in the morphology of the corpus callosum. But this does not make the theory false, because once again scientists are not sure which measurements to take: they might get different results if they counted the number of fibres rather than measured the gross size. What is clearer is that girls become more developed in their left hemisphere (for verbal skills), and boys in their right (for visual-spatial skills). This is why more men are left-handed: the right hemisphere of the brain controls the left side of the body, so if your right hemisphere is dominant you will have more control over the left side of your body.

There is nothing accidental about this, because it is part of a general, if rather mysterious, difference between the sexes, which I have not yet mentioned. If you could find some way of measuring and weighing separately those parts of your body which come in pairs, the chances are that you would find that those on one side of your body were consistently larger than those on the other. Women tend to be left-sided generally, and men right-sided. The reason for this appears to be that the male hormone testosterone favours development of the right side of the body at the expense of the left. There is a striking illustration of this. In Chapter 1 we saw that very occasionally children are born with genitals which are half male and half female; in these cases, it is usually the left side which is female and the right which is male.

This is fascinating stuff, but what we are interested in is whether these biological influences have any effect on spatial ability. We might expect hormones to be involved, because it is at puberty that differences in visual-spatial ability appear. There is indeed medical evidence to suggest that testosterone is an important factor. Men with the condition *idiopathic hypogonadotropic hypogonadism* produce abnormally small amounts of testosterone and have impaired spatial ability. This is because male hormones have a permanent organizing influence on the brain—particularly the right hemisphere, where spatial functions are located—before and at puberty in boys. The more male hormone a foetus is exposed to, the more masculine it will grow up to be in looks and behaviour. And one aspect of this behaviour is good performance on spatial tasks.

So does this mean that girls cannot have good spatial ability because they do not have male hormones? Of course not—remember that a normal female foetus is also exposed to small amounts of male hormone. But some—those with Turner's syndrome—are not. The brain of these foetuses is therefore allowed to develop in a fully female pattern, accentuating feminine behaviour and the comparative mental strengths and weaknesses. Adults with Turner's syndrome tend to be placid, shy and retiring, and are much more likely to withdraw from attack than to defend themselves. As for their intellectual abilities, they are particularly weak at mathematical and spatial tasks. On the other hand, girls with an excess of male hormone (for instance, because of *congenital adrenal hyperplasia*) show significantly better spatial ability than their unaffected female relatives. They also show more masculine behaviour in other areas.

Testosterone is obviously important for good spatial ability. But boys with very high amounts of testosterone do not show better spatial ability, and male patients with *congenital adrenal hyperplasia* do not show the advantage that female patients do. In fact, spatial ability is better in androgynous than in very masculine men. So it looks as if spatial ability depends on a balance of male and female hormones. This can explain the common regression in spatial and mathematical ability in female teenagers after puberty. But if the balance of hormones in a girl's brain is tilted towards the male hormones, the brain concentration of female hormones is kept within the range for the optimal expression of spatial ability. This is why late-maturing, androgynous girls tend to show higher spatial ability than their more feminized counterparts.

But this explanation is not the only one for findings like that of a British researcher, who reported that girls who take maths at A level are unusually tough-minded and radical, and also obtain low scores on a test of traditional feminine attitudes. It may be that girls who have excellent visual-spatial ability spend more time in the company of boys and acquire more masculine characteristics by association. In any case, the biological perspective cannot provide the whole story. There may be biological factors which underlie sex differences in cognition, but gender differences, where noted, are small, and are almost certainly exacerbated by social factors. So for anybody who is bad at maths or reading, the fact that there are biological factors involved does not mean that it is pointless to try and improve. Women's visual-spatial skills can be improved without tampering with their hormone levels, by simply giving them appropriate training.

There is a way of examining the effects of different hormone levels in women without provoking a public outcry. So far we have just established that hormones can have a *permanent* effect on the brain and spatial processing abilities. A group of Swiss psychologists wondered whether circulating levels of hormones can have a *temporary* effect on these sorts of functions. They investigated hemispheric superiority in women at different stages in their menstrual cycle, when the levels of female hormones vary. The women in the experiment had to perform two tasks, one verbal (deciding whether a group of letters presented made a word or not) and one non-verbal (recognizing whether the pattern shown was a face or not). They showed the usual left-hemisphere bias for the verbal task (making a quicker, more accurate response when the stimulus was flashed in the right visual field) and this asymmetry did not change during the menstrual cycle. However, they showed a significant right-hemisphere advantage for face perception only in the menstrual phase. This is the relatively male pattern of lateralization, so it is interesting that it is found when the amount of female sex hormones is very low. This superiority disappeared during the menstrual cycle and even shifted in the premenstrual phase (when female hormone levels are high) to a small left-hemisphere superiority. This supports the theory that the left hemisphere is particularly responsive to female hormones, and shows that the effects of hormones on the brain and behaviour can be temporary.

So women with high levels of female hormones might be expected to perform badly on a visual-spatial task because they use the left hemisphere instead of the more suitable right hemisphere. Two Canadian psychologists have confirmed that women with a normal menstrual cycle perform worse in a perceptuo-spatial task when their female hormone levels are high. In contrast, they found that performance on speeded manual and articulatory tasks is actually enhanced during this phase. So the influence of hormones on cognitive functions is not unidirectional, but seems to favour some skills at the expense of others.

This research is important because it shows that hormones might influence the balance of hemisphere activation. This influence might be partially responsible for the contradictions between different experimental studies on the question of whether men or women show greater asymmetric functional organization of the brain. It seems that brain organization is a dynamic process, shaped by many interactive forces, a key one of which is the influence of hormones.

We have seen evidence of some intrinsic biological factors underlying sex differences in cognition. These are exacerbated by social factors, and because of the huge differences between individuals, the small but significant gender differences in ability should not bar women from certain male-dominated professions. Biological considerations make an important contribution to our understanding of the differences and similarities between women and men. The key message from the evidence in this chapter is that that *brain sexing, and therefore gender, is a matter of degree*—the more male hormone a foetus is exposed to, the more it will grow up behaving and looking male. Everyone is influenced by both male and female hormones, and the optimal performance on many tasks is attained when there is a happy balance of the two. Since brain sex is just a difference of degree, generalizations about the differences between men and women are not going to be very useful in predicting the behaviour of any one person.

Men, women and science

The difference between the sexes in visual-spatial ability is some-times put forward as the reason why professions such as science and architecture are dominated by men. But a moment's thought (and a swift calculation) shows that this cannot be the whole explanation. If it were, we might expect to find approximately one woman scientist or architect to every two men on the basis of the scores of the two sexes on tests of visual-spatial ability. In fact, the ratio is more like one woman to every hundred men in these and other professions like engineering and surgery, which seem to involve visual-spatial ability—though it has never actually been proved that they do. However, it would be unfair to place all the blame on the professions for not employing more women. A large gap opens up between the sexes in scientific achievement long before they get to the stage of applying for jobs, as can be seen from Figure 7. This is based on the results of a large study in which thousands of fourteen-year-old boys and girls in different countries were given a standard test of their scientific ability. Japanese boys come out top, followed by Hungarian and Australian boys. Then come Japanese girls, well below Japanese boys, though ahead of both English and American boys. I have not introduced this chart to make international comparisons, revealing though these may be. The point I want to make is that the gap in scientific achievement between the sexes seems to be universal, and by the age of fourteen it is already far too large to be explained simply by differences in visual-spatial ability.

In England and Wales in 1990, nearly twice as many boys as girls attempted maths A level, and nearly twice as many boys as girls passed. In physics, the sex ratio was even more distorted-boys outnumbered girls by over three to one. But amongst can-didates as a whole, the relationship between exam attempts and passes was not just a simple one—although fewer girls attempted A levels, more girls than boys actually passed. What makes a girl so reluctant to chance her arm at maths or science? In primary school, girls are just as successful as boys at maths. But even at this stage they are the victims of a preconception which both they and their teachers share, that maths and science are masculine subjects—despite objective evidence to the contrary. In an experi-ment carried out in a London infant school, in which children were asked to build something with Lego, the structures produced

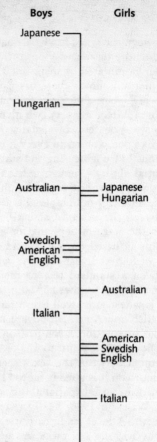

Figure 7. *Average scores of boys and girls on a standard test of scientific achievements (Kelly, 1978)*

by girls were just as complex and original as those constructed by boys. Their teachers, however, had previously told the experimenters that they had no chance of persuading the girls even to take part in the experiment!

Playing with construction sets is probably the easiest—and most enjoyable—way for a child to boost his or her visual-spatial skill. But such toys have a definite masculine image which can be broken down only by deliberate adult intervention. When this occurs, researchers find that girls are keen to play with them, even in the absence of adult encouragement.

Unfortunately, few teachers take the trouble to introduce girls to what they think of as boys' toys. In fact, research into what goes on in the classroom suggests that, however anxious they may be to avoid it, teachers are a powerful force in perpetuating the traditional sex stereotypes. For a start, they allow boys to talk and interrupt them more during lessons. This not only encourages boys to be more assertive but also ensures that more of a teacher's time is devoted to resolving their problems. This might be justified, in view of the developmental lag which operates against boys, were it not for the fact that teachers of mixed classes display a more subtle form of sexual discrimination which is less easy to excuse.

Research shows that boys are more often punished than girls, but usually for non-academic faults such as untidiness or misbehaviour. When girls are reprimanded it is almost always for academic mistakes. You might think that this would benefit a girl by focusing her attention on her work, but the problem is that when praise is given to a girl, it is generally not for work but for her appearance or conduct. So the lesson a girl learns is that what she is good at is being ladylike, while academic work is something which brings her criticism, when her efforts are noticed at all.

Teachers are even more at fault in the way in which they encourage children to react to their own mistakes. In studies of classroom behaviour, observers have noticed that when a boy gives the wrong answer, particularly in a 'masculine' subject like maths, his teacher is likely to keep at him, suggesting he tries new approaches to the problem until eventually he gets it right. He therefore learns to expect to get sums right, so long as he works at them hard enough. More generally, he will come to regard initial failure as a challenge to be overcome by trying again. But when a girl gets a sum wrong, the teacher's response is rather different. She is more likely to be told not to worry, and less likely to be encouraged to try again. The implication is that no one really expects girls to be able to do sums, and the more general lesson a girl will learn is that failure, especially in this area, is beyond her control and not really her fault. This attitude is known as *learned helplessness*. It is not, of course, confined to girls, but it seems to affect them more than boys, and it may go some way towards explaining why they take against maths and science when they get to secondary school.

That girls at secondary school react particularly badly to maths and science may also be a reflection of the way they are taught. Whereas in languages or history progress is made by building up more of the same sort of information while developing more sophisticated ways of handling it, most maths and science teachers in secondary schools present their subjects as a succession of quite different problems, each of which demands that a new technique be mastered. We inevitably make mistakes when first trying out new techniques, so it is not difficult to understand why boys, who have been taught to respond more constructively to their own mistakes, come to occupy most of the desks in science and maths classes in a mixed school.

Talk of mixed schools brings us to the final, and perhaps most important reason for girls' disappointing performance at maths and the 'hard' sciences (in biology, which is thought to be a 'softer' science than physics and chemistry, girls out-perform boys). This has to do with the importance adolescents attach to the notion of gender, and the fact that science and maths are seen as 'masculine' subjects. Even at primary school, when children are asked what they think about science and scientists, both sexes agree that science is a man's subject, and that scientists are grey-haired, scruffy and invariably male. Since they will have had little formal science education at this stage, their attitude is presumably shaped by comics, books and TV. The early years of secondary school are crucial in deciding a child's academic future, because this is when they decide which subjects they are good at, and their attitudes towards school and academic work in general begin to harden. But it is also the time when girls—but not yet boys—are beginning to be troubled by the doubts and uncertainty which mark the adolescent identity crisis, and are particularly anxious to establish their femininity. While the boys around her are still in the world of late childhood, cheerfully accepting things as they come and undisturbed by psychological concerns, the newly adolescent girl is eager to 'find' herself and to develop a consistent and pleasing personality.

Girls of this age in mixed-sex schools seem to be in a quandary. They want to please their parents and teachers by doing as well as they can academically, but they may be unhappy about doing better than boys in exams. The solution many girls adopt is to abandon masculine subjects like physics and maths as soon as they can and concentrate their efforts on safe 'feminine' subjects such as languages or biology, where boys are thinner on the ground and less likely to be offended by a girl who does well. Girls are much less aware of this problem if there are no boys around, which explains why they do significantly better at maths and science in single-sex schools, whereas boys do equally well in single-sex and mixed schools.

In mixed-sex schools, teachers might be expected to try to dissuade girls from abandoning maths and science. But it is not clear that they do. A remark overheard in a biology dissection class, and quoted in a recent publication of the British Schools' Inspectorate makes the point: 'Now which of you boys will do the cutting?', asked the teacher. 'Girls, let me know if you feel sick.' Bear in mind that this was a course in biology, which is regarded as the most 'feminine' of school science courses. Moreover, in all probability nine out of ten of the girls who were being encouraged to be squeamish would soon be dealing as a matter of course with childbirth and its aftermath.

Given the important role which fathers play in establishing their children's attitudes towards gender roles (see Chapter 1), it comes as no surprise to discover from a study of successful female mathematicians in America that paternal encouragement seemed to be a key factor in their choice of career. Without such encouragement, it must be difficult for a girl to follow a career in maths or science. What makes it even more unlikely is that she has to make a decision about what subjects to specialize in at exactly the time when she is most concerned about establishing her feminine identity. Whatever else the books and magazines she reads tell her about the image of the ideal woman, being scruffy, grey-haired and eccentric is no part of it. Adolescence sees a great female exodus from science courses, and as they abandon the subject at school, girls abandon the chance of gaining the qualifications needed for a scientific career.

This problem is beginning to correct itself—there is very recent evidence that gender stereotyping of school subjects is not as strong as it was. Pupils at a secondary school in the UK rated seventeen subjects on a seven-point scale, and only CDT (craft, design and technology), IT (information technology) and physics were regarded as significantly masculine. Subjects seen as significantly feminine were RE (religious education), typing and home economics, but the majority of non-vocational subjects (including maths) were clearly neutral.

In addition, subjects which have previously been considered 'masculine'—maths, science and games—were very popular with many girls. In fact, these were the subjects girls most often said they liked. But where gender stereotyping still exists, boys and girls have very different expectations of masculine and feminine subjects. Whereas boys tend to regard masculine subjects as interesting and feminine ones as boring, girls think of masculine subjects as difficult and feminine ones easy.

What are the practical implications of all this? Is there any point in trying to persuade more girls to persevere with maths and science in the hope that more of them will eventually end up in one of the visual-spatial professions? Judged from two different viewpoints, I think the answer to the question must be yes. From society's point of view, the general good is served by jobs being done by those able to do them best—and it doesn't take great visual-spatial ability to perceive the damage done by a round peg in a square hole. Taking account of the difference between the sexes in visual-spatial ability, we might be satisfied that the general good were being met if 40 per cent of engineers, architects, surgeons and physicists were women. But when the figure is only a tenth of this, we can be pretty certain that these professions contain a significant number of men doing jobs which could be done better by a woman with greater natural ability. So an influx of women could only improve the standard of work carried out in these professions.

It is especially intriguing to speculate on the effect of an upsurge in the number of women architects. Judging by what happened in early civilizations and in simple societies where the builders tended to be women, we could expect buildings to become oriented more to the user than to the designer, and to be more flexible and less geared to the profit motive.

In all these 'masculine' subjects, the waste of women must be an important consideration. Women who showed an early flair for science or maths, but gave them up at school for any of the reasons mentioned earlier, may later bitterly regret giving in to pressures to 'learn something more feminine', as they contemplate the careers closed to those without scientific or mathematical qualifications. Leaving careers aside, it is difficult to overestimate the inconvenience of trying to operate without technical skills in a technological society. The feeling of baffled rage when your car refuses to start isn't, of course, confined to one sex. But the gaps in women's education mean that they are more likely than men to find themselves helpless victims of uncooperative gadgetry, which reduces their effectiveness, as well as making them feel inadequate. It cannot be a coincidence that American researchers have found that young women with high mathematical ability have a significantly higher opinion of themselves and their ability to control their own lives than their less numerate contemporaries.

Strategies for encouraging more girls to pursue a scientific career follow naturally from what has been said. They need to meet or see films of women scientists, and to learn that women have made contributions no less significant than those of men in the areas of science which are not regarded as masculine territory. In psychology, for example, many of the most distinguished researchers are women; interestingly, nowhere is this more true than in the study of sex differences!

Perhaps we should also think again about the way in which science is taught in school, making an effort to relate the subject to girls' interests and experience, wherever these are significantly different from those of boys. It may be the case—as some researchers claim—that girls are less receptive to the formal and theoretical way in which science has traditionally been presented, but this is not the only way of teaching science. And if by adolescence girls have developed different interests from their male counterparts—for example, in home life and human relations—these should be valued as highly as boys' preoccupations, and built upon in science classes. Many domestic items could be used in experiments, and subjects like the chemistry of food-processing can easily be used to demonstrate the relevance of science to everyday life.

More radically, even if we are convinced that the social drawbacks of single-sex schools outweigh any possible educational advantages they might offer, especially to girls, there might be a lot to be said for subjects which have a distinct masculine or feminine image being taught to single-sex classes, by a same-sexed teacher. Girls contemplating a career in science need to see other women—their friends as well as their teachers—succeeding at it, and they should be allowed to do so without the distraction—or disapproval—of boys.

Teachers as much as the girls themselves have to be convinced that the fact women achieved so little in science in the past was not an inevitable consequence of being female, even if it was partly caused by trying too hard to be feminine. Social attitudes too will need to change. As one researcher has put it: 'Anyone is loath to admit that they are illiterate, but not innumerate. It is somehow feminine to say "I can't add up".' And as for younger children, there is no reason why compensatory science classes should not take their place alongside remedial reading classes; these might involve training in visual-spatial skills—which we know works—as well as playing with mechanical construction kits and so on.

We have seen evidence that some cognitive abilities can be described as 'masculine' (visual-spatial skills) or 'feminine' (verbal skills). Applying these labels does not mean that we can make predictions about the abilities of an individual, or even useful generalizations about men and women. This is because men and women have both masculine and feminine attributes, and are influenced by male as well as female hormones. The difference between men and women in intellectual abilities is already small, and although it is unlikely to be just the influence of social factors which is maintaining the gap, the removal of such pressures would allow everyone fully to develop his or her individual talents. The only people likely to suffer would be incompetent male scientists, engineers, surgeons and architects. Some tears may be shed for them, but not, I think, by those familiar with their handiwork.

Footnote   The answer to the puzzle depicted in Figure 4 is Block E.

5

WHO WANTS WHAT?

There is a puzzling discrepancy between the conclusions we have reached so far and one of the most striking aspects of the world we live in:. if women are not weaker, moodier or less intelligent than men, why do they get so few of the best jobs?

Feminists are in no doubt about the answer to this question. Until very recently, the upper echelons of the most prestigious professions were out of bounds to women, simply because they were women. Even now, when it is illegal to discriminate against a person on the grounds of his or her sex, it would be naïve to believe that the opportunities open to a man and a woman with the same qualifications are equal. In Britain, women judges are still a curiosity, women surgeons a rarity, and none of the major trade unions has ever been led by a woman. In professions based on traditionally feminine skills or in those dominated numerically by women, the position is often no better. Most of the leading chefs and fashion designers continue to be men, while the fallacy of equating power with numbers will be illustrated shortly.

As a general rule, the more prestigious a profession, the fewer women practise it; within a profession, the higher the rank, the fewer women reach it. If educational qualifications are the first step on the road to professional success, it must also be significant that only in the last two decades have the top universities in Britain and the US opened their doors to anything like as many women as men. So where the past and present are concerned, we may have to look no further than sexual discrimination to understand why men have left women so far behind in professional achievement.

Equal opportunity

If this is all that has been holding women back, we must expect some drastic changes in the future. Guaranteeing women equal

job opportunities by law may not eliminate sexual discrimination
in practice, but it is evidence of a change in society's attitude
towards women at work. And although girls may still find it more
difficult to fulfil their potential at school because less is expected
of them, particularly in science subjects, they are now closer to
achieving equal educational opportunities than ever before. In
Britain, more girls than boys enrol in further education on leaving
school, and while the majority of places in the most prestigious
forms of higher education (universities and polytechnics) are still
occupied by men, the most recent figures indicate that women
graduates find jobs more easily than men. (This may, however,
simply reflect the fact that employers are more willing to hire
women for non-graduate and part-time jobs and that women are
more prepared to accept them.)

The development of effective contraception means that women
can now opt out of child-bearing without being condemned to
chastity, and so can pursue a career more single-mindedly than in
the past. But there is still a clear division between the types of
profession which men and women graduates enter, as there is in
the salaries they can hope to earn. The stereotypes of women
teachers and businessmen still prevail, and they reflect the different subjects in which men and women choose to become
qualified. This is changing fast—the proportion of women enrolled
at Britain's first business school jumped from one in ten in 1966
to four out of ten in 1982, and women are rapidly achieving
greater representation even at the very top of better-educated
male-dominated occupations. In 1992, the British intelligence
service MI5 took on its first female head, a woman was appointed
as Director-General of the Takeover Panel, and ICI appointed its
first ever female board member. But these instances are news-
worthy precisely because they are exceptions.

Even once they get to such high positions, things are not easy
for women. A recent survey by Brook Street Employment Bureau
and *Elle* magazine found that women high-flyers have to pay for
their success with unhappiness in their private lives. They often
experience a feeling of isolation the higher they climb, with fewer
women to act as role models or confidantes. And, unfortunately,
it would be rash to assume that it is simply a matter of time
before women start to get their fair share of such high-status jobs.

For a start, history shows that an influx of women into a
profession does not necessarily lead to their joining its highest

ranks. Take the administrative grade of the Civil Service, for example, an élite in which the number of women has risen steadily over the years. But before the recent appointment of a female Director of Public Prosecutions, no women had reached the highest rank of permanent secretary. In other highly regarded professions which have been open to both sexes for many years, women have been conspicuously unsuccessful in achieving positions of power, and in some cases their numbers have actually fallen over the years. For example, Mrs Thatcher may have shown that it is possible for a woman to become Prime Minister, but women constitute fewer than 7 per cent of Members of Parliament.

Similarly, although women formed 10 per cent of the academic staff of British universities at the end of 1979, they accounted for a mere 3 per cent of those who had reached the highest grade of professor. And although four out of five teachers in London primary schools are female, women occupy only half the headships.

The same pattern is shown in Britain's National Health Service, where women now represent four-fifths of the workforce. But only one of the fourteen regional health authorities and only three of the first fifty-seven NHS trusts are chaired by women. And while in 1991 the number of women entering medical school in Britain was higher than the number of men for the first time, less than 1 per cent of consultants and general surgeons at this time were women. The overall picture is no better: while women make up 44 per cent of the labour force in Britain, and are expected to account for 50 per cent of workers by the end of the 1990s, they hold only 11 per cent of managerial positions. The picture gets worse as they clamber up the promotional ladder: only 9 per cent of senior managers are women, only 5 per cent of directors, and fewer than one chief executive in a hundred is a woman.

History provides another reason for being cautious about women's chances of achieving high professional status. In the days when most schoolteachers in the US were men, teaching was a highly regarded profession. But now that it is a predominantly female occupation, it has lost much of its status. The same thing has happened in professions as diverse as medicine in the former Soviet Union and growing cassava in Nigeria, which suggests that women who pursue professional status may find that they are hunting a chimera—how can they ever achieve it if any profession in which they become successful automatically loses its status as a result of their success? On the other hand, the lessons of history do not always apply to the future. Perhaps we are now prepared to accept—as we were not in the past—that jobs at which women can be successful may still be worth while.

This is the optimistic feminist's view of the future, and it rests on two assumptions: that there is no difference in what men and women are capable of achieving, and that the only reason why women have achieved so much less in the past is that they have been victims of unfair discrimination. How convincing is this argument? Certainly, women have been discriminated against, and it is inconceivable they would not have accomplished more had this not been the case. Moreover, the evidence discussed in the first half of this book seems to support the view that men and women have very similar natural ability. Where the feminist argument falls down is in failing to acknowledge that ability alone is no guarantee of achievement. To succeed at something you not only have to be able to do it, you must also *want* to succeed at it, and some psychologists believe that this is where women are lacking. They claim that although the two sexes have equal ability, they have different needs and ambitions, and that the reason men and women differ so much in their achievements is that they want different things.

Ambition and achievement

Like the alleged differences in ability between men and women we looked at earlier, the suggestion that the two sexes differ in motivation comes complete with a biological justification. As before, the starting-point is the observation that, from a biological point of view, the most important achievement of any species is its own continued survival. What could be more natural, the biologists argue, than that women, who make by far the more important contribution to this goal, should have a little something built into them which ensures that they stick to it instead of getting side-tracked into activities which might divert them from their essential task, and which anyway can be done equally well by men? Leaving aside for the moment the question of what this little something might be, we can see here the basis of a justification for the traditional division of labour between the sexes, as well as an implication that women who seek professional success are doubly misguided. From the biological perspective, it is women rather than men who are the more successful sex, for it is they who keep the species going. So a woman who abandons her traditional role of bearing and rearing children is not only acting against the 'little something' in her nature but is also reducing her own importance in the biological scheme of things.

Many people find this argument reassuring, but it runs into practical and empirical difficulties. The first problem is that, however warmly nature may look on women who confine themselves to the traditional role of wife and mother, society takes a very different view. In industrialized societies, looking after children—whether your own or someone else's—is an occupation which carries very little status. As long as this remains the case, women cannot be expected to settle happily for the traditional role if they have the qualifications to pursue a career which would bring them more social approval, not to mention financial reward. As things stand, those who do stay at home to rear children are diminished in their own and the world's eyes, and this could lead to a situation where the only women who do this are those who cannot find a more interesting job. This would mean that the genes of the most able women would not be passed on, which must be to the species' disadvantage. There are three possible solutions to this problem, which confronts all the technologically advanced countries of the West. The first is to try to turn the clock back by asking women to forget the advances they have made towards equal professional opportunities and simply to accept their traditional role. The chances of women going along with this are negligible, and the second solution—paying women the same salary for raising a family as they would have got at work—would not solve the status problem. The last solution is to develop working practices that are friendly to women, by offering crèche facilities and flexible working hours, and even changing the culture of working patterns. This might also be welcomed by the many men who do not want to work excessively long hours either. It would also be necessary to reorganize the career structure of high-status professions in such a way that women's advancement is no longer automatically blocked by extended periods away from work. Companies are becoming more and more aware of the need to think about changes favouring women, because women are expected to take up 80 per cent of all new jobs in the UK over the next few years. An increasing number of women with family responsibilities are considering a return to full-time work, and 60 per cent are resuming management jobs. I am pessimistic, though, about the chances of this happening—for reasons that will be discussed in the next chapter.

Meanwhile, we must see what evidence there is to support the idea that men and women want different things out of life. There are several ways in which the two sexes may differ in motivation. One suggestion is that women have a positive maternal drive to bear and bring up children, and as a result have less motivational energy left for other activities than men, whose desire to get on in the world is not diluted by an equivalent paternal drive. Most people seem to believe in a maternal drive, though, as we shall see in Chapter 6, the evidence for its existence is actually not very impressive. In the present chapter, we shall examine the other half of the proposition: that there is something about women's motivation which makes them less interested than men in achievement for its own sake.

If women really do have a 'little something' in their biological make-up which prevents them from doing as well as they could, it is remarkably well disguised. At school, for example, you might expect it to make girls do less well at tests and examinations, but this is the opposite of what actually happens. Girls in fact get slightly better marks than boys throughout their school careers, despite the fact that they are no cleverer, and may actually be at a disadvantage because of their inferior visual-spatial ability. Amongst children in England and Wales in 1990, for example, girls out-performed boys at O Level and CSE in virtually every subject except maths, physics, geography, and computer studies. Even in such male bastions as technical drawing and woodwork, the few girls who were bold enough to compete obtained higher average grades than boys (the girls involved, however, may well have been unusually gifted).

Such sweeping superiority suggests that if anything it is girls who take the greater pride in their own accomplishments. Examination results are an indirect way of telling how anxious someone is to succeed. There is, however, a more direct way of assessing this, by showing people pictures which can be interpreted in different ways, and asking them to make up stories based on what they think is going on in each picture. The idea behind this test is that since the pictures are ambiguous, what each person reads into them will give us a clue as to his or her preoccupations and underlying motivation. For example, one picture might show a young man and a middle-aged man talking to each other, with neutral expressions on their faces. If in response to it you wrote a story in which the young man was an employee trying to persuade his boss (the older man) that he was due for promotion, you would be given a higher need-to-achieve score than somebody else in whose story the two men were father and son exchanging holiday reminiscences.

When boys and girls of secondary-school age are given this test, it is the girls whose stories show more themes concerned with achievement, though if boys are put into a competitive frame of mind before doing the stories test by being asked to carry out a short test to assess their leadership potential, their need for achievement scores can be boosted to reach the girls' level. In fact, girls might be even further ahead of boys in achievement motivation than studies using these tests suggest, because it is common practice to show girls pictures in which the central characters are female, while boys are shown pictures of male characters. Since both sexes get lower achievement scores when they are asked to write stories based on pictures of women than they do when the characters are men, the girls' achievement scores may be artificially lowered. The fact that girls' writing contains fewer achievement themes when their stories are about women presumably means that although they themselves may have a high need to achieve, they have a pessimistic view of what other members of their sex actually manage to accomplish.

Research into achievement motivation in children points to the conclusion that girls take at least as much pleasure in their own achievements as boys do and are no less anxious to be successful. However, although measuring his need to achieve may tell us all we need to know about the extent to which a teenage boy is affected by the success motive, it may not do justice to the more complicated position in which an adolescent girl finds herself. We saw earlier in the book that she is particularly concerned with establishing her femininity, and that intellectual achievement is associated with masculinity. So she seems to be in a predicament, torn between her desire to do well and the fear of appearing unfeminine, especially if she is rash enough to do better at work than the boys in her class. This has led some psychologists to suggest that even though women may be just as anxious as men to succeed, in their case the need to achieve is more likely to have to play second fiddle to a diametrically opposed motivational force—the fear of success.

The will to lose

What evidence is there that women are more frightened than men of being highly successful? The first person to test this idea experimentally was Matina Horner, who asked men and women students to write a story about a successful member of their own sex, and then deduced how frightened they were of success by counting how many unpleasant personal characteristics they attributed to the successful character and how many misfortunes befell him or her in their stories. The students at an American medical school were supplied with the first line of the story, which was as follows for women: 'After the first-term examinations, Anne finds herself top of her medical school class.' For men, the first line of the story was the same except that the central character was called John rather than Anne. When the stories were analysed for images thought to indicate their writers' fear of success, there was found to be an enormous difference between men and women students. More than 90 per cent of the men responded favourably to their hero's success—they said that John had worked hard and predicted a glittering future for him. But Anne fared much worse at the hands of the women students, 65 per cent of whom showed their feelings about successful women by describing Anne as ugly and unloved, and predicting for her a career without marriage which might end in a nervous breakdown or even suicide!

When these results were first published in 1969, they were widely hailed as the definitive explanation of why it is that women achieve less than men even when they have the same jobs and similar qualifications: women dare not do too well for fear of being thought unfeminine, whereas success can only enhance a man's masculinity. Because it sounded intuitively reasonable and also explained a vexing difference between the sexes, the concept of 'fear of success' caught on quickly with psychologists, and follow-up experiments have been carried out all over the world. Unfortunately, it seems as though we are going to have to look for a different explanation of why men and women differ in what they accomplish, because no one has managed to reproduce the enormous difference between men's and women's fear-of-success imagery which Horner found. If all the studies are taken together, there is a slight tendency for women to score higher than men on fear-of-success motivation. But more than a dozen studies—including one carried out in the same room, at the same time of year, with a similar experimenter and subjects, a few years after the original experiment—have found exactly the opposite result: that it is men who are more frightened of success.

It looks as though the students' replies reflected a realistic assessment of a woman's chances in the American medical profession rather than a deep-rooted difference in motivation between the two sexes, because women show much less fear of success imagery in their stories if Anne is not described as a medical student or if the opening of the story states that half of the students in her year were women. Even if it were true that fear of success affects women more than men, it is not at all certain that this would explain why women achieve less in their careers, because some psychologists believe that women who are most afraid of success also tend to have a high need for achievement, and to be high achievers, despite their worries about being successful. Far from being opposites, motivation towards achievement and fear of success may actually go hand in hand.

Most of the studies mentioned so far have been carried out on children or students. So there is still a possibility that something happens to women when they take up a career which dampens their need for achievement. If this were the case, then the fact that women achieve less professional success might after all be due to a difference between the sexes in motivation. It might even still be possible to maintain that this difference was biologically based if we made the assumption that women begin to be affected by the maternal drive only in the years after they have finished their education. But in fact there is no need to entertain this hypothesis, because so far as we can tell, women are no less motivated to succeed in their careers than men, when both are doing the same jobs.

Surprisingly little research has been carried out on this question, but what evidence there is does not suggest that a gap opens up between the sexes in motivation to succeed. Among college students about to enter the job market, there is a tendency for men to be more interested in the promotion prospects a job offers, whereas women seem to be more concerned about job security. But among working men and women of roughly equal status, there seems to be little difference in the scope of their ambitions. For example, a recent study of male and female accountants who worked for a large international company discovered no sex differences in any aspect of work motivation. And a survey published in 1987 comparing male and female managers showed that, if anything, women are more career-oriented and ambitious than men. It is significant that this difference appears at the management level—women in high-status positions may have to be more motivated in order to gain high-status positions, because of the greater obstacles and prejudices that they have to deal with.

Most studies of motivation at work have investigated what is called 'motivation to manage' rather than the need to achieve. This is measured in a similar way to the fear of success. You are given the first words of a sentence and asked to complete it. Your score depends on how you shape up on five of the attributes known to be characteristic of highly motivated and effective managers. These include a positive attitude towards authority and competition, willingness to be assertive and impose your wishes, how prepared you are to stand out in a group, and a positive attitude towards routine administration. Most of these are thought to be masculine attributes. But when the test was given to a group of men and women managers in their thirties working for one of the American car-manufacturing giants, there was no significant overall difference between the sexes in their willingness to manage. There is no comfort here for people who believe that the reason women fail to get top jobs is that they don't want them. Notice, however, that the women in this study were already junior managers, which made them unusual, especially in that sector of American industry.

When men and women are selected at random and asked if they would like to be promoted, their replies usually do show a difference between the sexes. A typical survey found that two-thirds of the men but only half of the women questioned said that they would like promotion, while slightly more women than men attached importance to such factors as working with friends and in pleasant surroundings. It has been found that people's desire for promotion is directly linked to their chances of actually being promoted, so the fact that women are less interested in promotion than men is probably just a consequence of the fact that more of them have dead-end jobs. Men in such jobs are found to have the same attitudes as women, so that is no evidence of a sex difference in motivation here. Once again, it is merely a reflection of the fact that men and women tend to do different kinds of jobs.

Although men and women may have equal needs for achievement, there may be other differences in motivation between them. For example, they might have different ways of achieving their ambitions, and we still have not ruled out the possibility that men and women get different satisfactions from achieving the same things. Another way of deciding how anxious someone is to achieve a goal is to see what risks he or she is prepared to take in order to accomplish it, and here it looks as though there may be a sex difference. In one situation which tests their willingness to take risks, children are seated in front of a row of nine levers, eight of which when pulled result in the child receiving sweets. But one of the levers is a disaster switch: when this is pulled, the child loses all the sweets so far accumulated. The children never know which of the levers is the disaster switch, but they do know that the more levers they have pulled successfully, the more likely it is that the next one will bring disaster. They also know that they can stop the game whenever they want. Up to the age of eleven, there is no difference between the sexes in the point at which they decide to quit: both are equally prepared to risk everything they have achieved in the hope of winning another handful of sweets. But from eleven onwards, boys are significantly more willing to take the risk, and consequently come away from the experiment with fewer sweets than girls do.

There is some evidence that in adulthood men are more prepared than women to take risks (accident statistics certainly support the idea), and this may be one reason why they achieve more. Whether willingness to take risks is really a quality we should be looking for when promoting people is another matter, but it may be one of the characteristics which enable men to overtake women in the race for top jobs.

Do men and women have different reasons for seeking achievement and success? It has been suggested that although men and women may work equally hard at a given task, a man is more interested in the task for its own sake while a woman works in order to gain social approval. Some psychologists have developed this further, and suggested that one of the most important differences between the sexes is that men are more interested in things and women in people. This sounds quite plausible, but like so many other plausible-sounding ideas, it does not survive scientific testing. Many experiments have been carried out in the laboratory in which tasks have to be performed purely for their own sake and without any social approval being given for success. There is no evidence that males do them better, either as children or as adults. Nor do women out-perform men when they have to carry out tasks in company or with the prospect of receiving social approval. One study, which is often cited as evidence that men are more interested in things, showed that between the ages of three and six, boys are more interested than girls in exploring an exciting toy they have never seen before. But this difference is specific to those three years, and it may just reflect the fact that at that age boys are slightly more impulsive than girls.

Of course, just because differences haven't been found does not mean that women don't care what others think—these studies may not be the right way to tap those differences. The social aspect is very important to women, who have usually been more interested in communicating with people from birth, and place more importance on working in a friendly environment. Women do care about what other people think, and there is evidence that they are more deflated than men by hostile criticism.

But so far as the desire for social approbation is concerned, it is actually boys and men whose behaviour changes more when they are being watched by others. As we saw earlier, the need for achievement scores of male students were boosted dramatically when they were encouraged to think competitively, and studies also show that little boys have a greater tendency than little girls to show off in the presence of other people. Maybe this is because girls have already learned that people tend not to take as much notice of their achievements as they do of boys', so they cannot expect to get as much social reward. In any case, the idea that women do as well as men only because they are desperate for social approval does not seem to be borne out by the facts.

Confidence and self-esteem

That men but not women perform better in competitive conditions brings us to perhaps the most influential of all the popular beliefs about the motivation of men and women. This is the idea that men are more successful than women professionally because they think more highly of themselves and are more firmly convinced that they can handle the top jobs, whereas women are said to be haunted by doubts about their own value and ability to cope with positions involving real responsibility. But do women in fact have a lower opinion of themselves than men, and are they really less confident in their abilities?

This sounds like a simple yes/no question, but it actually turns out to be nothing of the sort. So far as self-esteem is concerned, there is some evidence that from an early age women think less highly of their own sex than men do of theirs. When researchers asked a group of kindergarten children if they would like to have been born into the opposite sex, one in five of the girls were ready to change while none of the boys showed any enthusiasm for the idea. However, this does not necessarily imply that the girls thought their own sex inferior. In answer to another question, none of the girls who were prepared to change sex thought that boys of their own age were cleverer than they were, though more than half of them said they thought their fathers were cleverer than their mothers. So it may just be that the little girls had already worked out that it is a man's world.

In another experiment, when teenagers were asked to assess a piece of written work, both boys and girls gave it a higher mark when they were told it was written by a man than when they believed it to be the work of a woman. But this experiment has been repeated, with children and adults, and the results are not always the same. Some researchers have found that women rate an article *more* highly when they believe its author to be a woman, while others have found that the sex of the author has no effect on what people think of the piece. More convincing support for the view that women have a lower opinion of their own sex than men comes from the observation made earlier in the chapter that women seem to expect nasty things to happen to other women who have become successful, while men take a more sanguine view of other men's success. Moreover, several studies show that both men and women rate the qualities they associate with the ideal male more highly than those of their ideal female.

So if women do have a lower opinion of their own sex than men, this may just be a reflection of the general devaluation of what women say and do. A lack of respect for women, even those in positions of authority, is learned quite early, as we can see from studies of the behaviour of British schoolchildren. Some educationalists have suggested that female teachers may experience more disruptive behaviour from boys than male teachers do, and boys seem to work harder for male teachers. This pattern continues at college: a review of recent research shows that students tend to expect higher standards and have different expectations of female academic staff, challenge their authority more, are more rude and aggressive to them, and evaluate them more harshly.

On balance, it looks as though women do tend to have rather a low opinion of other women generally, and it would seem to follow from this that individual women must think less highly of themselves than men do. This assumption has been tested directly, by getting people to fill in questionnaires about themselves, and indirectly, by asking them to estimate what other people think of themselves. In fact, the two methods produce the same result, and it is not at all what you would expect: individual women do *not* seem to value themselves less highly than individual men, whatever they may think about their own and the other sex generally. In childhood, any difference between the sexes in self-esteem actually tends to be weighted towards girls: a few studies have found that they value themselves more highly than boys do, despite the fact that they are more willing to admit to their own failings. Parents tend to describe their sons and daughters as equally satisfied with themselves, while in one study teachers rated the girls in their class as having higher self-esteem, though there was no difference between the sexes in the way the children rated themselves.

Later in life, it is no easier to show that men and women differ in self-esteem. Most studies find that they value themselves equally highly as individuals, and when there is a difference between the sexes, it can go either way. A study carried out on men and women in late middle age who had been exceptionally gifted as children offers some support for the popular view: the women admitted to more feelings of bitterness and disappointment than the men. But another study, carried out on people between the ages of twenty-five and forty, found just the opposite: it was the women who were more optimistic than the men about their future personal and professional prospects. A third study, of retired academic and professional people, found men and women to be equally happy with their lives and satisfied with themselves.

It is a confusing picture, but the evidence does not seem to support the common assumption that the average woman's opinion of herself is lower than the average man's is of himself, even though she may not think as highly of her own sex as he does of his. This is a surprising finding: not only does it contradict a widely held assumption—that women tend to be less satisfied with themselves than men are—but it points as well to a curious inconsistency in their attitude. It is also a booby-trap, because it encourages us to draw what turns out to be another erroneous conclusion. The fact that women think just as highly of themselves as men do seems to imply that they must have just as much confidence in their own ability. But the evidence is overwhelmingly against this assumption. For once, experimental studies support popular wisdom. It may seem paradoxical, but despite the fact that men and women are equal in ability, equally anxious to succeed, and have much the same opinion of their own value as individuals, when there is a job to be done, men are much more confident than women that they will be able to do it and much more satisfied with their actual performance. This difference in self-confidence is the most striking difference between the sexes in motivation, and it applies even when the task is one in which women usually do better than men—solving anagrams, for example.

Outside the laboratory, the position is exactly the same: several studies have found that when students are asked to forecast how well they will do in an examination, men on the whole expect to do as well if not better than they have done in the past, whereas women tend to predict that they are going to do worse than their past performance would suggest. In one typical study, American women students were much more pessimistic than their male colleagues in predicting what course grades they would be given, although in the event they actually did better than the men. Similarly, in a survey of 5,650 second-year students in more than a hundred British universities, polytechnics and colleges, 64 per cent of men questioned said they thought they would get first- or upper-second-class honours compared to only 48 per cent of the women, and the men were also much more confident than the women of obtaining a suitable job after graduation.

Your first reaction to this finding may be that it must be due to the fact that men are more inclined to boast. But the difficulty with this explanation is that the measures of self-confidence were taken in private, so whom were the men trying to impress, except perhaps themselves? And if men are more inclined to boast to themselves, surely they would score more highly than women on the measures of self-esteem, and we know that they do not. Another possible explanation is that women deliberately under-estimate their chances for fear of tempting fate. This would certainly be in keeping with another popular belief, that women are the more superstitious sex. There is some empirical support for the idea, though a study carried out recently amongst London students casts doubt on it. So how can we explain men's greater— and unjustified—self-confidence? The answer to this question actually lies not in men's arrogance but in women's lack of self-confidence, and to understand this we have to look at an aspect of personality we have not yet considered.

Although the two sexes are fairly equally matched in their achievements at school and at college, it seems that men and women explain their own successes in different ways. When you succeed at something, you can either take the credit yourself or you can put it down to luck or some other factor beyond your control. For example, after doing well in an examination, you could either point out that you were good at the subject and had worked hard, or else you could say that by some lucky fluke the examiners had set all the questions you had revised. People who usually take the credit for their own success are said to have an *internal locus of control*, which means that they believe that they can generally control by their own actions what happens to them in life. But if you are one of those people who brush aside any success which comes your way by saying that the task was unusually easy or that luck just happened to be on your side that day, then you have an *external locus of control*. Most of us fall into one or other of these categories, and so can be described as either internalizers or externalizers. During childhood, equal numbers of boys and girls fall into the two categories, but by early adulthood more women than men are found to have an external locus of control. This suggests an explanation for the fact that women tend to be less confident than men when asked to predict how well they are going to do at some future task. It may well be that women are more pessimistic in their prediction because they are more inclined to dismiss their previous success as a matter of luck, which is unlikely to be on their side again.

You can test the idea that women believe more in luck and men in their own skill the next time you go to a fair. Observe who plays what game, and you will probably find more women playing games of luck like Bingo but more men shooting ducks or playing other games which call for skill. A psychologist who observed this had the bright idea of inviting people into her laboratory and offering them a choice of games which they could play. She found that 75 per cent of the men chose a game which required skill, while 65 per cent of the women opted for a game of chance. The same investigator then asked a group of top men and women managers why they thought they had been so successful. The women did not put it all down to luck. But they were more inclined than the men to stress how hard they had worked to get to the top, whereas the men were more willing to attribute their success to natural ability, which suggests that it is not just male students who are blessed with greater self-confidence than their female contemporaries.

The fact that women have less confidence in themselves than men do may lie at the heart of many of the sex differences which have been observed in adult behaviour: for example, the fact that women are more inclined to use the 'don't know' option in opinion surveys, and that more women than men believe in God. It may even explain why women have a greater tendency to vote Conservative, since psychologists regard a Conservative vote as a sign of anxiety in the face of uncertainty!

Being self-confident and in control of your fate seems to be an important part of the stereotype of masculinity, and it is not difficult to see where boys get these characteristics from. Read a few children's stories and one of the first things that will strike you is the difference in the extent to which male and female characters are in control of their lives. According to the results of a recent detailed analysis of the content of children's stories, when pleasant things happen to a male character, he is usually responsible for bringing them about. But when they happen to a female—which is much less often—she usually has someone else to thank for her good fortune. After years of reading such stories, watching television programmes in which men act (often to startling effect) while women watch and wait in admiration and hope, and observing that men hold the vast majority of positions of power and responsibility, there is nothing very mysterious about the fact that more women than men tend to become externalizers. And because of this perceived lack of control, it is not surprising that more women feel helpless in the face of difficulties and are more likely to suffer from depression, as we saw in Chapter 3.

What is surprising is that the sex difference in locus of control does not appear earlier. But when we look at other measures which have been used to assess a person's feeling of his or her ability to influence events, it becomes clear that boys do become very much more confident than girls in this respect by the age of six, if not earlier. In fact little boys tend to see themselves as being more influential than they really are, in much the same way as they later tend to be over-optimistic when asked to predict how well they are going to do—or have done—in an examination or some laboratory task. Since it has also been found that men are less deflated than women by hostile criticism, one reason why they feel more self-confident and in control of their lives may be that they are better at ignoring unfavourable comments from other people and at erasing the memory of past failures.

If you look back over the evidence in this chapter, you will find little support for the suggestion that men and women want different things out of life. Both sexes seem highly motivated to achieve similar objectives, and although men may be more willing to take risks to get what they want, there is no evidence that they are more interested than women in doing a job for its own sake, or that a woman's main reason for wanting to be successful is that she craves the social approval success brings. It is true that competition galvanizes boys more than it does girls, but it brings them only up to the level of motivation at which girls operate without the extra spur. Men and women have an equally high opinion of themselves as individuals, even though women tend to think less well of their sex as a whole. Men do tend to be more optimistic than women that they are going to succeed at a task— though this optimism is often misplaced—and more men than women believe that they are in control of their destinies. But this is not enough to explain why women's achievements in spheres other than the domestic should drop off so sharply once they have finished with education, or why men should be so much more successful professionally. So we are left with the question with which we began: why is it that men get all the best jobs?

What holds women back?

One possible explanation stems from the difference between the education years, when women do as well as men, and the years at work, when they don't. The argument is very simple. When you are at school or at college, your life is highly structured and you have comparatively little choice about how you spend your time or what your objective should be—it is usually the next set of exams. But things are rather different later in life: you have to set your own goals and decide how to achieve them. So a man's greater self-confidence and his belief that he can control his destiny now gives him a distinct advantage.

There may be something in this argument, though I think it underestimates the extent to which college students have to organize their own lives, and exaggerates the freedom of action most people have in their working lives. There is also less pressure on women to become mothers when they are students than in later years. But the suggestion that men do better than women at work because of a difference in personality is less plausible than it sounds, because although the two are related, the relationship is actually the other way round: researchers find personality has comparatively little to do with what sort of job a person is likely to get, whereas the job someone does can have quite a marked effect on their personality and attitudes.

Nor do I know of any evidence which supports the idea that there is something about women's personalities that makes them worse bosses than men. Women who have become managers themselves are sympathetic in their assessment of other successful women, according to the results of a study carried out in Canada in the late 1970s. Women workers too tend to be comparatively well-disposed towards the idea of women as employers. Male employees, however, are less charitable, especially if they have had experience of working for a woman boss. Why should this be so?

One reason is that women are often portrayed as being weak and indecisive, unable to make the tough decisions that a good boss needs. But it may just be that women take account of more information, instinctively keeping several factors in balance— they are particularly good at perceiving the human dimension of any problem, like the female architects we talked about in Chapter 4. These sorts of qualities should not be seen as a weakness in a manager—in fact, the human factor may increasingly become an advantage in business, as will be discussed in Chapter 8.

The two complaints most frequently made about female bosses is that they are less good than men at getting people to carry out their wishes (though this, if true, might tell us more about the position of women in society than about deficiencies in an individual woman), and that power turns women nasty. These attitudes came out very clearly in a survey I carried out. A young male accountant stated his views succinctly: 'I've worked for several women, and some of them have been real sods.' However, he then rather spoilt the effect by adding: 'Just like some of the men I've worked for!' He continued: 'With a bloke you can have an argument and get it out of your system. But with a woman nothing is said . . . You're forever trying to be a clairvoyant, and that's worse than saying nothing because it never actually comes out what you've done wrong.'

But is this feeling about women bosses justified, or is it just that maltreatment by a woman boss is more likely to stick in the mind than similar treatment from a man, because she is that rare bird—a boss who is also a woman? Laboratory studies with students confirm the popular belief that women resort to emotional outbursts and to appeals based on their own helplessness more often than men when trying to get their own way, while men rely more on reasoned arguments. They also show that the 'feminine' strategy, though it may work in the short term, is less effective than the male approach over a period of time, and is damaging to the self-esteem of the person using it.

But these studies were carried out on students who had no authority over the people they were trying to persuade, and there is no evidence that women who become bosses use this strategy. In fact, studies of leaders in real-life organizations have found no difference in the strategies male and female bosses use to impose their wishes, and they also show that women bosses are no more unpleasant to their employees than men are, so long as they have real authority. It seems that the worst boss to work for is one with an impressive title but no real power—'paper tigers' vent their frustration on weaker animals. But this applies to both sexes, and the bad reputation women have as bosses probably stems from the fact that it is more common for them to be fobbed off with token authority. When they are given real power, there is no evidence that women behave any worse—or any better, it has to be said—than men.

It is very difficult to discover to what extent the woman boss has become accepted. It seems to vary enormously according to country, region and type of job, not to mention the personalities of everyone involved. But the conclusions reached by researchers who investigated the question among American library staff are not untypical. They found that women preferred to be supervised by another woman, that women with male supervisors seemed to get on less well with their fellow workers than women supervised by other women or than men with male supervisors, and that women supervised by other women experienced greater job satisfaction than men with male supervisors.

But what sort of women achieve authority at work and how are they affected by their success? There are so many different levels of power at work that it is impossible to establish general laws. However, there are some straws in the wind. For example, personality tests and attitude surveys point to the unsurprising conclusion that successful working women are more eager for responsibility and more willing to take risks than others. In New Zealand, where women occupy a much smaller proportion of senior positions than they do in either Britain or the US, it appears that female managers are more likely to have been brought up either in big cities (which are challenging) or on isolated farms (which seem to provide a spur by being a background to be escaped from at any price!). In New Zealand at least, small towns are an unpromising breeding-ground for successful career women, because they combine a low level of stimulation with a tolerable level of comfort and amenities.

More than half of the women involved in this ambitious attempt to provide a biographical profile of the female manager were single or separated, and exactly half of them had no children. Apart from their shared geographical backgrounds, they also had in common the fact that nearly two-thirds of them had been elected class leaders at school. A less expected bond which linked them was the fact that most of them had passed their driving test soon after reaching the age at which they were allowed on the roads, which may be interpreted as a practical manifestation of having a high internal locus of control.

There is evidence that women in senior positions tend to work harder than their male colleagues. Not invariably, however: a study of British MPs carried out during the 1970s revealed that women politicians, far from being more conscientious than their male colleagues, actually had noticeably poorer attendance records at committee meetings. But there is abundant evidence that successful career women who have families work very much longer hours than those who do not (using 'work' in a technical

sense, to refer to any activity we feel duty-bound to carry out,
however entertaining the diversions we are offered may be—
which for most mothers will include housework and child-care).

In one study of American academics, a 107 hour working week
was fairly typical of those women who combined a successful
career with domestic chores, as compared with a week of 78
working hours for those without family responsibilities. But the
most striking finding in this study was the fact that the former
group were no more willing to admit that they were overloaded
than the latter. The most likely interpretation of this finding is
that the working mothers did not regard child-care as work. I shall
have more to say about this in Chapter 6. An alternative explanation is that the women were deceiving themselves by making
light of their work-load in order to avoid finding themselves in a
position where it became necessary to make a choice between
their dual careers.

These findings hardly support the suggestion that women suffer
from any lack of motivation. There is, however, one well-
publicized trap into which at least some successful professional
women fall. This is known at the Queen Bee syndrome. Having
succeeded in what is still largely a man's world, the successful woman may feel well-disposed towards the system and her
usually congenial male colleagues, and come to identify herself
with them rather than with other women. Indeed, Queen Bees
sometimes come to despise less successful women more than
men do, and become overtly hostile to the feminist cause, arguing
that since they have made it to the top, women who fail to do so
have only their own feebleness to blame. As the former Prime
Minister Margaret Thatcher was fond of saying: 'What's the
women's movement ever done for me?' They may even conspire
with male colleagues to keep other women out of important jobs,
while strongly denying that sex discrimination exists—how could
it, since they have made it to the top? But although Queen Bees
can become as bad as men in this respect, there is no evidence
that they are any worse to work for, and the attitudes of the
Canadian women managers mentioned earlier serve as a reminder
that by no means all successful women become victims of the
syndrome.

Why then do so few women get to the top? Women do find
it easier than men to express their lack of self-confidence and
emotions, they may have slightly different cognitive abilities, and

certainly choose to study different subjects at school. But some women are undeniably more intelligent than most men, and their superior sensitivity, verbal ability and interpersonal skills could make them better doctors, priests, judges or managers than many men. Although we have seen that the popular belief that they simply are not equipped for the job is based on a series of misconceptions, there can be no doubt that aspiring women professionals still have to contend with a formidable barrier of sexual prejudice.

There is some evidence that this is directly linked to a woman's attractiveness: the more pleasing she looks, the more hostility she must expect at the selection stage. But women in non-managerial positions may have the opposite problem. One American study has shown that although attractiveness is disadvantageous for female bosses, it is an advantage for women in non-managerial roles. Additional results show that while attractiveness makes women seem more feminine, it does not enhance the perceived masculinity of males. So attractiveness seems to influence how well we think a woman can do a task by affecting our view of how feminine she is—we assume that a very feminine woman will be less suited to masculine tasks. According to the stereotype, feminine women make very efficient secretaries, but less competent managers.

If a woman's chances of professional advancement rest in the hands of a man, she has at least two hurdles to overcome which have nothing to do with her objective suitability for the job. He may feel threatened by the knowledge that she will have had to work harder than a man to get where she is and is therefore likely to be of disturbingly high calibre. There is also a very high probability that he will follow one of the most fundamental principles of selection—the tendency to hire one's own kind. The only consolation women can derive from this is that as more of them make their way up management hierarchies, the principle may be working to their advantage—unless, of course, they become victims of the Queen Bee syndrome!

But leaving prejudice aside, there may still be two ways in which being a woman constitutes a serious obstacle to professional success. The first concerns an aspect of personality I have deliberately avoided in this chapter. It is widely believed that, however similar the two sexes may be in other respects, men are naturally more aggressive and more willing and able to fight their way to the top—literally, if necessary. We shall examine the evidence for this claim in Chapter 8. But we cannot leave the subject of motivation without commenting on the fact that while a man can pursue professional success with single-minded determination, a woman usually has to divide her time and energy between her job and a second career, that of housewife and mother.

Getting married has a very different effect on the career prospects of a couple who take the plunge together: it reduces the time a wife can devote to her career, while it may actually increase the working hours available to her husband. Surprising though it may seem, sociologists find that technological progress has had no discernible effect on the time a housewife spends on housework. The average American housewife today spends the same number of hours—fifty-three a week—on domestic chores as her grandmother did, and there is no reason to think that the position is different in other countries. Moreover, despite the demand that men should share the burden, there is little evidence that this is happening. Even when they have no children, working wives still tend to do the bulk of the shopping, washing and cleaning. When there are children, it is found that a husband's contribution to the running of the house actually declines with each child, while the housework done by his wife increases by 5 to 10 per cent for each child. These statements are based on the observations of a team of social scientists working in twelve different countries, in Eastern and Western Europe and in North and South America, and they found surprisingly little variation between one part of the world and another.

Perhaps the major obstacle to any change in the traditional division of labour—and balance of power—between the sexes is the finding that although both men and women seem to be coming round to the idea that women may achieve equality at work one day, the corollary—that men should accept an equal share of domestic duties—is much less widespread, and it is very difficult to see how the first could ever come about without the second. But at least we have found an answer to the question we began with. Since nine out of ten women get married, and the great majority of them have babies, it seems reasonable to assume that the main reason why men get most of the best jobs is that women simply do not have the time and energy to compete for them, let alone do them. They have other things to do.

6

DUAL CAREERS

Nothing in the evidence we have discussed so far suggests that biology is responsible for the fact that we live in what is patently a man's world. Perhaps it can explain how and why men got the upper hand in the first place. But we have yet to identify any aspect of human behaviour essential to success in the modern world in which men have the edge on women by virtue of their being men. The greater physical strength of men now seems to be irrelevant—it is, in any case, offset by their being more vulnerable to disease—and we have seen that men and women are fundamentally very similar in intellectual ability, ambition to succeed, reliability and other aspects of personality which might be involved in getting on in the world. Of course, we have not yet exhausted the catalogue of popular beliefs about the difference between the sexes. There are still two old favourites waiting patiently in the wings: the widely held beliefs that men get to the top jobs either because women are more squeamish about fighting for power (men are more aggressive), or because women are so bruised by their sexual encounters with men that they become resigned to male domination in other areas of life (men want sex, women need love). In the last two chapters of the book, we shall see how well these stand up to advances in our knowledge about human behaviour.

But if we asked the proverbial visitors from Mars to observe life on this planet and tell us why they thought men get most of the best jobs, I doubt if they would mention any of the matters we have been discussing. Instead they would surely say that there is nothing in the least surprising that most of the positions of power in public life go to one sex, since the majority of members of the other sex either withdraw altogether from the competition or at best devote only part of their energy to it, at a stage in their careers where progress is crucial to ultimate professional success.

This sounds like a fair analysis of the present situation, and it is only recently that women have entered the competition at all. A hundred years ago, there was nothing unusual about a woman having twelve children, half of whom might have survived to become adults. If she breast-fed them for eighteen months each, she would have been either pregnant or nursing for virtually the whole of her adult life, given the average life-expectancy of those days. Although things are very different now, many of our contemporary attitudes about what jobs are suitable for women and how much women can be expected to achieve at work seem to date from a time when the vast majority of the work-force was male. It is surely significant that women are more easily accepted, and prosper accordingly, in the newer professions—computer-programming and market research, for example—than in older professions such as medicine or law, which still seem to be dominated by attitudes formed in the days when only menial jobs were open to women.

Women and work

Only one British household in twenty now conforms to the traditional pattern in which the husband goes out to work while his wife stays at home caring for two small children. Women now form more than 40 per cent of the work-force in Great Britain (in Europe, only Danish women are more actively involved in the national economy), though in 1989, four out of ten of these are part-time (whereas only one in ten employed men had part-time jobs). A woman's decision to have children usually leads to a significant gap in her career. Although the hiatus need be no more than a matter of months, the average woman takes about seven years out of employment to raise a family. This period may change in the future with fluctuations in the birth-rate and in the number of women who decide not to have children at all—according to the Director of Population Research in the US, we can expect the proportion of women who make this choice to rise to as much as a third in the near future. It must be remembered that predictions about population trends are notoriously unreliable, and I shall leave speculation about the future of women's dual roles as worker and mother until the end of the chapter.

The changes that have occurred over the past hundred years have been made possible by technological progress: for the first time in history, we can reliably control how many children we have, and, appropriately enough, since they are more affected by the birth of children, the most effective methods of contraception are at the disposal of women. The average woman now has only two children, and goes back to work when they are quite young—the 1991 General Household Survey reported that 59 per cent of employed women have dependent children. But she still accepts the primary responsibility for bringing them up, which affects the type of job she can do and the energy she can devote to it. In 1988 11 per cent of women with children under four were in full-time employment, and a further 25 per cent in part-time employment. Taking a part-time job may look like the ideal solution for a woman who wants or needs to go to work as well as to bring up a family. But part-time jobs tend to offer low pay and low status, and this may contribute to women's inequality in the work-force.

Women with dual careers may deny that they are overloaded, but it is difficult to believe that the demands of motherhood really have no effect on their chances of achieving success at work. Comparisons of successful women with children and those without children produce conflicting results. The attitudes of the Canadian women academics mentioned in the last chapter are not unique: many professional women claim that they find motherhood 'relaxing', and feel that the experience gives them more rather than less energy at work. Remember too the medical evidence discussed in Chapter 3, which suggests that the dual role can be beneficial—staying at home with the children makes women vulnerable to depression.

Is there any way of changing the status quo without causing damage to children? For example, can fathers bring up children as well as mothers, or are women biologically prepared for the task by having a maternal instinct men cannot hope to match? Before trying to answer these questions, we must realize that we are dealing here with an area of human behaviour in which we cannot turn the clock back and settle for the traditional way of organizing our lives. Advances in medical technology have not only made it possible to limit the number of children born, but also made it essential that we do so. Infant mortality has been greatly reduced—by the development of antibiotics, for example—which means that far fewer children need to be born to ensure the survival of the species.

Biological and social considerations make it undesirable for women to function as a non-stop production line for making babies, and technology has provided them with the means for bringing about this change. As a result, they have had to find some other way of occupying their time. But neither biology nor technology can explain why they have chosen to fill the gap by joining men at work. Some writers have suggested that human beings have an innate biological need to work, but it is impossible to reconcile this with the fact that many men and women survived happily on a modicum of work in societies where slave labour was available. So far as the influence of technology is concerned, one of the characteristics of most jobs created by technological innovation is that they can be done equally well by men and women—provided that they have had the right training. But the overall effect of technological progress is to reduce the number of jobs which need to be done by human beings, so technology can hardly be held responsible for the rise of the working woman.

So what did drive women to work? Some of the impetus undoubtedly came from women themselves. The demand for greater professional opportunities was one of the rallying cries of the founder members of the Women's Movement, who realized that men owed much of their superior status to the fact that they held all the positions of power in public life. This may be one reason why women demanded the right to work, but they were granted it only as a result of historical events over which they had little control. Ironically, it was war—one of the few activities for which men seem better suited than women, as we shall see in Chapter 8—which first forced men to relax their stranglehold on jobs which carried prestige. Before this century, wars were usually fought between small professional armies, and so it did not require any drastic redeployment of personnel to keep public life going. But the advent of conscription changed all that, and it was during the two World Wars that large numbers of women enjoyed their first taste of work which carried responsibility and prestige.

The importance of these wars in bringing women into the work-force is sometimes exaggerated, however. Nearly four out of ten women in Britain were already working before the 1914–18 war. Indeed, in 1911, they accounted for nearly one in five of all white-collar managers and administrators, a degree of power-sharing it took them nearly seventy years to re-establish! Any gains they made in the years of the Great War were lost when peace was restored. Many women had to give up their jobs to the returning heroes, while others were forced to keep house for their husbands because of the sharp decline in the number of women prepared to work as domestic servants. But women had shown that they could do 'men's jobs' perfectly adequately when the need arose. The two sexes had worked together, and the ground had been prepared for the massive influx of women into the labour-force which occurred much later, in the 1960s and—especially—the 1970s: the number of women at work increased by more than a third between 1951 and 1981, but almost 40 per cent of that number joined the work-force during the period 1971–6. And while the number of women at work has increased, the number of men at work has decreased. This effect is most dramatic for men and women aged between twenty-five and forty-four. In 1971, over 95 per cent of men in this age group were in paid work, and this figure had dropped slightly by 1990. But at the same time, the proportion of women in this age group who were employed rose from just over a half to nearly three-quarters.

In Chapter 5, we were concerned almost exclusively with women at the top end of the job market. But no more than one woman in five holds a management job (in industry, the figure falls to less than one in ten). Unlike men, working women tend to be concentrated in a small number of professions, most of them poorly paid. Two-thirds of all women currently employed in Britain work in just ten occupations. This explains not only how it is that we can speak of whole professions having low status (see page 117), but also why it is that, for all the increase in women's employment, their earnings stubbornly refuse to catch up with men's. Figures released in autumn 1982 showed that whereas only one man in ten was earning less than £90 a week (the official definition of low pay), half the adult women workers in Britain qualified as low-paid. Women constituted two-thirds of all full-time low-paid workers, and at that time no fewer than nine out of ten low-paid part-time workers were women.

As their economic activity has increased over the last few decades, it has also become more socially acceptable for women to go to work. In the sixties, 78 per cent of women questioned thought that mothers with young children should not work under any circumstances. In 1988, this figure had fallen to 45 per cent, although nearly one in three still thought that mothers should work only in cases of financial necessity. The feeling that a woman's place is in the home is particularly strong amongst the elderly and amongst skilled workers of both sexes. But it is a

theory that few people can afford to put into practice in the
present economic climate, even if they wished to, because in the
average household, the wife's earnings now make up a quarter of
the family income. However, we still seem to have great difficulty
in coming to grips with the notion of women as a significant
economic force: according to a study carried out in the 1970s,
only three British husbands out of ten told their wives what they
earned—this at a time when one married woman in ten earned
more than her husband (the figure is now estimated to be one in
seven)!

Although a significant number of women earn more than their
husbands, the great majority earn less. Department of Employment figures released in September 1991 showed that the average weekly wage for women is £222, £97 less than the £319 a
week that a man can expect to get. And when overtime pay was
excluded, although the average pay gap between men and women
was the smallest since records were started twenty years ago, the
average woman's salary was still only 78 per cent of the average
man's.

And yet women show no sign of becoming disillusioned with
working. On the contrary, surveys suggest that four out of five
women with children still say they would certainly carry on
working even if they became millionaires overnight. Although we
have seen that they no longer work for pin-money, women have
obviously learned to appreciate the psychological fringe benefits
of employment—status, friendship and so forth. It therefore
seems very unlikely that they will voluntarily agree to leave
the work-force *en masse*, however much such an eventuality
may appeal to politicians seeking to reduce the level of male
unemployment.

This is why it is crucial to study that comparatively new breed,
the Working Woman, if we are to understand the similarities and
differences between men and women. In this chapter, we shall try
to discover what effect working has on a woman, on the man (or
men) in her life and—very importantly—on any children she may
have.

The maternal instinct

Let us first look at what happens to women who decide to devote
themselves exclusively to their careers, and to opt out of mother-

hood altogether. It is difficult to estimate how many women fall into this category at present or are likely to in the future, though we know that the proportion of American women aged twenty-nine who had not yet given birth rose from one in eight in 1965 to more than one in five in 1976. We also know that in 1975 17 per cent of unmarried American women students who took part in one survey and 15 per cent of married Dutch women who took part in another, declared their intention not to have children. It seems, then, that a significant minority of women remain voluntarily childless, that their numbers are unlikely to decline, and that those who do not have children are more likely to achieve positions of power in public life than those whose energy is divided between their jobs and the demands of motherhood.

But what are they like, these harpies who prefer the rigours of office life to domestic bliss? According to popular belief, a woman who does not have children is not fulfilling her natural role, and so is bound to be frustrated and miserable. This is supposed to apply to men who remain childless as well, but to a much lesser extent, because there is thought to be no male equivalent of the maternal instinct which is alleged to nudge women into motherhood and to ensure that they love and treat properly any children they may have. But is there such a thing as the maternal instinct, and are women naturally better equipped than men to rear children?

Where other animals are concerned, there does seem to be biological instinct at work. Virgin female rats, for example, show very little interest in other rats' pups, but they become much more maternal, building nests or retrieving pups when they wander off, when they are given a transfusion of blood taken from a rat which has recently given birth. This suggests that rats have a maternal instinct, and that it is under hormonal control. But it is not just *female* rats which can be prodded into protecting the young by being given the appropriate hormones. Male rats too, whose interest in their offspring is usually confined to attacking them, show some signs of maternal behaviour when saddled with new-born pups which no one else will look after. If they are injected with hormones, they will even build nests for them, but surprisingly, it is testosterone rather than female hormones which turns them into makeshift mothers. So although there may be a maternal instinct in rats, it is not confined to females, nor is it exclusively under the control of female sex hormones.

The position is much more complicated when it comes to monkeys and humans. Although hormones are involved in the process of giving birth—there are hormonal changes just before birth, and the sucking of a mother's breast by a new-born baby stimulates hormones which cause her uterus to contract and expel the afterbirth—female primates cannot function adequately as mothers unless they are given the opportunity of learning how it is done. A female monkey who is separated from her mother at birth and so deprived of first-hand experience of mothering, refuses to look after her own first child, though she gets better with practice and can learn to rear later children adequately. The tendency for mothers to love their children may be biologically inspired in many animals, but it cannot be a very strong drive, because it often requires only a brief separation after birth for the mother to show no response to her offspring when it is returned to her.

Where human beings are concerned, the evidence for a maternal instinct is rather flimsy. Girls play with dolls and show maternal behaviour more than boys, and so seem to practise motherhood from a very early age, but whether this is due to biological instinct is not clear. The argument in favour of it, like so many of the arguments we have examined, began in the mists of time. Some biologists maintain that caring for children must have been bred into women, and bred out of men, for the species to have survived for so long. They argue that since primitive children would have been entirely dependent on their mothers' milk, only those with the most nurturant mothers could have survived, and so the genes of non-nurturant mothers must have died out. Men, on the other hand, would have been most likely to pass on their genes by impregnating as many women as they could lay their bodies on. So it would have been the genes of the nurturant, stay-at-home men which would have died out, and those of the hit-and-run Don Juans which would have been most likely to be perpetuated.

It is impossible to prove that this story is fiction. But we could write it very differently, and no less plausibly. We might, for example, argue that it would have been counter-productive for a primitive man to sire large numbers of children, because he would have been unable to provide food and protection for all their mothers. As a result, many of them would have died. Prolific fathers would also not have been available to stand in for their children's mothers when they became ill, so we could make a perfectly respectable case for saying that it would actually have been the stay-at-home man who had the best chance of being survived by children carrying his genes. This implies that evolutionary considerations would have favoured the development of an instinct to produce and rear children in both sexes, and, as we shall see later in the chapter, there is very little about the way in which mothers and fathers treat their babies—or the way in which babies respond to their parents—which suggests that any instinct we may have to bring up children is the prerogative of one sex rather than the other.

Perhaps the most frequently heard argument in favour of a maternal instinct stems from there having been very few societies in which women have not been responsible for child-care. This has led to the assumption that they are uniquely well equipped for the role. In fact it proves nothing of the sort. People who argue in this way are merely putting themselves in the position of the disc jockey who says, 'A million people have bought this record, so it must be good', and you have only to listen to some of the records which sell a million to see how shaky this proposition is! They are also guilty of a logical error known as the naturalistic fallacy—the belief that the way things are is the way they ought to be—which commits them to the view that any change must be for the worse. It requires only one instance of a historical change which has been for the good of mankind—the abolition of slavery, for example—to prove them wrong.

While we are looking at history, it is important to record the fact that although women have always looked after children, they have also been responsible for most of the violence which children have suffered. In societies which permitted infanticide, it was often women who performed the grisly task. Even when it was not sanctioned—in Victorian England, for example—women have been prepared to murder their illegitimate children rather than face social ostracism. No doubt they felt remorseful and deprived as a result of their action. But an 'instinct' which is subordinate to economic and social pressures looks increasingly suspect, especially in the light of baby-battering. The factors which cause parents to inflict deliberate physical damage on their children are still something of a mystery. But we know that mothers are far more often involved than fathers (unsurprisingly perhaps, given the relative amounts of time the two sexes spend in their children's company), and that the phenomenon has reached disturbing proportions in recent years.

According to popular wisdom, however, motherhood comes naturally to women. On becoming pregnant, a woman is gripped by a primeval instinct which ensures that she will love, cherish and instinctively recognize the needs of her child after it is born. It may seem churlish to question so attractive a picture, but several lines of evidence suggest that it reflects at least a degree of wishful thinking. For a start, recent surveys have shown that only about half of all women feel an immediate sense of love for their babies. Four out of ten first-time mothers recall that their predominant emotion on holding their baby for the first time was indifference. In the huge majority of cases, however, this is replaced by love and affection within a week of delivery, and it should be said that an early lack of affection is often linked to some understandable cause such as difficult labour, unusually large doses of pain-killers, or depression which existed before the child was born.

The condition of post-natal depression, which affects a significant number of new mothers, is less well understood. Contrary to what many doctors believe, it does not seem to be caused by hormonal irregularities, and is not confined to the weeks after giving birth. It is unknown in most non-industrial societies, especially in those where long-established custom removes the need for parents to make decisions about how to rear their children. Post-natal depression may well be the price of individual freedom and responsibility in this aspect of living. But it is another phenomenon which suggests that we should re-examine one of the two most important implications of the maternal instinct hypothesis: the notion that all women take to motherhood as easily as ducks take to water.

Its second implication—that all normal women must want to become mothers—has led to a great deal of misery, not only among women who have been unable to have children, but also for those mothers—and their children—who had babies as a result of social pressures rather than from a positive desire to do so. Since there is no convincing evidence that women are governed by an instinct to have children, I think we should abandon the notion of a maternal instinct, while acknowledging that the experience of being a mother is one which the great majority of women still prefer not to miss.

But I see no reason to be apprehensive about the well-being of those who decide not to have children. Indeed, the results of a survey carried out in the Netherlands suggest that both men and women can be just as happy without children as with them. A large and representative sample of men and women between the ages of twenty-five and sixty-five answered questions about their satisfactions and fears, and their replies offered no support whatever for the view that having children is a recipe for happiness in either sex. Parents in the sample were no happier than non-parents—if anything, the reverse was true—and older people without children were found to be no more anxious about old age or death than those who had children, nor were they more doubtful about the purpose of life. All these findings applied equally to men and women, so if either sex has an innate need to produce children, it seems that a significant proportion of the Dutch population is frustrating it without suffering any obvious ill-effects!

These results are surprising. We might have expected to find that at least the older members of the sample were regretting that they had never had children. But they tie in with the findings of surveys carried out in several countries on the attitudes of parents approaching the time when their children leave home to begin independent lives. It is commonly believed that parents become depressed at this point. There is even a name for the malaise which is supposed to afflict them—the Empty Nest syndrome. But this is the opposite of what researchers have actually found. Most of the couples they have talked to seem to be positively looking forward to life without their children (many of them spontaneously describe it as a bonus for reaching middle age!). If we take these results in conjunction with the finding that 42 per cent of British working-class mothers who are confined to their homes with young children suffer from clinical depression, and that up to the age of thirty-five women without children are less prone to neurotic disorders than those who have them, the conclusion seems inevitable: it is impossible to maintain that a woman who decides not to have children must necessarily be less happy than one who makes the opposite decision.

Working mothers

Women may be able to survive without having children, but the great majority of them want to experience motherhood and I very much doubt whether this will change. What *has* changed is that most women now want to combine being a mother with having a career. This brings us to a very important question: is it damaging for children to be brought up in a home where a mother is at work? A report put out by the World Health Organization (WHO) forty years ago produced the axiom that mother-love in infancy is as essential for normal psychological development as vitamins are for normal physical development. The principal author of the report subsequently made it clear that he did not believe that only a child's biological mother was equipped to bring him up, or that her absence—for any length of time, and for whatever reason—must inevitably harm him. But these were the ideas that took root in the public consciousness.

The practical consequences of the report were enormous. Welfare agencies based their policies on the assumption that it must be less damaging for a child to be brought up by incompetent—or even downright malevolent—parents than by foster parents or in an institution. More importantly, mothers of that generation were led to believe that it would be irresponsible for them to return to work until all their children were at school, however pressing the economic or personal reasons for their wanting to take a job earlier.

Most psychologists now agree that the WHO report which introduced the concept of *maternal deprivation* greatly overstated its effects. This was not, as some feminists have suggested, part of an international conspiracy to keep women out of the labour-force at a time of high unemployment, but simply because the report was based on incomplete information, and was too strongly influenced by the results of studies of children who had been brought up in institutions in which the quality of child-care fell far below modern standards. Unfortunately, the report was produced before child psychologists had developed techniques for studying the detailed workings of the relationship between a baby and his or her parents, at a time when we knew much less about how successful child-rearing is carried out, let alone why it sometimes fails.

Partly as a result of interest generated by the report, the relationship between human babies and their parents has been examined in minute detail over the last twenty years. Child psychologists have spent many thousands of hours observing how parents and their babies behave towards each other, and we are now in a much better position to assess how much a baby is likely to be affected by having a mother who works, and to look again at the all-important question, Are women uniquely well equipped to bring up their own children? I call this question all-important because the fact that women are men's equals in so many respects will count for very little—and may well be a source of frustration—if it really is true that children inevitably suffer when their mothers are not present all the time throughout the pre-school years.

We saw earlier that there is not much evidence that women have an irresistible biological instinct to produce babies and must suffer if they deny it. But it is still possible that when a woman does have a baby, biological factors make her the best person to bring it up. We know that the maternal behaviour of a female rat is at least partly controlled by its sex hormones, and we also know that the production of oestrogen in pregnant women is stepped up during the five weeks before they give birth. It has not yet been proved that this has any effect on the way they treat their babies, but we might take it as evidence that mothers are biologically prepared for the birth of a child, and perhaps as an indication that they are likely to be the best person to look after it. It would not, however, prove that they are the *only* people who could do the job, and there are two qualifications which have to be borne in mind when trying to gauge the significance of a mother's hormones for the well-being of her child.

The first is that, even in rats, hormones influence maternal behaviour only before and for a short period after giving birth. The female rat soon comes to rely on the presence of her pups to remind her to behave in a suitably maternal fashion, and there is convincing evidence that a human mother, too, often finds it difficult to form a close relationship with a baby who is taken away from her at birth and placed in an incubator, because it has been born prematurely or as a result of some other complication. Interestingly, fathers are also more likely to play a major role in looking after a child if they have been present when it was born, and during the first days of its life.

The second thing to bear in mind is that by no means all mothers in industrialized countries breast-feed their babies (in

Britain, figures released in November 1982 suggest that about a third do not). Since we know that the act of breast-feeding produces a physiological response even in adoptive mothers, we must assume that mothers who do not breast-feed thereby reduce any impact which hormones might otherwise have had on their behaviour.

There is some evidence that breast-feeding strengthens the emotional bond between a mother and her child. But the fact that so many mothers form a perfectly satisfactory relationship with their children without breast-feeding them, while the relationship can break down when breast-feeding is employed, argues against attaching too much importance to this aspect of a mother's rapport with her child. It is also striking how quickly and easily adoptive parents take to their new role, even though the adoptive mother has not been pregnant with the child, and so will have neither experienced the hormonal changes of pregnancy nor breast-fed the child.

There is no way of being certain how much—if any—of a mother's behaviour towards her baby is innate, and how much the result of learning. John Watson, the founding father of behaviourist psychology, spent some time observing young mothers and concluded that nursing is the only ready-made activity. As he put it, 'The mother is usually about as awkward as she can be. The instinctive factors are practically nil.' Other observers have disputed his view. Most mothers seem to have a standard way of touching their new-born babies, beginning with the arms and legs and then stroking the back and stomach. They also tend to hold their babies so that they can look into each other's eyes. When holding or feeding the baby, they bring its face to within about a foot of their own, which happens to be the distance at which a new-born baby's eyes focus best. More significantly, even adults without children consistently hold babies at a distance at which the baby's—though not necessarily their own—eyes are best in focus. Mothers also pitch their voices higher when talking to their babies, and we know (though mothers may not) that babies are more responsive to high-pitched sounds.

However, the fact that mothers everywhere seem to treat their babies in the same way in many respects does not prove that the behaviour is instinctive. And even if it is, there is evidence that fathers too behave in a fairly standard way when first confronted by their own children, which suggests that it is not just mothers but *parents* who are biologically programmed to treat babies in a certain way. Nor do we have to wait to become parents before our biological response to babies manifests itself. American researchers introduced a group of eight- to fourteen-year-old children of both sexes to a young baby, and then observed their reactions while they watched a film of the baby lying in its cot. The results were extraordinarily revealing. At a physiological level, girls and boys were equally affected by the sight of the child smiling or crying. Their heart-rate tended to slow down when it smiled, and they became physiologically aroused when they saw that it was crying. But it would have been impossible to tell that they shared the same gut reaction from the way they behaved. The girls looked much more interested while the boys pretended to ignore the baby's distress, a sex difference which was much more marked among the older than the younger children. This is a classic demonstration of how a basic biological similarity between the sexes can be turned into what looks like a significant sex difference in behaviour, presumably as a result of the pressure to conform to different gender roles.

Fathers and their children

The fact that it is usually the mother who plays the major role in bringing up a child seems to be the result of economic rather than biological necessity. Someone has to go out and earn the money, and since most husbands earn more than their wives, partly because they tend to be older, it usually makes economic sense for them to sacrifice her salary rather than his. But very few husbands today follow Oscar Wilde's prescription for fatherhood ('Fathers should be neither seen nor heard; that is the only proper basis for family life'). In fact, we know that men can rear children, in a slightly different way from mothers but—so far as we can tell—no less effectively.

A recent series of experiments shows that even the male rhesus monkey, who is usually an aggressive and inflexible creature not given to nurturant behaviour, is capable of rearing a child when encouraged to do so in the laboratory. In these experiments, a baby monkey was taken away from his mother a month after being born and placed first in the cage next door to an adult male, and then—for a very short time—in a small protective cage inside the adult's. This was a necessary precautionary measure, in view of the fact that male monkeys normally have little to do with the young, and sometimes attack or even kill them. Once the adult had stopped making threatening gestures, the baby monkey was released from the small cage and soon approached the adult and tried to cling to him. At first he was repulsed angrily, but after a while the adult began to groom him—an important ice-breaker in the social life of rhesus monkeys—and from then on the two became steadily more attached to each other. In fact they became closer than most rhesus *mothers* and their children, and remained so long after the time when young monkeys usually break with their mothers and start to lead an independent life. Their relationship was not the same as that of the typical rhesus mother and child—they went in for more rough-and-tumble play than female monkeys will tolerate—but the younger monkey developed into a perfectly normal adult male and remained on excellent terms with his foster-father.

I pointed out in Chapter 1 how dangerous it is to assume that what holds for other animals must hold for humans too. But the fact that a male rhesus monkey, who would normally be indifferent or hostile towards his offspring, can find within himself the ability to rear a baby gives us a powerful incentive to look at the results of studies in human infants, in order to investigate the role which human fathers play in child-rearing and to see what happens when the father replaces the mother as the principal caretaker of a young child.

This is an area of great theoretical interest to psychologists, but it is also a matter of considerable practical importance. There are already couples where the man assumes the major responsibility for bringing up the children, usually because the woman earns a higher salary than he does and they are not prepared to entrust the task to a hired help. The arrangement is probably most common in Sweden, where child-care is regarded more as a public responsibility, and either parent is entitled to seven months off work after the birth of a child at 95 per cent of their full salary.

More than half of the women and 43 per cent of the men in the survey of *Cosmopolitan* readers mentioned earlier said that they would like this system to be introduced in the UK. But a complete reversal of roles will probably never appeal to more than a small minority of couples, and may just be unrealistic. Even in Sweden, where public policy and ideology support gender equality in the family, and men are more involved in child-care, domestic chores continue to be allocated mainly on the basis of gender.

This is less important than the fact that, in countries where maternal employment is both acceptable and encouraged, the feelings of guilt and conflict which are often reported by working mothers in Britain are much less common. The rapidly increasing number of women who want to share responsibility for child-rearing with their husbands or professional child-minders in order to pursue their careers would obviously feel better about doing so if they knew that mothers do not occupy a uniquely important position in their children's lives.

Fortunately for their peace of mind, this is exactly what the evidence suggests. The most striking finding to emerge from the scientific analysis of a baby's world is that mothers are less important figures than we thought, and that fathers play a vital role—particularly when they are at hand all the time, but even when they are not. Careful observation of couples who both participate in looking after their children reveals that when both parents are present during the first three days of life, it is fathers who spend more time stimulating their babies by holding and rocking them, though mothers smile more at their babies. The father may be the main source of stimulation, but it is the mother who assumes the bulk of the caretaking duties such as cleaning and feeding, even though most babies feed just as well when their father is holding the bottle, and fathers are just as good as mothers at interpreting a child's distress signals. By the time a baby is three months old, its parents have often swapped duties: when both parents are present, he now does more of the caretaking while she provides more stimulation, by playing with the child. A year later, the mother still tends to be the child's main playmate, though this changes later: at eighteen months, both parents share the privilege, while by the age of three, most children prefer to play with their father.

When both parents are involved in child-rearing, their roles are not interchangeable. We saw earlier in the book that fathers tend to be more physical when they play with children, while mothers favour conventional games like peek-a-boo, and they also provide them with more intellectual stimulation by reading to them or encouraging them to manipulate objects. During the first year of their lives, children tend to laugh and smile more at their fathers, but are more likely to turn to their mothers for reassurance when threatened or in distress.

The quality of a child's relationship with his or her father seems to be the most important factor in deciding how he or she will respond to the rest of the world. For example, an experiment carried out on six-month-old boys found that those who had most contact with their fathers were least disturbed when a stranger of either sex picked them up. Similarly, a recent American study shows that the less frequently babies of both sexes are dressed and bathed by their fathers, the longer they cry when they are left alone with an adult they don't know.

Nor is social development the only area in which fathers make a significant contribution. The rocking, talking and touching that fathers provide in response to their children's signals teaches a baby that it can affect other people by its actions, and encourages its intellectual curiosity. As a result, research shows that the more contact a child has with its father, the more advanced it is likely to be. This effect is more marked for boys, though other aspects of a father's behaviour can also have a direct effect on a daughter's intellectual development: more specifically, it seems that fathers who are imaginative at playing have the most advanced sons, while those who are generous with their praise and good at responding to a child's initiatives do most to accelerate their daughters' development.

Children seem to seek different things from their parents: security from their mother, friendship and stimulation from their father. But they do not show a consistent preference for either until they are about a year old. By the time they are one, however, most children have become more attached to one parent than to the other, though they have usually formed an important relationship with both, and perhaps with other adults as well. Roughly a half of children show a marked preference for their mother over their father; they are more distressed when she leaves the room, and they spend more time with her when both parents are present. But about a quarter of children (mainly, though not exclusively, boys) show a marked preference for their father, while the remaining quarter seem equally attached to both parents.

The picture is more complicated than I have painted it here: for example, the sex of a child is significant, as is the amount of time an individual father spends with his children. But that only one child in two would rather be with its mother than its father makes it very difficult to maintain the view that biology dictates that mothers must occupy a unique position in the life of their children. Where once it seemed that babies must form a unique

bond with their mothers to have any chance of developing normally, psychologists now believe that what matters is that they
should form at least one close relationship with someone.

It seems to be beneficial for young children to spend time with
and become attached to more than one person, because this
makes them less concerned about being left with a stranger. If
more than one person is responsible for looking after them, they
get used to adults coming and going. As long as there are not so
many caretakers that the child is unable to form a close relationship with any of them—four is acceptable, but a dozen too
many—the chances are that he or she will be less affected by
separation trauma and spend less time in the 'clinging' phase.
In societies where fathers have virtually no contact with their
children when they are young, babies start to show distress at
being separated from their mothers at a younger age and in a more
extreme form than in a society such as ours, where most fathers
participate to some extent in the task of looking after their children. It is also, of course, extremely useful for a child to be
attached to more than one person if its 'favourite' has to go away
or if the child has to go into hospital and be looked after by
unfamiliar people. In these circumstances, the child who is used
to being looked after by more than one person—whether it is its
father, granny or a regular baby-sitter—has a distinct advantage
over a child looked after solely by its mother.

We have seen how important a father can be to a young baby
when he is prepared to play his part to the full. But how much
time does the average father spend with his children when they
are young? Estimates vary enormously, but even progressive,
middle-class American fathers spend no more than an average of
eight hours a week with their children, according to the results of
a survey carried out in Boston in the early 1970s: three-quarters
of the fathers in this sample, whose children were about nine
months old, said that they did no regular caretaking, and only half
of them had ever changed a nappy! There were large individual
differences between the men—one spent an average of seven
minutes a day with his child, another as much as four hours—
but their involvement was surprisingly modest, in view of the
importance which babies seem to attach to them. Research
carried out on first-time fathers in London ten years later suggests
that little has changed, despite the fact that so many more women
are now at work: it was found that only one father in twenty

made a convincing claim to share child-rearing duties equally with his wife, while two-thirds had never bathed their babies.

Some researchers have come round to the view that paternal deprivation is just as serious a threat to children's welfare as maternal deprivation, a suggestion which must be taken seriously, since we know that children—especially boys—who are brought up in the total absence of a father are more likely to become delinquent and tend to do less well at school (interestingly, it is their visual-spatial ability which is particularly affected).

Since children obviously enjoy and benefit from the company of their fathers, it is important to establish why most fathers spend so little time with them. The answer to this question is vital for women too. If it is really true that nurturance is a quality which has been selectively bred out of men, in accordance with the biologists' argument outlined earlier in the chapter, then the outlook is bleak for women who hope to solve the problem of combining motherhood with a career by asking the father of their children to make a greater contribution towards bringing them up. Fortunately for them, the evidence is overwhelmingly against the proposition that men simply cannot rear children. We have already seen that a male monkey can do it, and we know that a man who is present at the birth of his child will hold, look at, talk to, kiss and imitate the baby as much as—if not more than—the child's mother. And although it is girls who are brought up to expect that they will become mothers and have to look after babies, most boys, even when they are in the roughest stage of their development, enjoy holding and playing with their baby brothers and sisters.

One scientist, Richard Dawkins, suggested that the instinct to look after your children is driven by the overriding natural desire to preserve your genes. This theory provides an interesting explanation for why men in promiscuous societies are very close to their sisters' children. A man's nieces and nephews are definitely genetically related to him, because he and his sister both inherited their mother's genes. But the children of his own wife may not have any of his genes, if she has had many sexual partners (that is, they may not be his children). So in order to ensure the survival of his genes, a man is better off protecting his sister's children than his wife's.

The most likely reason why men spend so little time with their children has nothing to do with biology. It is simply a matter of the way in which our society is organized, as we can see by looking at what happens when the rules are changed, or by examining other societies which have different traditions of child-rearing from our own. It is still too early to assess properly the success of the Swedish experiment with paternity leave mentioned earlier, although we do know that, five years after it was introduced, approximately one couple in eight was taking advantage of the scheme, though this figure was much higher among professional public-sector workers. (Another provision of the Swedish legislation was that both sexes should have an equal right to take time off to look after sick children: within two years of its inception, almost two-thirds of Swedish men were taking more than seven working days off each year for this reason, which was only slightly lower than the figure for Swedish women.) There are, however, enough instances of children in Europe and America being brought up primarily by their fathers for us to be fairly certain that it is no more damaging for a child to be raised in this than in the more traditional manner.

Where the children of single-parent families are concerned, we know that they run a greater risk of getting into trouble than other children. But the dangers do not seem to be greater when the single parent is a father rather than a mother. Compared with single mothers who do not go out to work, single fathers are found to be much less anxious about making alternative caretaker arrangements, and less bothered by the possibility that their children will be distressed at being left. They are also less likely than single mothers to blame themselves for any unhappiness their children may experience, and they give a greater priority to their own personal needs. When the comparison is made between single fathers and working single mothers, all these differences are much less marked (interestingly, it seems that single mothers are less likely to take a job if they have a boy to look after). Nevertheless, it sounds as though children looked after by a single father should be more at risk. But this does not seem to be the case. Generally speaking, the finding is that children in one-parent families appear to suffer least by living with a parent of their own sex. Boys living with their fathers tend to be more mature and sociable, and to rate higher on self-esteem than those reared by their mothers; for girls, the opposite seems to be true.

The fact that children brought up by only one parent are more at risk than those from homes where both parents are present, of course, reinforces the point that it is not just mothers who benefit when fathers are willing to make a contribution to bringing up children. But perhaps the most convincing evidence that men could play a much greater role in child-rearing comes from observations made by anthropologists. Although women are responsible for child-rearing in most societies, there are a few in which men play a much greater role. Western societies place a uniquely heavy burden on the shoulders of the mother: for example, in most primitive societies all the villagers feel responsible for any child they see playing, whereas in our society mothers cannot rely on this kind of help. In at least one language the word meaning 'to give birth' applies to both sexes, and in many societies the custom known as the Couvade operates: when a mother becomes pregnant both she and her husband jointly observe certain rituals, such as avoiding some types of food, and when she goes into labour he may take to his bed too. If you are tempted to dismiss this as no more than a quaint primitive custom, bear in mind that more than half of the husbands in a survey carried out in Britain had experienced mysterious symptoms when their wives were pregnant. They defied rational explanation, but cleared up as soon as their wives gave birth!

The future of parenthood

Some social historians believe that the minor role which men at present play in child-rearing in our society, far from reflecting a biological difference between the sexes, is actually a fairly recent development, dating from the Industrial Revolution. It is only since then that a rigid distinction has been drawn between home—where women and children belong—and work, where men go to earn the family's living. If they are right, it does not require great powers of foresight to predict that this division of labour and allocation of roles between men and women may not last much longer. Not only have women's aspirations changed, but the question is how our daily life is going to be organized in the future. Technological progress probably means that there is going to be less work for people to do, and advances in telecommunications will make it possible for many of the remaining jobs to be carried out at home rather than in an office. Two consequences of these developments are that men will have a great deal more leisure time than they have had since the Industrial

Revolution, and that the distinction between the office and home will become much less clear.

We can be reasonably confident that these changes are going to take place; but what effect they will have on the position of men and women is anybody's guess. According to one school of thought, they will inevitably lead to a final battle between the sexes, in which women will be forced to abandon the progress they have made towards equal professional status and return to their 'traditional' roles of housewife and mother, driven back by men prepared to exploit their greater aggression (of which more in Chapter 8) in order to increase their share of the jobs which remain. At the opposite extreme, there are those who believe that men will see the extra leisure time at their disposal as a golden opportunity to spend more time with their children, and willingly accept an equal share of the responsibility for bringing them up.

My own guess as to what will happen falls between the two. People's worries about being unemployed will not disappear overnight, even if those who work are to be paid no more than those who do not. As long as dignity and status depend on what work we do, and as long as the job market continues to contract, there will be pressure on women to abandon the idea of a career. Against this background, we must expect opposition to schemes based on the suggestion put forward in Chapter 5, that the career structure of high-status jobs should be reorganized so as to avoid frustrating the ambitions of women who want to combine motherhood with a successful career. As a result, a significant number of women will choose not to have children. Many investigators have found that women who go out to work have fewer children than those who do not, and statistical analysis suggests that working may actually reduce a woman's fertility, though we do not yet understand the mechanism behind this.

Other women will certainly continue to combine a career with motherhood, sharing the responsibility of child-rearing with their husbands, other relatives or professional baby-minders. Children do not seem to suffer from being brought up by professional child-minders. Indeed, there is some evidence that they can profit from it. Both their social and language development appear to benefit from the company of other children; and although it has been found that children at day-care centres are more given to temper tantrums than those reared at home, they do not seem to have a worse relationship with their parents nor are they more prone to long-term behaviour problems.

According to one American study, working mothers are if anything more closely attached to their children and slightly stricter with them than non-working mothers. Perhaps as a result, their children were found to be more independent and socialized, and better adjusted and behaved. All these differences were small, however, and the issue is too important to risk making a generalization on the basis of a single study. The same reservation must be made about a very recent study which suggests that there is at least one respect in which the children of working mothers are very different from those of non-working mothers: the researchers found them to be much less sexually stereotyped in their attitudes.

When it comes to deciding who will work and who will not in the future, I suspect that the individual characteristics and qualifications of a particular man or woman are going to matter more than what sex he or she happens to be. Women have acquired a taste for work, and the proportion of them who receive higher education is rising steadily. If they can be persuaded by arguments such as those presented in Chapter 4 to abandon their traditional preference for arts subjects, I see no reason why they should not play an increasingly important role in public life, and am cautiously optimistic that the child-rearing card need not always be the joker in the hand which nature has dealt them.

7

SEXUAL BEHAVIOUR

Woman wants monogamy;
Man delights in novelty.
Love is woman's moon and sun;
Man has other forms of fun.
Woman lives but in her lord;
Count to ten, and man is bored.
With this the gist and sum of it,
What earthly good can come of it?

Dorothy Parker

So far this book has been rather like *Hamlet* without the Prince.
We have looked at many different aspects of human behaviour
and found that men and women seem to be much less different
from each other than is generally assumed. There are some differences, but we have so far failed to find any convincing proof
that men must inevitably have the upper hand over women as a
consequence of the biological differences between the two. But
we have said virtually nothing about the one area of human
behaviour where the difference between the sexes is literally
all-important—sexual behaviour itself. Not even the most committed opponent of sexual discrimination can deny that men and
women have completely different genitals, and in this chapter we
are going to see what effect the difference in this small but vital
part of their anatomy has on the way that the two sexes feel
and behave. We shall also see whether there is any truth in
the suggestion that the difference between men's and women's
attitudes towards sex is such that men dominate women in sexual
relationships, and that this effect is so marked that it spills over
into the everyday, non-sexual encounters between the two, thus
explaining why it is that women tend to be the losers in the battle
of life.

History and biology

The popular belief about sex differences in sexuality is easily stated: men enjoy sex more than women do. Since human beings are quite active sexually, it looks as though men tend to get their way, which leads to the suggestion that women get used to giving men what they ask for in bed, and so are prepared to defer to their wishes, and accept that they must have what they want, elsewhere. The first thing to be said about this description of male and female sexuality is that it would have seemed very odd to many of our recent ancestors. Ancient literature is full of complaints about women's excessive sexuality, while a text on witchcraft written in the fifteenth century blamed the fact that most witches were female on women's insatiable sexual desire, which allegedly made them more susceptible to the devil's blandishments. In many of the comedies written in the seventeenth and eighteenth centuries, the plot hinges on the efforts of one person to lure another into bed, but it is by no means always a man who is the predator. The idea that only men like sex seems to date from the Victorian era, when doctors urged husbands to trouble their wives as rarely as possible, and a mother could advise her daughter to lie still, close her eyes and think of England on those occasions when her husband could contain himself no longer and presented himself in her bedchamber.

History suggests that women's sexuality has had its ups and downs over the centuries, but this has not prevented some biologists from claiming that men are naturally sexier, and that it is an aberration for matters to be otherwise. Their argument starts from the assumption that our bodies—like those of all other species—are geared to the preservation and proliferation of our genes, and that the difference between male and female reproductive systems is such that men and women must have very different attitudes towards sex in order to have the best chance of perpetuating their genes.

The most obvious strategy—to have as many children as possible—works only for men, according to the biologists. A man can produce millions of sperm, each with the potential to produce offspring, so he need not be too particular where he deposits each batch, since he knows that there are plenty more where that came from. The more women he makes pregnant, the more likely it is that his genes will be carried on, so men can afford to develop a taste for novelty, and work on the assumption that there is strength in numbers. Women, on the other hand, have incomparably fewer chances to reproduce themselves. They have a limited supply of eggs, available for fertilization at the rate of only one a month, and once they become pregnant, they are out of circulation for nine months, or much longer if we take into account the fact that breast-feeding can suppress ovulation. A woman therefore needs to be altogether more choosy about the person with whom she has sex, since the biological imperative dictates that she must make sure her precious eggs are not wasted on sperm from anything less than prime breeding-stock.

But there is new evidence that some female animals may actually benefit if they are promiscuous. This is because they can use multiple mating as a method for choosing the best genes for their offspring, so on meeting a male with better genes the inferior stored sperm can be swapped for his. In a fascinating field study on adders, some Swedish scientists claimed that having lots of sexual partners and avoiding mating repeatedly with the same male increases the genetic variability of the stored sperm and increases a female's reproductive success.

This theory does not apply to human beings, who, unlike adders, cannot store sperm for months before ovulation. A man's sperms stay alive for only twelve hours, so a woman would have to have sex with several different men within this time period to use 'sperm competition' as a method of selecting the best genes. Anyway, the adder's method seems no better than the one described above which filters out poor-quality males by refusing to mate with them—and this way there is no chance of getting the genes from inferior males. Maybe female adders just cannot discriminate between males, and have to rely on sperm competition to make the choice for them.

I have argued throughout this book that although biological arguments can sometimes give quite a plausible account of how we might have come to behave as we do in the first place, they rarely do justice to the subtle social pressures which have come to influence our behaviour as society has evolved, and which now seem to have a much greater effect on our lives. Later in this chapter, we shall see that although the sex instinct may be essential to the survival of the species, biological factors—including the cyclical fluctuations of our sex hormones—have surprisingly little influence on our sex lives. But first we must see

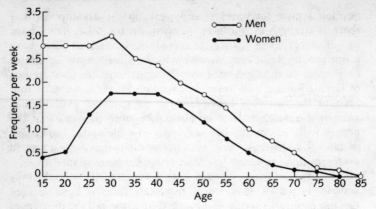

Figure 8. *Frequency of sexual outlets (by whatever means) for men and women at different ages (Kinsey, 1948; Kinsey et al., 1953)*

what predictions the biological argument makes about human sexuality. It clearly implies that women should be less promiscuous than men, and that they should get less pleasure from the sexual act itself, to reduce the likelihood of their being tempted to risk wasting an egg when there is no suitable breeding-partner available. It also suggests a basis for the popular belief that the two sexes take a different approach to sexual liaisons—men want sex, women love—with the man being less involved, more likely to bring the affair to an end, and generally the dominant partner.

Are any of these claims true? The first almost certainly is: surveys of sexual behaviour are virtually unanimous that the average woman has fewer sexual partners during her lifetime than the average man. This is only one aspect of a more general difference between the sexes in sexual activity: however you measure it, men get slightly more sexual activity—heterosexual, homosexual and masturbatory—at every age. This can be seen from Figure 8, which is based on the most comprehensive study of human sexual behaviour ever undertaken—Alfred Kinsey's epic eighteen-year survey of the sexual habits of more than 10,000 American adults. But these findings do not mean that we have to accept the biological explanation, because they are open to an equally plausible alternative interpretation. This does not rule out the influence of biological factors; but it explains the sex difference in sexual behaviour in terms of the observable experiences of individual men and women today, instead of making guesses about how our ancestors may or may not have behaved.

Adolescence—a turning-point

Many sex researchers have now come round to the view that the pattern of an adult's sex life is set by his or her adolescent experience of masturbation, and that the reason why men are more sexually active than women is that boys masturbate more than girls in the years before they start having sexual relationships with other people. Before they reach adolescence, there is very little difference between the sexes in sexuality. All children seem to derive erotic pleasure from handling their genitals from a very early age, and both boys and girls go through a stage—usually between three and six—of 'practising' for adult sexual behaviour: they flirt with adults, impersonate the romantic behaviour of elder brothers and sisters or TV actors, and may even play-act love affairs with their friends. After the age of six, both sexes enter a phase of inhibition and extreme modesty about their own and other people's bodies—especially their genitals—though their private thoughts and fantasies suggest that Freud was wrong to claim that sexuality is dormant during these years.

With the arrival of puberty, children have their attention drawn to their genitals as a result of the anatomical and hormonal changes described in Chapter 2. At this point the experiences of the two sexes diverge sharply. When a girl begins to menstruate, she may feel proud to be grown-up at last, but the physical changes she undergoes are not likely to bring her obvious sexual pleasure. A boy, on the other hand, starts to have erotic dreams and frequently finds himself with an unsolicited erection. Like it or not, he can hardly fail to be aware of his genitals or of their potential as a source of pleasure. Not surprisingly, boys develop a lively interest in their own and their friends' genitals. They are a favourite topic of conversation amongst boys who have recently reached puberty, and words often lead to deeds. Masturbation contests and mutual masturbation are commonplace amongst boys of this age, and there is no reason to suppose that either practice is necessarily bad for those who take part.

Girls are very different. Though they may have erotic dreams, they are not constantly having their attention drawn downwards by the unexpected but not unwelcome discovery that they have an erection. Being internal, their genitals are less obtrusive than a boy's, and to the extent that adolescent girls are competitive about their physical development, it is their breasts which are the focus of attention and, for early maturers, of envy. While adolescent boys are learning about physical sex, girls are reading about love and romance, fashion and beauty. There is not the same tradition amongst girls of discussing with their friends the development of their genitals or sexuality, so for biological and for cultural reasons, a girl is less likely than a boy to discover and practise masturbation, and if she does so, it is likely to be on her own.

So the fact that men seem to be more interested than women in sex may be a result of the biological differences between the two sexes, but not in the way suggested by the biologists. The influence is also greatly enhanced by the traditions handed down from one generation of adolescents to the next, with older boys and girls setting different examples to children who have just reached puberty. This suggests that the gap between the sexes in sexual activity will become narrower, since the taboo against women masturbating is disappearing rapidly. As late as the 1930s, medical textbooks were prescribing cauterization of the clitoris for girls caught masturbating. But now women are encouraged to masturbate even by quite staid magazines, and it is right that they should be, since research shows that a woman who masturbates is much more likely to reach orgasm during sexual intercourse than one who does not. However, despite the steady flow of propaganda in favour of the practice, recent surveys find that the proportion of women who masturbate—about 60 per cent—has not risen significantly since Kinsey carried out his research. There does seem to be a trend towards women starting to masturbate at an earlier age and doing so more frequently. But the fact that nearly 40 per cent of women still deny that they have ever indulged in what is virtually a universal practice amongst men raises again the spectre that women find sex intrinsically less pleasurable than men do.

Sexuality and hormones

The average woman, despite her much publicized ability to experience multiple orgasms, actually has many fewer orgasms

Sexuality and hormones 169

during her life than the average man, a fact often produced by biologists as a decisive argument in favour of their view that women are so constructed that they cannot enjoy sex as much as men can. According to Kinsey, the average American man in 1948 had 1,523 orgasms under his belt before he got married, compared to the 223 of the average American woman. The difference is probably very much smaller today than when Kinsey published his findings. I have already mentioned that women now start to masturbate at a younger age, and surveys carried out in many countries confirm what everybody assumes: that there has been an enormous increase in premarital sexual activity over the last quarter of a century, especially amongst women. In Kinsey's day, a bride was twice as likely as her bridegroom to be a virgin; now, men are still more likely than women to have had sex before marriage, but the gap has narrowed considerably, and it has almost ceased to exist amongst the middle-class young. According to a more recent British survey of teenage sexuality, teenage girls, although less likely than boys to have lost their virginity, tend to be more sexually active, and to be more likely to have lengthy sexual relationships once they do so.

Nevertheless, it remains true that many women have to wait until they are years into a relationship before they experience their first orgasm—a feat achieved effortlessly, sometimes spontaneously, by virtually all boys in adolescence—while a significant number of them (perhaps 12 per cent) go through life without ever having one.

To understand this difference between the sexes, we need to answer two questions: what purpose do orgasms serve, and why is it that women find them more elusive than men do? According to the biologists, we should view orgasms as nature's way of ensuring that we continue to reproduce ourselves. Unlike other species, we are not forced to copulate by irresistible hormonal changes. Whereas a female rat in oestrous can no more resist the attempts of males to copulate with her than she can stop herself drinking when she is thirsty, human sexual behaviour seems to be almost entirely unaffected by hormonal changes. This is rather surprising, because sex is the one area of behaviour where you might have expected us to behave like other animals—after all, our need to reproduce ourselves ought to be no less urgent than theirs, and all women and some men have a regular hormone cycle which, at least in the case of the menstrual cycle, is bound up with the reproductive function.

Hormonal changes do affect the sexual behaviour of some people. According to one study, about 6 per cent of women are more likely to have intercourse in the middle of their cycle than at other times of the month (that is, at the time when they are most likely to conceive) even when they do not wish to conceive, while a small percentage of women show a regular peak of sexual activity just after menstruating. But these changes, where they are noticed, are not thought to be due to the effect of female hormones on the *woman's* behaviour. Instead, some scientists argue that female hormones affect sexual interaction by altering the woman's sexual attractiveness, probably via *pheromones*. The female odour varies during the month, and men who are sensitive to this (not all are, and probably none is consciously aware of the effect) seem to be more likely to initiate sex at particular points during the cycle.

But the majority of women do not have a regular pattern of sexual activity linked with their menstrual cycle, and if they disrupt their natural hormonal cycle by taking an oral contraceptive, the effect which this has on their sexual behaviour is unpredictable. Some women report that they become more sexually active—and enjoy sex more—when they are on the pill, whereas others complain of reduced libido. The only general effect the pill has on women's sex lives is to remove peaks and troughs when these exist, eliminating the last traces of cyclicity in sexual activity.

Although many researchers have tried to prove otherwise, there seems to be very little connection between the female sex hormones and sexuality. Oestrogens are involved in lubricating the vagina, but removing a woman's ovaries and hence the source of female hormones generally has very little effect on her sexuality. There is a slight decline in women's sexual activity after the menopause, when hormone levels drop. But the capacity to have an orgasm is not necessarily affected, which suggests that social rather than biological factors are at work here. The male sex hormones cannot be dismissed quite so lightly: there is a connection between sexual behaviour and androgen levels in both men and women. If the adrenal gland (which produces and controls the flow of testosterone) is lost, then libido collapses. So testosterone seems to be the sex hormone for both men and women, and we might therefore expect men to want sex more than women, since after puberty they have twenty times as much testosterone in their bodies as women.

But human beings are not as simple as lower animals, and hormones do not *cause* sexual behaviour. In fact the *cognitive* aspect has a huge influence on sexual behaviour and the resulting subjective pleasure. Alcohol plays an important role in many types of sexual activity—it has many romantic connections, is a powerful tool of seduction and is also correlated with many forms of sexual aggression. But scientists have shown that it actually *suppresses* physiological sexual responsiveness—the more alcohol in the bloodstream, the longer it takes to reach orgasm. The effect of alcohol, then, is presumably a *psychological* one, removing feelings of anxiety or guilt and giving sexual courage (and perhaps making us, like animals, more under the control of our hormones). Two researchers tested this by observing the responses of people who thought they were given an alcoholic drink (vodka and tonic) when in fact it was non-alcoholic (tonic only). They found that even when the subjects had no alcohol, the belief that they had was enough to enhance both subjective pleasure and objective arousal. The researchers concluded that alcohol does remove psychological sexual inhibitions, helping to overcome insecurity or shyness, which may detract from sexual pleasure. But their experiment showed that these effects are cognitive and so could be achieved without alcohol.

So psychological influences can importantly affect sexual behaviour. But these tend to be much harder to measure than physiological factors like the amount of hormones in the blood. For instance, according to one study, the likelihood of a couple having intercourse at any particular time is at least partly a func-tion of how much testosterone the woman has in her blood-stream: the more she has, the more likely it is. Since the decision as to whether or not intercourse will actually take place is more usually made by the woman, it is not surprising to find that the man's testosterone level does not seem to affect the outcome. But this is not to say that testosterone has nothing to do with male sexuality. It almost certainly has, judging by the observation made by a scientist that his own beard grew faster towards the end of a period of sexual abstinence, in anticipation of the return of his regular sex partner. Since beard-growth is a measure of the level of testosterone being produced, there obviously can be a connection between testosterone and male sexual behaviour too. But it is a complex one. Male impotence is often associated with low testosterone production, and flagging libido in both sexes can sometimes be revived by injections of the male hormone. How-

ever, in those countries where persistent sex offenders can choose
to be castrated, this treatment—which cuts off the supply of
testosterone—does not invariably lead to the loss of sexual
responsiveness. And when sex offenders are given oestrogens to
reduce their sex drive, it seems to be the cognitive aspects of their
sexuality, such as the amount of time they spend thinking about
sex, which are affected, rather than the physiological aspects—
their ability to get an erection, for example.

Intercourse and orgasms

The extent to which our sexual behaviour is affected by sex
hormones is still hotly disputed by experts in the field, though
there seems to be a consensus that male sex hormones are the
more important, but that their influence is greater on *women*
than on men. However, it is absolutely certain that hormones
do not make us copulate, which means that there must be some
other reason why we are prepared to fall in with nature's wish
that the species should continue. This brings us back to the
biologists' suggestion that orgasms are simply a device to ensure
that we carry on copulating, by means of the pleasurable sensation
they provide as a reward for engaging in sexual intercourse. This
is an important argument, because it may mean that men and
women must inevitably have very different sexual experiences.

The crux of the matter is the ease with which men and women
reach orgasm. According to the biologists' rather bizarre view of
human sexual activity, it is vital that men reach their climax
first, because otherwise intercourse would be completed as often
as not before the male had reached ejaculation, and hence be a
waste of time and energy from the biological viewpoint, since
no sperm would have been produced. On this analysis, during
intercourse men reach orgasm first—and women are often denied
orgasm—as a matter of biological necessity, so it is inevitable
that men have more orgasms than women. Since these are the
sensations which make sex a pleasurable activity (in the biologists' eyes, at least), it is also inevitable that sex is a more
pleasurable activity for men than for women, and that whenever a
couple decide to have intercourse, it is always the man who is the
major beneficiary and the woman who is putting herself out to
provide him with enjoyment.

Like so many of the biologists' explanations, this argument has a very dated ring to it. It is also a grossly inadequate account of human sexuality, since it ignores some of the most important findings which have been made since Kinsey published his pioneering reports. It would be silly to deny that the desire to reach orgasm is one—though by no means the only—reason why we devote a considerable amount of time and energy to copulation and its preliminaries, which include most aspects of the dating and mating game. Nor would I dispute the results of a host of surveys which have found that, in our society at least, sex is more important to men than it is to women: the average man thinks about sex more and claims to get more pleasure from it than the average woman, and he also has more orgasms. But the biologists' interpretation of this difference between the sexes is riddled with flaws. The first problem is that sexual intercourse is not the only, nor even the most efficient, way to achieve an orgasm. If the only point of the orgasm is to ensure that we reproduce ourselves, then nature would hardly have arranged things so that we could achieve the same sensation by masturbating.

More importantly, the fact that it takes women longer than men to reach orgasm during intercourse probably tells us more about the act of sexual intercourse than it does about the ability of the two sexes to reach their climax. Although only four out of ten of the women in Kinsey's sample almost always had an orgasm during intercourse, 95 per cent of those who masturbated reported that they could achieve one regularly by this means. What was even more striking was the speed with which they could do so—a matter of less than three minutes for almost half of them.

So the biologists are wrong to say that women always take very much longer than men to reach orgasm. A more plausible explanation of the difference in their experience during intercourse is that the position most favoured for intercourse in our society might almost have been chosen to minimize the pleasure a woman can derive from the act. The missionary position is so called because missionaries tried to impose it in place of what they regarded as the sinful position—the man squatting on his heels and the woman lying on her back with her thighs spread across his—adopted by Australian aborigines and other primitive societies. In the missionary position, the juxtaposition of bodies is such that comparatively little pressure is applied to the most sexually responsive area of a woman's body—her clitoris—

because the bulk of a man's weight falls elsewhere, and it is difficult for either partner to stimulate the clitoris by hand, since it is covered by the man's body. Almost every other position for intercourse and all other types of sexual activity avoid this problem, and it is a telling comment on the imbalance of power between the sexes that women have for so long put up with the form of sexual activity least likely to bring them pleasure.

The great vaginal–clitoral debate about the site of the female orgasm has subsided since Masters and Johnson's exhaustive—and often exhausting—investigation of the physiology of the human sexual response. By using an artificial penis, Masters and Johnson were able to take detailed recordings of the changes which occur throughout the pelvic region of a woman who is sexually aroused, and they found clear evidence that, wherever and however she is stimulated, the clitoris is the primary—though not the only—source of a woman's sexual response. This is not in the least surprising since the interior of the vagina—though equipped with muscles admirably suited for the task of providing a man with sexual satisfaction—is a comparatively insensitive area of the body. The clitoris, on the other hand, is the only organ in the animal kingdom which has the sole function of giving its owner sexual pleasure. Though small, it contains as many nerve endings as a penis—we saw in Chapter 1 that the two organs develop in the foetus from the same unisex *tubercle*—and the fact that they are concentrated in a much smaller area in a woman increases sensitivity and perhaps contributes to her ability to have several orgasms in quick succession. Even if there were no other evidence, the sexual anatomy of the two sexes would be enough to make nonsense of the claim that men have a greater capacity for enjoying sex than women do.

But it is not only women who have benefited from nature's largesse when it comes to sexual anatomy. As can be seen from Figure 9, the human male has been provided with a penis bigger than that of any of his near relatives in the animal kingdom, and far larger than is strictly necessary for the functions it has to perform, though his testicles are more modestly sized than those of a chimpanzee. This anomaly has had the biologists scratching their heads, but they have finally come to the conclusion that since there is no human society in which the penis is used as an offensive weapon or even as a threat, the generous proportions of the human male's penis are designed either to attract females

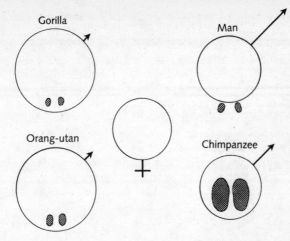

Figure 9. *The female's view of the male, indicating the difference between the sexes in body size, the size and position of the testes, and the size of the erect penis (Short, 1979)*

or to increase his capacity for sexual enjoyment. Since several surveys have shown that the size of a man's penis ranks very low amongst the features which women find attractive in men, it is probably safe to conclude that this quirk of natural selection is another of nature's tricks to make sure that men do not shirk their sexual duties. The unusually generous proportions of women's breasts, on the other hand (see Figure 10), may well be designed to attract the attention of the opposite sex.

The sexual revolution

The nuts and bolts of human sexuality have been described in great detail by many other authors, so I have only touched on those aspects of Masters and Johnson's research which throw light on the suggestion that women are by nature less sexually responsive than men. All the evidence suggests that this is not so. Indeed, Masters and Johnson frequently comment on the similarity between the orgasmic responses of the two sexes, the main difference lying in the fact that while some women can have many

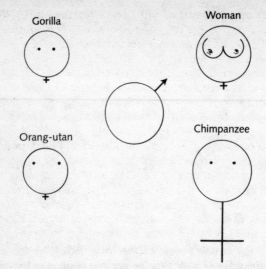

Figure 10. *The male's view of the female, indicating the difference between the sexes in body size, and the relative development of the mammary glands and the external genital area before the first pregnancy (Short, 1979)*

orgasms in quick succession, men have a *refractory period* after they ejaculate, during which they are unable to muster another erection, however much they are stimulated. As well as this difference in quantity, there is also one of quality: women's orgasms seem to vary more than those of men. As Masters himself put it, the male orgasm is a rose-is-a-rose-is-a-rose sort of thing, while the female goes all the way from poppies to orchids.

Perhaps the main interest of Masters and Johnson's work is the effect it has had on people's sexual expectations, via its popularization in books and magazine articles. As long as sex was thought of as an essentially masculine preoccupation, each act of sexual intercourse could be regarded as a small victory for the male partner, since he had 'persuaded' the woman to co-operate in a venture likely to bring him more pleasure than her. Now that the myth of woman's inferior sexuality has been exploded, and we have all become do-it-yourself sexologists, it seems that people are becoming dissatisfied with sex lives they might once have found perfectly adequate, and the evidence is mounting that it is men who are suffering most from the contemporary explosion of knowledge about sex.

The proportion of patients at sex clinics who are men has risen sharply in the last few years, and they are echoing the ancients' complaint about female insatiability rather than their great-grandfathers' frustration at their wives' lack of sexuality. Three-quarters of the men in Kinsey's sample reported that they usually reached orgasm during intercourse within two minutes, which suggests that there will need to be a dramatic improvement in men's sexual technique if they are to satisfy the first commandment of the new sexual order—nice guys finish last. Sex therapists are losing some of their enthusiasm for the sexual revolution started by Kinsey and Masters and Johnson. They are now starting to talk about sexual tyranny as couples come to them for treatment not for frigidity or impotence, but because she is having 'only' one orgasm during intercourse, or because he wants sex 'only' once a night. The problem is that many people believe that Masters and Johnson have told us how we all ought to be behaving sexually, whereas they were actually concerned with the limits of human sexuality—what is the most we are physiologically capable of?

The increase in female sexuality is not just a figment of the media's imagination, or a case of sex therapists protesting too much about the boom in their business. Nor is it just confined to well-educated, middle-class women, though there is some evidence that it is most marked here. A large number of surveys all point in the same direction: the gap between men and women in sexual activity has been closing steadily since Kinsey's reports were published. We saw earlier that women have almost caught up with men in premarital sexual activity, and the same applies to extra-marital affairs: whereas Kinsey found that wives had only a third of the number of extra-marital flings their husbands had, a survey published in the 1970s suggested that the figure had become nearer three-quarters—striking evidence that the double standard which used to apply to sexual behaviour was becoming an anachronism. However, women may still be more choosy than men in their extra-marital as in their premarital adventures: twice as many husbands as wives in this survey admitted to more than six extra-marital encounters, so the general rule that men are more promiscuous still seemed to hold. Interestingly, it applied to homosexuals as well. The same survey found that eight times as many male as female homosexuals had had eleven or more partners, which suggests that biological sex is more important than sexual orientation in determining the pattern of our sex lives.

Another change since Kinsey's day can be seen in women's response to erotica, and even in that last-resort sexual activity—graffiti. In complete contradiction to Kinsey's claim that graffiti are a predominantly masculine form of expression, researchers who perused the walls of boys' and girls' cloakrooms in Cincinatti high schools made the startling discovery that nine out of ten graffiti on display were written by girls, with the most explicitly sexual material being found in schools favoured by the middle classes!

Kinsey's observations about the way in which men and women react to erotic pictures or stories may also no longer apply. Whereas four times as many men as women in his sample admitted that they were excited by this type of sex at a distance, most recent research suggests that this is another sex difference which has disappeared. When women are asked how they feel while watching pornography, they still seem to be more reluctant than men to admit that they are sexually aroused. But when sexual arousal is measured physiologically, for example by monitoring blood pressure in the penis or vagina, women are found to react no less strongly to the sight of a couple copulating on film. Since it makes no difference to their reaction whether the film portrays the couple as being in love or as complete strangers to each other, we may conclude that the sight of sex—with or without love—can be just as arousing to a woman as it is to a man.

Indeed, when a different set of researchers asked male and female students how sexually aroused they felt after watching film of a man or a woman masturbating, the highest levels of arousal were reported by women—apparently, though rather surprisingly, because the men experienced more guilt than the women at the sight of a member of their own sex masturbating. But virtually all of the recent studies on the effect of pornography on sexual arousal have been carried out on college students. Since Kinsey worked with a much larger and more heterogeneous sample, the difference between his results and those I have mentioned here may be more apparent than real. American college students are in the vanguard of the sexual revolution, and they are certainly not typical of the population, in America or elsewhere.

This criticism cannot be levelled against a final body of research findings which show that there have been changes, especially in the sexual behaviour of women, since Kinsey's day. When Kinsey turned his attention to the role played by sexual fantasies during intercourse, he found that here too there was a difference between the sexes, with more men than women admitting that while making love to one person they would be having erotic thoughts about another. At the time, this practice was still frowned upon in women, since it was regarded as a sign of neurosis or frustration. Now, however, surveys carried out in Britain and America show that two women out of three fantasize during intercourse, and there is evidence that the practice adds to their enjoyment. Researchers who have explored the content of women's sexual fantasies find that being overpowered and reliving previous sexual experiences are two of the most common themes.

Sex in relationships

The research we have been discussing strongly suggests that the difference in sexuality between men and women is much smaller than we once thought. So where does this leave the old idea about men wanting sex, and women love, and what effect is the change in women's sexual behaviour having on the balance of power between the sexes? According to the traditional view, men get more than women out of a sexual relationship, for a smaller investment. As a result of their different experiences in adolescence, women are alleged to be more starry-eyed and romantic about their attachments, whereas men are hard-hearted and rational. He makes the running sexually, while she may fall in with his wishes, but only if she is in love with him. Since a woman attaches more significance to a relationship than a man does, she is less likely to end it than he is, and she will suffer more when it is over. This is the old-fashioned view, and if it is (or was ever) an accurate description of how men and women conduct their relationships, it is not difficult to see where male domination came from, or to understand how men have managed to get most of the best jobs. After all, if the relationships a woman has with men in her private life always end in (her) tears, how can she expect to get the better of them at work?

But is this how men and women conduct their relationships? As far as marriage is concerned, we saw in Chapter 3 that men do indeed seem to be into a better thing than their wives are, although both married men and women tend to be healthier than those who are not married. But the reasons that marriage is even more beneficial for men are probably social and economic rather than sexual, which is why sexual relationships outside marriage are a more fruitful source of information about the effect which sex has on what men and women think of each other.

How do we choose our partners in the first place? There is plenty of evidence that men place greater value on physical attractiveness than do women, as we see from questionnaire results, analyses of lonely hearts advertisements and studies correlating attractiveness with opposite-sex popularity. Once they have made their choice, men seem to be more inclined to stick with it.

A very wide-ranging investigation of what actually goes on in the sexual relationships of unmarried couples was carried out between 1972 and 1974. A group of American psychologists interviewed 231 couples, all of whom were at college in the Boston area and went out with each other for at least part of this period. It is usually a disadvantage to take such an unrepresentative sample as this, and of course the results of this survey do not give us a picture of the dynamics of 'typical' relationships. But the characteristics which make this sample untypical make it ideal for answering the questions we are concerned with here. Because both partners were young, middle-class students, economic and social factors would have had much less significance for these couples than they do in most relationships. Since they were both students, they would have had roughly the same degree of financial independence and job status, and since very few of them had concrete plans for getting married, we can assume that this study will give us an idea of how men and women behave in a relationship when the cards are not stacked in favour of the man and when both partners are in it for emotional and sexual, rather than economic or social reasons.

The couples were given extensive questionnaires, covering many aspects of their relationships, on three separate occasions. Each partner was interviewed separately, and given a firm assurance that nothing he or she said would ever be revealed to the other partner. The three issues of most interest to us are: loving and leaving, the balance of power, and the decision about whether and when to have sex. According to the traditional stereotypes, it is the woman who loves and the man who leaves. The Boston study found exactly the opposite. It was the men who tended to subscribe to romantic ideas about love at first sight and love overcoming all barriers, and when asked why they started the relationship, they were more likely than women to say that they wanted to fall in love. When each partner was asked how much he or she was attracted to or in love with the other, it was found that men were giving more than they were receiving—again, the opposite of what is popularly believed.

Almost half of the couples had broken up by the end of the survey. When the researchers looked at how the relationships had ended, conventional wisdom was once more turned on its head, because it was the women's rather than the men's feelings which decided whether or not a relationship would survive. When a relationship broke up, the chances were that the woman had had reservations about it from an early stage, and her ardour cooled more noticeably than his as the relationship moved towards its end. In keeping with the results of several other studies, it was also more often than not the woman who precipitated the final break-up. One reason for this may be that the women were better than the men at forecasting what was going to happen, and so perhaps had more time to prepare themselves for falling out of love. This may also explain two other findings of the study: men were harder hit than women by a relationship coming to an end, and a couple was more likely to remain friends afterwards if he rather than she had precipitated the break-up.

These results show that, in this sample at any rate, men fall in love more quickly and easily than women, while women have a cooler, more rational view of relationships. But it would be a mistake to jump to the conclusion that there has been a complete reversal of roles in premarital relationships, and equally rash to assume that there is a monster loose on the north-eastern seaboard of the United States—the New American Woman, who lives only to break men's hearts and avenge the indignities her predecessors have been subjected to by men over the years. Other aspects of the Boston study suggest that traditional sex roles are far from dead. For example, when couples were asked the question, 'Who do you think should have more say about your relationship, your partner or you?', 95 per cent of the women and

87 per cent of the men replied that both partners should have an equal say. But when the researchers probed more deeply into the relationship to see who really held the power, they discovered that fewer than half the couples were practising what they preached. Amongst the others, it was usually the man who more often got his way.

In those couples where the woman tended to get her way, the couples were often not sleeping with each other. Which brings us to one of the most important findings of the Boston study: for all the convergence in their sexual behaviour, men and women still seem to have different attitudes towards sex, and different ways of turning it to their advantage in a relationship. In keeping with the results of the surveys discussed earlier in the chapter, the Boston women students were less interested than their boy-friends in sex, and more likely than them to be virgins at the beginning of the study, though this may just have been a reflection of the fact that the men were on average a year older. Just under half of the couples who were sleeping together reported that both partners were equally keen on sex. But where one was more interested than the other, it was the man in three-quarters of the cases, and the woman in only a quarter. One in five of the couples did not sleep together, and only five couples out of the forty-two in this category gave the man's reluctance as a major reason for their abstinence. The woman's attitudes and sexual experience were also the most important factor in deciding how early in their relationship a couple decided to take the sexual plunge. So in at least one respect traditional sex roles are flourishing, even in this untypically young, intelligent and progressive sample. Men still try to exert their authority by initiating sex, while a woman has to rely on negative control, which she can exercise by rejecting her partner's advances or slowing down the pace at which their sexual intimacy increases. An intriguing footnote to this is provided by researchers who studied a different group of American student dating couples in 1980. They discovered that men who felt they were getting more out of a relationship than their girl-friends found the sexual side of it more satisfying than those in partnerships which were equally rewarding to both sides.

If women can enjoy sex just as much as men do, why does the traditional pattern of male initiative and female resistance survive? It can no longer be just that women are more frightened by the consequences of an unplanned pregnancy. Indeed, the

Boston study found that it was men who were more worried about this. One possible explanation is that our idea of our own sexuality and that of the opposite sex is formed in the late teens, when men are at the peak of their physical sexual capacity. Women of this age are perfectly capable of enjoying sex, but most of them do not reach the peak of their capacity for sexual pleasure until a full decade later—further evidence that a woman's sexual enjoyment is not inextricably linked to her fertility. It is not clear whether this lack of synchrony between the sexes serves any useful purpose or whether nature is merely being mischievous. The result is frustration, not only for eighteen-year-old men but also for thirty-year-old women, who complain that their husbands are losing interest in sex just as they are coming to their sexual prime. The traditional pattern of male initiative and female resistance applies most strongly to young couples—like those in the Boston study—and there is some evidence that it disappears or is even reversed in older couples.

Another explanation of the traditional pattern is that it is just a matter of convenience. All our dealings with other people are conducted within a framework of unspoken rules and conventions. Without it social life would be virtually impossible, since it would be even more difficult than it now is to know what the person we were dealing with was after. Sexual relationships are amongst the most fragile and delicate of all our social encounters, and the great advantage of traditional sex role-playing is that it gives both partners a familiar, understandable and well-rehearsed set of guide-lines as to how each should behave towards the other. A couple may be desperate for clues as to each other's feelings and intentions, especially at the beginning of a relationship, before they know each other well as individuals. It is obviously much easier for them to avoid embarrassing misunderstandings which might bring their relationship to a premature conclusion if they are both reading from a well-thumbed script rather than trying to improvise an experimental drama.

As a couple come to know each other better, each will develop idiosyncratic rules for interpreting the other's behaviour, and sexual role-playing may decline. A significant number of married couples actually seem to reverse sex roles during the second half of their life together. But in less well-established relationships, especially of the sort we have been discussing here, even the most egalitarian and sexually liberated couple will find life easier

if they go along with the traditional sex roles, and one partner may be disconcerted if the other steps out of line. This is most noticeable when women start taking the sexual initiative, for although men often complain how unfair it is that they always have to make the running sexually, it is still rather a rare man who actually likes it when he is dragged into bed by a woman on their first date. Not only does this break the rules, it also assaults his ego by questioning the masculine role which is part of his idea of himself. So the chances are that he will protect himself against this happening again, by convincing himself that she is not his type of woman.

Although there has been a dramatic change in woman's sexual attitudes and behaviour, especially since the introduction of the pill and other reliable forms of contraception, the basic script followed by a couple having a sexual relationship seems to have remained much the same, at least in the early stages of their relationships. So there may be some truth in the suggestion made at the beginning of this chapter: one reason why so many women are still resigned to deferring at work to men no more qualified than they are is that this is what they are used to doing out of office hours. But why women should accept being dominated by men *anywhere* remains a mystery, which we must try to unravel in the final chapter.

8

AGGRESSION AND THE
BALANCE OF POWER

Once a woman is made equal to a man she becomes his
superior.

Sophocles

Perhaps the most popular of all the beliefs about the differences
between the sexes is that men are more aggressive than women.
Not only do most people—scientists included—believe this, but
they also attach great importance to it, particularly when trying
to explain why it is that men are the dominant sex. When I talk
about dominance, I mean that men have higher public status (that
is, they get the best jobs and are responsible for making decisions
which affect other people's lives), higher domestic status (they are
the formal head of the family), and also that they win the lion's
share of whatever commodity happens to be most in demand in
the society in which they live, whether it be money, sexual
partners, alcohol or whatever. Wherever anthropologists have
carried out their investigations, they have found male domination
to be the rule, at least in public life (domestic power is more
evenly distributed in societies like our own). This domination
seems to be based on two factors: women's involvement in child-
bearing and child-care, and the belief that men are the more
aggressive sex.

In this final chapter, we are going to see what evidence there is
for the view that men are more aggressive than women, and then
consider whether such a difference can really be responsible for
the imbalance of power between the two sexes. But first we have
to decide what aggression is, and what it means to call somebody
aggressive. The word is applied to an enormously wide range of
activities—everything from a campaign to sell toothpaste to a

declaration of war—so it is not just semantic nit-picking to insist on a definition. Aggression is usually defined as an unprovoked attack, but this definition gets us into trouble when dealing with children's behaviour. Many of the unprovoked attacks little boys launch on their friends are no more acts of aggression than the playful, velvet-paws 'fighting' of kittens, so I think it is wiser to describe as aggressive only actions which are intended to cause injury, whether physical or psychological.

Measuring aggression

Having agreed on a definition, we now have to decide how and where to measure aggression. There is no shortage of laboratory studies. But on this occasion, for reasons which will become clear later, I propose that we look first at the real world. One obvious starting-point is the observation that wars are always fought between armies of men. The romantic myth of the Amazon warrior turns out to be just that—a romantic myth. Even in Israel, where all available human resources are involved in some form of military activity, women are not drafted into front-line combat units, though they are trained to use weapons. One reason for this may be that the physical differences between the sexes make men better equipped for hand-to-hand combat. Even amongst the Burundi, an African tribe where the women are in some respects stronger than the men and are less good at controlling their tempers, men still tend to get the better of their wives when they come to blows, because of their greater agility. But the fact that warfare is a male activity may not tell us anything about sex differences in aggression. War is usually an act of political calculation rather than an assertion of national aggression, and the soldiers who do the actual fighting do not seem to be motivated primarily by feelings of aggression.

Crime statistics are another possible index of aggression. They too are often cited as evidence that men are the more aggressive sex, because the great majority of crimes involving violence are committed by men. But it would be wrong to assume that aggression is always the sole—or even the most important— motive for a crime of violence. Very often it has an economic objective, and the fact that it is committed by a man may just reflect the fact that men tend to be the major bread-winners. Moreover, there are some types of violent crime—for example, non-lethal violence within the family, including child abuse—where wives come very close to matching their husbands. And if you look at the figures for violent crime amongst young people, you will see that girls seem to be catching boys up: in 1950 only 1.3 per cent of violent crimes committed in Britain by people under seventeen were the work of girls, but by 1977 the figures had shot up to more than 16 per cent. The picture is much the same elsewhere: in the US, for example, the number of women arrested for serious crimes like robbery and burglary quadrupled between the 1930s and the 1970s. But between 1979 and 1989, the increase in female crime was not significantly different from the increase in crimes committed by men.

The dramatic earlier change may be due partly to the fact that policemen became less inclined to be lenient with female delinquents. But there is some evidence that fighting and other forms of aggressive behaviour are on the increase amongst teenage girls, especially in mixed-sex schools. It has been suggested that the Women's Liberation Movement was to blame for the rise in female crime. However, a study of women prisoners in a New Jersey gaol found the inmates decidedly unliberated in their attitudes. In fact, the majority of them felt strongly that women should conform to their traditional role, and seemed to despise themselves for being unfeminine.

Turning from warfare and crime to the study of aggression by ordinary people in everyday life, we come up against an unexpected difficulty. According to such writers as Konrad Lorenz and Desmond Morris, human beings are naturally aggressive. If this is so, the socialization process must be extraordinarily effective, because the most striking thing about acts of aggression by adults is their rarity. Many people go through their entire adult life without being involved in either a serious physical fight or a real insult-hurling verbal punch-up. This is not to deny that minor rows and arguments are an accepted part of our everyday existence. But if you count up how often you have set out to inflict real damage on another person, by blows or words, you may be surprised to discover how infrequently you behave aggressively.

Not only is this surprising, but it can also be rather frustrating for scientists who have a professional interest in aggression. They are often stymied by the fact that children—like adults—very rarely assault each other with intent to cause grievous bodily harm. They do, however, engage in a great deal of mock fighting, or rough-and-tumble play. This leads us to one of the very few clear-cut differences in behaviour between the two sexes: whenever and wherever they are observed, boys engage in more rough-and-tumble play than girls.

In a typical study, four-year-old Californian children were invited to play in groups of three—all of the same sex—in a room containing a trampoline, and their behaviour was monitored through a one-way mirror. The researchers' original aim was to test the widely believed idea that boys are more active than girls. No evidence of a difference in overall activity was found. But a clear sex difference emerged in the *way* boys and girls played, especially in the incidence of rough-and-tumble play. About a quarter of the boys engaged in fairly extreme types of horseplay, piling on top of each other on the trampoline or rushing into each other and collapsing in shrieks of laughter. None of the girls played really boisterously, although some of them took part in a more decorous type of high jinks. About a quarter of the girls went to the other extreme, organizing a rota system in which they went on the trampoline one at a time, while the two other members of the group watched and waited their turn. None of the groups of boys organized such a system.

A similar difference can be observed in the games boys and girls play with a ball. In girls' games, the emphasis is usually on keeping the ball going back and forth amongst the group; boys, on the other hand, tend to invent rules which ensure plenty of physical contact and an eventual individual winner. Interestingly, this difference between co-operative and competitive styles of playing is greatest between the ages of twelve and fourteen, when concern about gender role is at its peak.

There does seem to be a sex difference in children's games, but two points must be borne in mind. The first is that even the most exuberant boys in the California study were only fighting in fun, so it would be rash to treat this as evidence that boys are more aggressive than girls. The second point, though slightly more technical, is even more important. It was made earlier, in Chapter 4, and it applies to virtually every sex difference there is.

When the average rough-and-tumble-play scores for boys and girls are worked out, the boys' average is higher. Moreover, all the children who behaved really exuberantly were boys, which makes it very tempting to say that rough-and-tumble play is 'typically' boyish behaviour. But of course this is untrue, because three-quarters of the boys did not show this wild behaviour; in fact, they showed the same amount of rough-and-tumble play as most of the girls. So the sex difference in rough-and-tumble play is actually due to the behaviour of a small group of untypical boys, and exactly the same reservations apply to the claim that it is typical for girls to play co-operatively or for men to have superior visual-spatial ability. In every case, the difference between the sexes is one of degree and it is caused by the behaviour of a small, untypical group of males and females.

If children laugh or smile as they fight, the chances are that they are not being aggressive. But sometimes children look as though they really want to hurt each other, and on these comparatively rare occasions, it is usually boys who are involved, both as aggressor and as victim. Not all studies find a difference between the sexes in this aspect of behaviour. But whenever there is a difference, it is always boys who are found to be more aggressive than girls, never the other way round. This is also the case when we turn from observational studies of behaviour in real life to the results of laboratory experiments in which children have been encouraged to behave aggressively. One way of doing this is to let them watch other people behaving aggressively and see what effect this has on their behaviour. For example, they might be shown a film in which an adult is warmly praised for attacking a large inflatable doll which rights itself after being punched, and then left to their own devices in a room containing a similar doll, having been told that they can do whatever takes their fancy. In these circumstances boys tend to punch the doll anything up to five times more often than girls do, which has been taken as evidence that they are more aggressive than girls.

Many researchers are sceptical about this conclusion, and about the experiments on which it is based. The problem is one which was raised in the Introduction: the situation in which the children are placed is so unreal that it is impossible to know how to interpret their behaviour. However, I do not think we should call it aggressive, since they are attacking an inanimate object with adult approval, and seem to regard the experiment as a huge—though incomprehensible—adult joke. Talking to them afterwards, several researchers have formed the impression that children punch the doll simply because they perceive that this is what is expected of them, and think it only polite to humour an adult who has obviously taken a lot of trouble to set up the game!

An alternative—if ethically rather dubious—way of studying aggression in children is to create a situation in the laboratory where they think they have the means of inflicting pain on another child without any risk of retaliation, and then give them a reason for using their power. In one such experiment, a group of eight-year-olds were told that a child in the next room was working on a set of arithmetic problems, and asked to help him learn by punishing him every time he got one wrong, by pressing a button which would cause him to be struck by a punching-machine. The punching-machine was real enough—the children had played with it—but the child next door was imaginary. The children were simply told from time to time that the 'victim' had made a mistake, and encouraged to press one of ten numbered buttons, with button one supposedly delivering a soft punch, button five a medium punch, and button ten a hard one. In a similar experiment with eleven-year-olds, children had to choose which of a series of progressively more unpleasant loud noises should be used to punish an imaginary opponent whom they thought they were competing against. In both experiments, boys chose to inflict significantly more pain than girls did on their non-existent victims.

As you can see, it is not at all easy to measure aggression in the laboratory, especially where children are concerned. It would be unethical to try and provoke them into behaving really violently, and there is the additional problem that they must be confused by an adult who tolerates—or even encourages—behaviour which most adults tell them is wrong. The situation is so artificial that it may be quite wrong to draw analogies between the way children behave in these experiments and what they get up to in real life. But it has to be said that, in at least one respect, the results of laboratory studies of aggression in children are very similar to observational studies of children in real life: roughly half of them find that girls are no less aggressive than boys, while almost all the rest have found boys to be the more aggressive sex (one or two studies in both categories have found more aggression amongst girls).

There is, of course, another way of approaching the problem: we can ask children what they think instead of watching what they do. Rating scales and questionnaires of the type discussed in Chapter 3 tend to provide a much clearer difference between the sexes. In two-thirds of the studies using these measures, boys have appeared to be more aggressive than girls, while the opposite has never been found. So it seems that boys certainly *think* more aggressively than girls, and have a more aggressive image of themselves.

Adult aggro

Most of what has been said about aggression in children applies to adults as well. More than half of the laboratory studies carried out have failed to find any difference in aggression between men and women, while most of the rest show men to be the more aggressive sex. As with children, the sex difference is much more marked in answers to questionnaires than in actual behaviour. Judged by their thoughts—and by how they see themselves—men are much more aggressive than women. But judged by their deeds, the two sexes are not so dissimilar.

Gender differences in aggression are small in magnitude in the first place, but seem to get even smaller in adults. This may just be because males become better at controlling their aggressive impulses as they get older. But the older groups usually looked at in these studies are college students, who do not make up a random sample. On top of this, the experiments used on the different age groups may measure different types of aggression. Whereas tests involving college students typically assess their willingness to give someone else an electric shock, researchers tend to focus on physical aggression in pre-school children.

Why do men behave more aggressively than women in some experimental situations but not in others? One possible explanation is provided by the popular belief that women are less given to physical expressions of aggression but are more willing to engage in verbal aggression ('cattiness'). This is almost certainly false. Women *are* less prepared than men to deliver intense electric shocks to people who have provoked them, but they are also less willing than men to match insult with insult.

In one experiment, when women were told they had the choice of retaliating either by giving shocks (electric shocks are never actually given in these experiments) or by returning an insult, it was found that they preferred the former, apparently because they regarded face-to-face insults as more aggressive than the impersonal delivery of an electric shock by a machine. Amongst children, too, boys are found to be at least as verbally aggressive as girls. Fighting is usually accompanied by threatening and insulting words, and it is probably a mistake to regard words and blows as alternative ways of expressing aggression. Nor is there much evidence to support another widely held belief, that women who have been provoked are more likely than men to displace their aggressive feelings, for example by abusing an innocent third party, pouring scorn on the experimental situation, or else by becoming angry with themselves. Many experiments show that men and women are equally likely to do this; when there is a difference, it is men who are found to be more prone to displace their aggression.

Perhaps the most interesting thing to emerge from laboratory studies of aggression in adults is that the sex difference is most marked in experiments when subjects are required to act aggressively without any good reason for doing so. For example, when people are asked to deliver a shock every time someone else makes a mistake on a learning task, and are given a choice between intensities of shock, women tend to deliver significantly milder shocks. The difference between the sexes is even more marked when the person delivering the shocks meets the 'victim' at the beginning of the experiment and has to watch him or her gasping or groaning as he or she pretends to receive the shocks. This procedure is calculated to make people taking part in the experiment feel sympathy for their victims and guilt about their own part in the proceedings, and it seems that these are the two factors which lie at the heart of the sex difference in aggressive behaviour.

Some research has suggested that a woman is less likely to be aggressive because she thinks more about the consequences—someone will get hurt, which will make her feel guilty and maybe anxious that the victim will retaliate. But when women behave less aggressively than men, it is not only because they are more frightened of the prospect of retaliation. In experiments where the aggressor and his or her victim change places half-way through, or when the laboratory set-up is such that it would be physically possible for the victim to get at the tormentor, it is *men* who seem to be more daunted by the prospect. What really seems to hold women back is that they feel much more strongly than men that they ought not to behave aggressively, and become more anxious after behaving aggressively unless they have some justification for their action.

It is very striking that in experiments where people are offered a good reason for inflicting pain, women are prepared to deliver just as powerful electric shocks as men are. This is particularly so when they are led to believe that their actions are in some way good for the victim. In real life, jury duty provides the perfect justification for meting out punishment, and although we do not know whether women jurors are more or less severe than their male colleagues in real trials, women are every bit as savage as men when taking part in simulated trials in the laboratory. Money, however, is not enough to override women's guilt about behaving aggressively: in experiments in which they are rewarded financially for delivering high-intensity shocks to victims who have done nothing to annoy them, women are more reluctant than men to give the order for the shock to be delivered.

What laboratory studies show is that men are slightly more ready than women to inflict pain on other people when they have no particular reason for wishing them ill, but that women are just as willing to do so when they are persuaded that it is helpful rather than antisocial to behave in this way. This fits very well with the findings of a large survey, in which adult Canadians, instead of being observed in the laboratory or given tests to measure how aggressive they were, were simply asked what they thought about aggression in other people and in what circumstances they themselves could be provoked into behaving aggressively. The results of this survey suggest that the two sexes have fairly similar feelings about aggression in other people: interestingly, there seems to be general agreement that it can have positive as well as negative aspects, whether it is a man or a woman who is being aggressive. But different things make men and women see red. When men become aggressive, it is usually because they have been provoked by another person, either at work, while playing a competitive game, or in an encounter with the opposite sex. But the circumstances in which women show aggression are very different; either there is a matter of principle involved, or else they see someone else being treated unfairly.

Aggression is another area of behaviour where the difference between men and women is much smaller in the laboratory than it is believed to be in real life. For once, though, I am not going to suggest that this means we ought to reject the popular belief: instead, I think we should be extremely suspicious of the claim that the laboratory is a suitable place to study aggression. Whatever instructions or reassurance they may be given, people tend to be on their best behaviour when they take part in experiments because they know they are being watched. For this reason, laboratory experiments on aggression—or any other aspect of behaviour people feel at all ambivalent about—are almost certainly doomed to failure. We can certainly show that one person is more willing than another to deliver an electric shock to an innocent victim, but there is no guarantee that this tells us anything about how aggressive he or she is. In the context, it may just mean that he or she is more easily won over by the authority of the experimenter.

Behavioural scientists have only recently come to realize the limitations of the laboratory as a place to study aggression. As a result, there have been very few real-life studies which test the belief that men are more aggressive than women. What naturalistic studies there are tend to show larger sex differences than experiments performed in the laboratory. We know, for example, that group violence—whether on the streets of large cities or on the terraces of football grounds—seems to be a predominantly masculine phenomenon, and that male motorists use their horns more freely than females when the car in front of them fails to pull away when the traffic-lights change. Most of the rest of the evidence involves indirect measures of aggression such as the way in which people answer questionnaires or react to aggressive jokes (the funnier you find them, the more aggressive you are supposed to be), and even the contents of day-dreams. Perhaps the most frequently used indirect measure of aggression is the projective test, which rests on the assumption that feelings we ascribe to others are a reflection of the way we ourselves feel. In a typical test item, you might be shown a picture of a motorist getting out of his car to speak to the driver of a vehicle which has just crashed into the back of his, and asked to guess what he is about to say. The more aggressive the words you put into the motorist's mouth, the higher the aggression score you would be given.

On all these tests, men emerge as significantly more aggressive than women. Similarly, experimenters who have explored people's reactions to overcrowding have found that women are less aggressive when their privacy is invaded, both indoors and when on the beach. So what evidence we have supports the popular belief that men are more aggressive than women. The studies on aggression seem to give inconsistent results, but a recent review of the research in this area shows that gender differences are more pronounced for aggression which causes pain or physical injury than for that which causes psychological or social harm. What is more, like many of the gender differences we have looked at, the differences in aggression are small and decreasing.

The origins of violence

But why should men be more aggressive than women? The male of a species is often the more aggressive sex, and is equipped with organs specialized for fighting, like the antlers of stags and the spurs of a cockerel. These masculine weapons, as well as the greater aggression shown by men, are influenced by biological factors. Like other basic motivational states (hunger and sex, for example), aggressive behaviour seems to be accompanied by activity in one of the oldest and most primitive parts of the brain, called the *hypothalamus*. The *amygdala* is another very primitive part of the brain, linked to the hypothalamus, and it is here that the *feeling* of rage is generated. We can identify which areas of the brain are involved in aggressive feelings and behaviour by seeing how an animal's behaviour alters when an electric current is passed through an electrode, the tip of which has been inserted into whichever part of the brain we are interested in. When the hypothalamus of a monkey is artificially stimulated in this way, it attacks another monkey much higher up the pecking order of its troupe, which it would never do in normal circumstances. Similarly, stimulation of a mouse's amygdala has been known to make it square up to a cat. And we know that these effects are not confined to sub-humans, because human patients report sudden, otherwise inexplicable, feelings of rage when they are stimulated in these—but not in other—areas of the brain while undergoing neurosurgery.

It is important not to read too much into the finding that the hypothalamus and amygdala are involved in aggression (and in other types of emotional behaviour) in species as diverse as rat and humankind. It does not mean that, where aggression is concerned, we are just like rats, because whereas these areas play a very important part in controlling how a rat behaves, in man they are subordinate to the influence of the newer and more sophisticated brain structures which have been superimposed on the primitive regions that form a large part of a rat's brain but are a relatively small component of ours. As a general rule, the higher up the evolutionary scale you look, the less control you find being exerted by regions of the brain like the hypothalamus and the more by higher centres such as the cerebral cortex.

Nevertheless, the hypothalamus and the amygdala *are* involved in human aggression. This suggests a possible explanation for any difference there may be between the sexes in aggressive behaviour. It has been suggested that the areas of the hypothalamus which are involved in aggression may be particularly susceptible to the action of male sex hormones, and that these hormones— especially testosterone—may in some way prime this area of the brain throughout development, so that it becomes more easily activated in men than in women.

There is quite a lot of evidence in favour of this proposal. For example, female monkeys whose mothers are injected with testosterone while they are pregnant later show the sort of aggressive behaviour usually associated with male monkeys. They are more threatening, and also engage in more rough-and-tumble play than female monkeys generally display. In humans, too, girls who accidentally receive a dose of male sex hormones before they are born tend to be more tomboyish than their sisters. But perhaps the most persuasive evidence came from the study of young Californian children mentioned earlier in this chapter. These children were part of a sample who had been studied since birth. In fact, researchers were present in the delivery room when they were born and took samples of blood from each child's umbilical cord, which were analysed to see how much male and female hormones they contained. When the children took part in the trampoline experiment four years later, it was found that the boys who showed the highest levels of rough-and-tumble play were those who had had the highest levels of male hormones at birth, while the girls who showed the least rough play were those who had had the highest levels of female hormone. Since there is also evidence that boys who are accidentally exposed to female hormones before they are born tend later to be less aggressive than most boys, it seemed at one point that we had at last found an area of behaviour where the two sexes not only differed, but did so from a very early age as a result of the biological differences between them.

However, thanks to the kind of twist in the plot with which followers of the sex differences saga are all too familiar, the issue is now open again. The California researchers, realizing the importance of the connection they were claiming between hormones and behaviour, repeated their experiment on a second group of boys, and failed to replicate their earlier finding. Other researchers have found signs of a link between testosterone and aggression in groups of men as diverse as hockey players, Swedish teenagers and Californian rapists. Female hormones (which neutralize the effect of male hormones) can prevent violent males from displaying extremely aggressive behaviour; indeed they are sometimes used to control the behaviour of male sex offenders. But we are still some way from being able to claim confidently that the relationship exists, and even further from understanding how it might operate. It is not even entirely clear what is the role of sex hormones in animals. We know that rats and mice given testosterone during the earlier stages of development and after puberty show the masculine higher levels of aggression. But in other species like the gerbil and hamster, *female* hormones are implicated in affecting aggressive behaviour. And even if there *is* a connection, it is clearly not just a question of Have Testosterone, Will Fight.

The latest idea seems to be that it is *high variability*, rather than a high absolute level of circulating testosterone that predicts aggressive behaviour in boys and girls. The relationship between hormones and behaviour is a two-way affair, with hormone levels influencing behaviour but also being affected by it. For example, the pecking order, or *dominance hierarchy*, amongst the males in a troupe of monkeys changes over a period of time, and researchers have found that when a monkey moves up the hierarchy by winning a fight with another monkey who was previously his superior, his testosterone level rises dramatically, while that of his defeated opponent drops. So although there is a connection between the male sex hormone and aggression, it is not simply a matter of testosterone causing aggression. The environment can affect the hormone, and there is no doubt that it also affects aggression. I mentioned earlier that boys treated a doll much more violently than girls after both had watched an adult being rewarded for roughing up a similar doll. But when the children taking part in this experiment were rewarded for copying the adult's behaviour, the difference between the sexes virtually disappeared. The girls fell on the doll with as much abandon as the boys when they were offered soft drinks or free stickers for doing so. If the children really were being aggressive by beating up the doll, the message seems to be that it takes very little encouragement to make girls behave as aggressively as boys.

However, even the suggestion that aggression might have a biological basis has led researchers to investigate the possibility that it may be inherited. But the evidence in favour of this notion is less than convincing. Criminal behaviour certainly runs in families, though it is difficult to disentangle the effects of genetic similarity from a shared environment. In the laboratory, a group of American experimenters recently compared the behaviour of pairs of identical and fraternal twins when they were encouraged to attack an inflatable doll. For all our reservations about this as a test of aggression, we might have expected the twins who shared the same genes to be more similar in their behaviour than those who did not, if this were really an area of behaviour in which heredity plays an important part. In fact, the identical twins were no more alike in this respect than the others.

But if it is not only biology that makes boys behave more aggressively than girls, what else is responsible? Studies show that neither sex is encouraged to show aggression by the person seen most often in the pre-school years. Mothers discourage aggression equally in their sons and their daughters. However, when fathers play with their children, they treat their sons and daughters differently, in a way which may exaggerate any biological tendency for males to be the more aggressive sex. Fathers are observed to play more roughly with boys than with girls, and to encourage their sons to tolerate more roughness, which may explain why boys later not only launch more attacks on their friends than girls do, but also are more often the target of other children's aggression. Moreover, when children have been naughty, it is twice as common for boys to receive physical punishment as it is for girls, who are usually punished verbally, by the threat of missing a treat or of losing their parents' affection.

One of the offences for which children are punished is being too rough. It may seem paradoxical that boys, who are punished more harshly than girls for this as for other misdemeanours, nevertheless become the more aggressive sex. One possible explanation is that boys get used to being hit and become less frightened by it, and also come to associate hitting and being hit with being masculine. Perhaps they also observe that hitting is an effective way for adults to impose their will, while girls learn from their different treatment that the appropriate way to resolve a clash of wills is by words rather than by blows.

But even in the battle of words, boys become the more aggressive sex from an early age. Analysis of nursery school children's conversation shows that boys tend to interrupt other speakers nearly twice as often as girls. This establishes a pattern that continues throughout life: at primary school, the ratio of male to female interruptions of a teacher in lessons is very much higher, while in adulthood it has been calculated that men are responsible for no less than 98 per cent of all the interruptions that occur in everyday conversation!

Although throughout childhood boys and girls do not tend to play together if they can avoid it, when they do so there is fascinating filmed evidence of the way in which boys seek to assert themselves. For example, they try to avoid playing in a Wendy house, as if already aware that the domestic arena is where male authority is at its shakiest. They also play at being the powerful father when girls are present, but not when they are playing with other boys.

Other aspects of the different ways in which boys and girls are treated may help to explain why boys get into so much more trouble than girls. For example, from a very early age boys are allowed to play in the streets while girls may only be allowed out to play in each other's houses. Girls are also expected to conform to stricter moral standards, and are subject to such subtle curbs on 'rough' behaviour as the demand that they—unlike boys—must not get their clothes dirty.

The media, too, exert a powerful influence throughout childhood and adolescence, encouraging the stereotypes of the active, aggressive male and the passive, docile female. Male heroes in literature and popular culture are often tough, violent and aggressive, and gender-stereotype research has found that these qualities are more desirable in men than in women. Analysis of the contents of short stories published by American women's magazines in 1975 revealed that two of the most popular themes were still the male who triumphs over female pride, and the heroine who chooses the dependable man rather than the lovable rogue.

In summary, it is easy to see how men might *become* the more aggressive sex, and I do not think that the deficiencies of laboratory studies of aggression are sufficient reason to reject the assertion that men are more aggressive than women in most circumstances. This brings us to one of the most crucial arguments in the whole debate about sex differences. It goes like this. Where the physiology of aggression is concerned, human beings are strikingly like other animals. In all other species where animals live in social groups with a dominance hierarchy, the position which an individual animal occupies in the pecking order is determined by its fighting ability. In human societies everywhere and (so far as we know) always, the dominant positions in public life are virtually all occupied by men, and the reason for this, the argument goes, is that men are more aggressive. This idea lies at the heart of all attempts to justify male supremacy— how often have you heard it said that you have to fight to get to the top, and women just do not have the necessary will to fight?— and if it is well founded, we may be forced to accept that women are destined to remain second-class citizens.

But is toughness really the ticket to the top for human beings? If you look at how young children organize their social groups, the parallel with monkeys seems quite apt. Dominance hierarchies can be seen in both sexes, though they are more stable amongst boys, and physical toughness and fighting ability are important for boys in deciding who comes where in the pecking order. But they are much less important in girls' groups and on the occasions when the two sexes play together. However, experiments carried out on four- to eight-year-olds show that when a boy and a girl are asked to draw a picture together and given different-coloured crayons, it is the boy's colour which tends to dominate the finished product. Other experiments confirm that boys of this age generally manage to establish dominance over girls when both are pursuing selfish goals. But in some situations the position is reversed. When a child seeks dominance not for his or her own ends but in order to stop someone else doing something stupid—for example, an older child telling a younger child to keep away from the fire— it is girls who more often accept responsibility, a state of affairs very reminiscent of the different situations which cause adult men and women to behave aggressively. One exception to the rule that boys tend to excel at 'nasty' and girls at 'nice' power games comes from the observation that girls are more unfriendly than boys when a newcomer (of either sex) tries to join in when two of them are playing together. But their hostility rarely lasts for long, and it may just reflect the fact that girls are more attached to small, exclusive groups.

Leadership and power

As children grow older, the similarity between their behaviour and that of monkeys begins to disappear. They come to realize that verbal persuasion is just as efficient and much less dangerous than fighting as a means of achieving one's ends. It is here that the fatal weakness in the biological argument used to justify male supremacy becomes apparent. Unlike monkeys, we do not choose our leaders for their toughness; in fact, aggressiveness is often a liability, best concealed by those who seek to reach the top. By the age of ten, boys and girls are equally good at persuading another child to do something he or she does not want to do, as you can see from the following experiment. Children were give a supply of bitter-tasting (though entirely innocuous) biscuits, and offered a small cash reward for every one they could persuade another child to eat. Although boys were no more successful at this than girls, the most successful girls and boys used noticeably different strategies to achieve their goal. Boys tended to favour coercion, threatening their victims if they judged this would work, or else telling blatant lies. For example, one boy who was obviously a born salesman used the following gambit: 'Do you know how Christopher Columbus got to America?' Long pause. 'By eating these ship's biscuits!' Girls, on the other hand, either offered to share the money they stood to win if the other child would co-operate, or else relied on the winsome, soft-selling technique: 'Go on, just for me. I promise it's all right.'

By the time they reach adolescence, when boys and girls are spending much more time in each other's company, it is the most persuasive rather than the most aggressive children who tend to become leaders. Those who set the style of the group and command the most respect are usually bright academically, good at games or physically attractive. Being aggressive is if anything a liability, because very aggressive children are shunned in groups of non-delinquent children. Even delinquent gangs are uneasy about 'nutters' who enjoy excessive violence for its own sake.

Before they reach adolescence, children's groups rarely have a single leader for all occasions, in the way that a troupe of monkeys contains one dominant male. The reason for this difference is that children's lives are very much more varied than those of monkeys. Outside school, they have an enormous number of options open to them in deciding how to fill their days. Different sorts of activity call for different expertise and hence for a variety of leaders. So the idea of a single dominant male is inapplicable in the human context, which further weakens the analogy between men and monkeys.

Adult life is even more varied and complex, and it is inconceivable that one person could combine all the qualities which would assure them automatic leadership in every situation. The autocratic boss may have to take orders from a junior employee when the two of them are playing for the office cricket team, and he may regularly have to defer to the legal expertise of the firm's lawyer. In marriage, although the husband is the formal head of the family, most couples work out a power-sharing arrangement, with each having the final say in his or her agreed areas of special competence. However, we saw in Chapter 7 that things are rather different in the earlier stages of a relationship, and even when a couple know each other well enough to have established who is best at what, it often turns out that the man has pre-empted the crucial areas of decision-making, leaving the woman to organize those aspects of their life in which he is less interested. But although it was not so long ago that a British judge ruled that it was part of the normal wear and tear of marriage for a woman to be punched and have her face slapped from time to time, the law now agrees that it is wrong for men to abuse women physically, even if they are married to them. In 1991 a man was convicted of raping his wife, making British legal history. Fortunately, brute force and physical aggression feature comparatively rarely in relationships between the two sexes, though we cannot rule out the possibility that fear of them may sometimes be at the back of a woman's mind when she allows a man to get his own way.

It is impossible to assess how common marital violence ('wife-battering') is, and almost as difficult to discover its origins. According to one school of thought, certain women are predisposed to become victims, as a result of their experiences in childhood and in previous adult relationships. A study of women in women's refuges in Sydney, Australia found little evidence to support this, however: fewer than one woman in ten involved had previously experienced violence. Nor did alcohol seem to explain their husband's behaviour. The only firm conclusion the investigators reached was that women with children and without jobs were most vulnerable to battering. A more disturbing note has been struck by researchers who studied the problem in Wales. They confirmed that alcohol seems to play little part in marital violence. But more than half of the women questioned in this study believed that their husbands had a right to beat them, which suggests that the idea that male supremacy stems from— and should be maintained by—sheer brute force cannot be dismissed as a thing of the past.

Outside married life, leadership goes either with formal status in an organization or according to social class, education, age and—especially—relevant expertise. When a group of strangers are thrown together and need to find a leader, the thought uppermost in their minds seems to be: who has the best qualities for the job in hand? They select the most aggressive person only if this is what the situation calls for. Otherwise, persuasiveness, the ability to reach a constructive compromise and inspirational flair seem to be far more useful attributes if you want to reach a position which allows you to exert authority. The ability to assert one's views is another very important ingredient in the success cocktail, but this is quite different from aggression. It does not have a biological basis, and although there is a great deal of evidence that women tend to be less assertive than men, it has been established that women who enrol in special training courses can learn to become more assertive.

Two American psychologists recently reviewed the research on the emergence of male and female leaders in groups which initially have no leader. The experiments they looked at were based in the laboratory as well as in 'natural' settings, and overall men emerged as leaders to a greater extent than women. But there did seem to be differences in the types of situations where men and women became leaders. Male leadership was particularly likely in short-term groups and in groups carrying out tasks that did not require complex social interaction. In contrast, women emerged as *social* leaders slightly more often than men.

Even if men are the more aggressive sex, this cannot explain why they get the best jobs, which raises the possibility that we have been barking up the wrong tree by concentrating on aggression. Perhaps we have been maligning men by assuming that they are hungry for power, and trying to discover what it is about them that allows them to be so successful in getting it. Should we have been thinking about women instead, and considering whether there are any 'typically' feminine characteristics which make them shy away from authority, leaving a power vacuum which men have occupied by default?

Looking back at the list of popular beliefs about 'typically' masculine and feminine behaviour we started with, there seem to be two obvious possibilities. The first is that women are naturally more compliant than men. Many studies show that girls are more obedient than boys from an early age, not only to their parents but to adults generally. But although we have seen that boys try to impose their wishes when playing with girls, girls do not always give in, and it is hard to believe that this explains why they are prepared to defer to their male contemporaries later in life.

The other possibility is that women are more easily influenced and suggestible. We can measure this in the laboratory by placing someone in a room with a group of stooges who have been secretly instructed to express a common opinion of a person they have all just met or an argument they have just heard. Alternatively, the experimental task may be to judge the length of a line or the area of a geometrical figure they have been shown, in which case the stooges are all briefed to make the same, slightly erroneous statement. In these situations, although some people succumb to group pressure and change their opinion, the great majority of the studies which have been carried out find both sexes to be equally suggestible. In a few cases, girls and women have been significantly more suggestible when their perceptual estimates have been challenged, but this probably tells us more about their inferior visual-spatial skills than their suggestibility. There is no evidence at all that they abandon their opinions about people or their position in an argument any more easily than boys or men do. Indeed, women are found to be *less* suggestible than men when the subject they are asked about is one they know well (for example, women's fashion). And they become even more independently minded if they are shown a short TV commercial in which a female character plays the dominant role—an interesting footnote to the evidence we discussed in Chapter 1, which showed how important a part TV plays in creating gender role stereotypes.

The occupations pursued by a disproportionate number of men, for instance in business and industry, are ones which require an element of aggressiveness. In contrast, women's careers tend to have the emphasis on giving help to others: women in professional employment are predominantly teachers and nurses. But it does not follow that it is a masculine trait to be aggressive, and a feminine one to be helpful. In fact, men are generally found to be more helpful than women, in studies of short-term encounters with strangers. The reason women are less likely to offer help to a stranger may also be why they tend to be less aggressive: they may be wary of strangers, in trying to avoid physical harm to themselves. But the traditional male role encompasses the norms of chivalry as well as of aggressiveness: men are expected to protect the weak and defenceless. So it does not look as if the division of labour is due to women being inherently helpful and men inherently aggressive. And even if men and women do have different strengths, this should not prevent them from doing the same jobs.

Many people have looked for evidence of sex differences in leadership style as an explanation for why more women are not in positions of authority. When the sample looked at is of people who have not been selected for leadership, there does appear to be a difference: there is a tendency for women to adopt a democratic or participative style, rather than the masculine autocratic and directive style. But these differences tend not to emerge between male and female managers within an organization, presumably because organizational roles override gender roles. This is another example of the phenomenon that keeps cropping up in this book: when men and women are equivalent in terms of status and power, they behave in a similar way. But because women are more often in positions with little power or opportunity for advancement, they tend to behave in ways which reflect their lack of power, and sex differences may appear substantial.

But the fact that powerful men and women behave in the same way is not necessarily a good thing, if it means that women are forced to adopt the macho male model of managerial behaviour and eliminate feminine traits in order to move up the organizational hierarchy. In fact, some organizational theorists and occupational psychologists have suggested that women conforming in this way may be detrimental to businesses. They suggest that women, because of their personality traits, are the natural business leaders of the future. Female managers are felt to be better listeners, and several studies have shown that women possess qualities which could improve communication, co-operation, commitment and team spirit—qualities which are necessary today for achieving excellence. Our understanding of what makes a good manager in the 1990s is veering away from the concept of a tough and aggressive heroic leader, and attaching more importance to someone who is an enabler, nurturing and supporting colleagues, and involving others in decision-making. This is because there is a trend for large organizations to become smaller, flatter and decentralized, relying on people working in project teams and having a more flexible functional role. In this sort of environment, managers will no longer be able to rely on the authority of status and position, and the emphasis will be much more on informal open communication. This style is a more feminine one: women may be better endowed with collaborative and interpersonal skills and could provide a better alternative to the macho management approach. Despite this, women are still held back by prejudices at work.

Explaining male domination

Since neither psychology nor biology seems capable of explaining male dominance, perhaps this is the moment to broaden our perspective and see if the riddle looks any less baffling from the more global viewpoint of the anthropologist. Anthropological evidence makes one thing very clear: the tendency for public life to be dominated by men is almost universal. But it would be wrong to conclude from this that there must be a single universal reason for this state of affairs, because anthropologists are adamant that there is no such thing as a universal male or female personality, or a single set of characteristics which everywhere are thought of as 'typically' masculine or feminine. In this chapter we have been evaluating the suggestion that men dominate our society because they are more aggressive than women. But if we had been considering, for example, the Masai, an African tribe, we would almost certainly have been testing a quite different proposition: that men dominate public life because they are more co-operative than women, since this is the quality on which Masai men most pride themselves. By far the most important generalization which has emerged from the anthropologists' study of men and women throughout the world is that although different societies have very different views about what qualities are masculine, such qualities are usually more highly valued than those thought to be feminine.

But is there any rational explanation for the fact that men

everywhere seem to end up running society? Many people believe that the key factor is that women have babies, which reduces their mobility and therefore makes it necessary that men should be responsible for activities like warfare which often take place away from the community. Being the war- and peace-makers, it is men who act as the community's representatives in the outside world. So only they acquire the sophistication and breadth of knowledge which equips them to be political leaders when they return home. There are at least two things wrong with this story, the first of which becomes apparent when we examine what happens in the few remaining societies which operate according to this primitive pattern. For example, amongst the Rendille (a primitive Kenyan tribe who live by herding cattle), the men are certainly more mobile, being away from home most of the time between boyhood and the age of about thirty. The women not only keep the home fires burning, they also build the houses and keep the villages running smoothly. But when the community is faced with an important decision, it is made exclusively by the men, who are transformed from herdsmen into village elders by a simple initiation ceremony, even though they may have virtually no experience or knowledge of how the village operates! The ability of men to absent themselves from the society for long periods of time is a very doubtful qualification for local politics. Yet the tradition lives on, and it is not only in primitive communities that retired generals make it to the top.

The other problem with this explanation of male dominance and female subordination is that it rests on the assumption that only women can bring up children, and we saw in Chapter 6 that this is not so. There have in fact been a number of societies in which child-care was delegated to wet nurses, nannies and foster-parents, and one reason why there has been so much controversy in our society recently about the unique significance of biological mothers may simply be that all we have left of the traditional division of labour between the sexes is that women tend to look after babies and men do not.

It is commonly assumed that if men and women do different kinds of jobs and have different status, there must be some inherent biological or psychological differences between the sexes which makes a division of labour and power inevitable. This is denied by the anthropologists, who believe that the two sexes are forced apart to meet the needs of the society they live in. They give a new slant to the biological imperative which has cropped up on several occasions in this book, by suggesting that what keeps men and women together—and hence ensures the survival of the species—is that they have become economically dependent on each other by accepting responsibility for different, but equally essential, types of work. This, according to the anthropologists, provides the basis for a stable society. But it does not explain why the contribution men make is valued more highly than that made by women, despite the fact that both are equally essential to the smooth running of society.

A matter of compensation?

At this point, it becomes a question of paying your money and taking your choice, because although there are several possible explanations, none of them is entirely convincing. One possibility, which will appeal to feminists, is that men seek (or are given) power as compensation for their lack of the obvious natural value which women have by virtue of their having babies. As Samuel Johnson put it, nature has given women so much power that the law has very wisely given them little. There is certainly a suspicion of false bravado about several aspects of men's behaviour we have discussed, which suggests that their superiority is far from effortless: their tendency to overestimate their own physical strength, for example, or their touching but misplaced faith that they are going to improve on their past performance in examinations. It has also been pointed out that men devise the most elaborate, exclusively male, rituals and have the most fierce code of masculine 'macho' in societies in which their superiority is most challenged, for example in the powerfully matriarchal Southern Mediterranean countries.

Nor is it just their inability to have babies which makes men a suitable case for compensation. We saw in Chapter 2 that men are more vulnerable than women to diseases and more likely to die at every stage of their life, and I suggested that this may be one reason why parents value boy babies more highly. From an actuarial point of view, it is more of an achievement for a man to reach adulthood than it is for a woman, which may be another reason why men are regarded as more 'special' than women.

There is a third explanation for the higher status of men which is less flattering to women where their past is concerned, but provides grounds for optimism about their future. This is the suggestion that women's lower status arose from social expedience. Society needed to bind warring factions together, and chose to do so by strategic marriages which resulted in children who were related to both factions. This system would work only if women did what they were told, and allowed themselves to be used as gifts to oil the wheels of society. If this was really the basis for women's inferior status, then the imbalance of power between the sexes can no longer be justified in societies like our own, where women tend to choose their own husbands.

But are things going to change? On the basis of the evidence discussed in this book, I have no doubt that women are capable of being men's equals, in the sense that there is no immutable principle of psychology or biology to stop them doing what men do, as well as men can. For a variety of reasons, there are many women who do not wish to compete with men and others who are unsuccessful when they do so. But there is nothing unnatural about the suggestion that men and women should at least be given equal opportunities. Male supremacy has been convenient in the past, but it has never come easily. On the contrary, it has always had to be reinforced by elaborate rituals—initiation ceremonies, for example—and a host of cultural buttresses, as can be seen from the fact that the Battle of the Sexes is a thread running through the entire history of literature.

Recent research in Britain conducted by the Henley Centre for Forecasting predicts that by the year 2000, half of the work-force will be women, and that three-quarters of the new jobs created in the nineties will be filled by women. The proportion of women in full-time professional occupations and senior management roles is expected to show a particularly dramatic rise. But there is no guarantee that this will happen—the influx of women may simply be accommodated by the low-paid, low-status end of the job market. How can we prevent this?

There seem to be two main ways to change women's inequality of achievement. The first is for them to mimic men—take more risks, be more aggressive and pursue power and dominance at the expense of personal relationships. Indeed, most successful top women managers do show a comparatively male personality pattern. This is almost certainly the easiest route to success in a man's world (remember, too, the evidence reviewed in Chapter 5 that attractive women managers may be at a disadvantage because they are perceived to be more feminine and hence less competent).

The second route is more idealistic, and requires us to broaden the definition of conventional success, to involve a wider set of achievements. For example, there is no reason why looking after a home and family should not be a fulfilling and rewarding occupation for both men and women. Men and women may bring different, often complementary skills to the jobs they do, and it makes sense to put the combined talents to good use, and value them equally. Sexual equality is not about identifying men's goals and men's methods as the ideal for women, but about allowing each individual to develop his or her talents without the constraints of an artificial gender role.

And even if it becomes generally accepted that there is no such thing as a 'man's job', we are still left with the problem of selling the idea that there should be no such thing as a 'woman's job' either, except of course giving birth to children. But those who seek to establish equality of opportunity between the sexes must realize that until such time as men accept an equal role in raising their children, any victories that women win will be hollow ones.

Further reading

The most comprehensive treatment of the subject is undoubtedly *The Psychology of Sex Differences*, by E. E. Maccoby and C. N. Jacklin (London, Oxford University Press, 1975). But this is written for psychologists, and the general reader may find *The Longest War*, by C. Tavris and C. Offir (New York, Harcourt Brace Jovanovich, 1977), a more acceptable overview of the subject. A list of other books of general interest is given below, followed by a list of the most important books and articles discussed in each chapter of this book.

General reading

Archer, J. and Lloyd, B., *Sex and Gender* (London, Penguin, 1982)

Lloyd, B. and Archer, J. (eds.), *Exploring Sex Differences* (London, Academic Press, 1976)

'Men and Women: The Balance of Power', special supplement in *New Society*, 18–25 December 1980

Oakley, A., *Sex, Gender and Society* (London, Temple Smith, 1977)

Ounsted, C. and Taylor, D. C. (eds.), *Gender Differences: Their Ontogeny and Significance* (London, Churchill, 1972)

Reid, I. and Wormald, E., *Sex Differences in Britain* (London, Grant McIntyre, 1982)

Singleton, C. H., 'Sex differences', in B. M. Foss (ed.), *Psychology Survey No. 1* (London, George Allen & Unwin, 1978)

Chapter 1   Men and women

Archer, J., 'Childhood gender roles: structure and development', *The Psychologist*, **9** (1989), 367–70

Broverman, I. K., Vogel, S. R., Broverman, D. M., Clarkson, F. E. and Rosenkrantz, P. S., 'Sex role stereotypes: a current appraisal', *Journal of Social Issues*, **28** (1972), 59–79

Davies, D. R., 'Children's performance as a function of sex typed labels', *British Journal of Social Psychology*, **25** (1986), 173–5

Downs, A. C., 'Sex role stereotyping on prime-time television', *Journal of Genetic Psychology*, **138** (1981), 253–8

Hargreaves, D. J., Bates, H. M. and Foot, J. M. C., 'Sex-typed labelling affects task performance', *British Journal of Social Psychology*, **24** (1985), 153–5

Harris, P. R. and Stobart, J., 'Sex-role stereotyping in British television advertisements at different times of the day: an extension and refinement of Manstead and McCulloch (1981)', *British Journal of Social Psychology*, **25** (1986), 155–64

Hines, M., 'Prenatal and gonadal hormones and sex differences in human behaviour', *Psychological Bulletin*, **92** (1982), 56–80

Hwang, C.-P., 'Mother–infant interaction: effects of sex of infant on feeding behaviour', *Early Human Development*, **2/4** (1978), 341–9

Kolbe, R. and LaVoie, J., 'Sex role stereotyping in preschool children's picture books', *Social Psychology Quarterly*, **44** (1981), 369–74

Livingstone, S. and Green, G., 'Television advertisements and the portrayal of gender', *British Journal of Social Psychology*, **25** (1986), 149–54

Lloyd B., Duveen G. and Smith C., 'Social representations of gender and young children's play', *British Journal of Developmental Psychology*, **6** (1988)

McCauley E., 'Disorders of sexual differentiation and development— psychological aspects', *Pediatric Clinics of North America*, **37** (1991), 1405–20

Maccoby, E. E. and Jacklin, C. N., *The Psychology of Sex Differences* (London, Oxford University Press, 1975), chapter 9

Manstead, A. S. R. and McCulloch, C., 'Sex-role stereotyping in British TV advertisements', *British Journal of Social Psychology*, **20** (1981), 171–80

Oakley, A., *Women Confined* (Oxford, Martin Robertson, 1980)

Parke, R. D., *Fathering* (London, Fontana Paperbacks, 1981)

Perry, D. G. and Bussey, K., 'The social learning theory of sex differences: imitation is alive and well', *Journal of Personality and Social Psychology*, **37** (1979), 1699–712

Scheibe, C., 'Sex roles in TV commercials', *Journal of Advertising Research*, **19** (1979), 23–7

Singleton, C. H., 'Sex differences', in B. M. Foss (ed.), *Psychology Survey No. 1* (London, George Allen & Unwin, 1978)

Smith, C. and Lloyd, B., 'Maternal behaviour and perceived sex of infant: revisited', *Child Development*, **49** (1978), 1263–5

Ullian, D. Z., 'The development of concepts of masculinity and femininity', in B. Lloyd and J. Archer (eds.), *Exploring Sex Differences* (London, Academic Press, 1976)

Chapter 2   Physical differences

Amos, A. and Bostock, Y., 'Policy on cigarette advertising and coverage of smoking and health in European women's magazines', *British Medical Journal*, **304** (1992), 99–100

Dyer, K., 'Female athletes are catching up', *New Scientist*, 22 September 1977, 722–3

Eisler, R. M. and Blalock, J. A., 'Masculine gender role stress— implications for the assessment of men', *Clinical Psychology Review*, **11** (1991), 45–60

Frisch, R., 'Fatness, menarche and fertility', paper read at Royal Society of Medicine Conference on Scientific Aspects of Obesity, Cambridge University, 25–26 March 1981

Hamilton J. B. and Mestler, G. E., 'Mortality and survival: a comparison of eunuchs with intact men and women in a mentally retarded population', *Journal of Gerontology*, **24** (1969), 395–411

Harrison, J., Chin, J. and Ficarrotto, T., 'Warning: masculinity may be dangerous to your health', in M. S. Kimmel and M. A. Messner (eds.), *Men's Lives* (New York, Macmillan, 1989)

Madigan, F. C., 'Are sex mortality differentials biologically caused?', *Milbank Memorial Fund Quarterly*, **35** (1957), 202

Moir, E., 'Female participation in physical activity—a Scottish study', unpublished paper, Dunfermline College of Physical Education, 1977

Ounsted, C. and Taylor, D. C. (eds.), *Gender Differences: Their Ontogeny and Significance* (London, Churchill, 1972)

Parkes, A. S., *Patterns of Sexuality and Reproduction* (London, Oxford University Press, 1976)

People in Sport (London, The Sports Council, 1979)

Rosen, B. N. and Peterson, L., 'Gender differences in children's outdoor play injuries: a review and an integration', *Clinical Psychology Review*, **10** (1990), 187–205

Seeman, M. V. and Lang, M., 'The role of estrogens in schizophrenia gender differences', *Schizophrenia Bulletin*, **16** (1990), 185–94

Stoney, O. M., Davis, M. C. and Matthews, K. A., 'Sex differences in physiological responses to stress and in coronary heart disease—a causal link?', *Psychophysiology*, **24** (1987), 127–31

Tanner, J. M., 'Physical growth', in P. H. Mussen (ed.), *Carmichael's Manual of Child Psychology*, 3rd edn. (New York, Wiley, 1970), vol. 1

Tanner, J. M., *Foetus into Man* (London, Open Books, 1978)

Waldron, I., 'Why do women live longer than men?', *Social Science and Medicine*, **10** (1976), 349–62

Whipp, B. J. and Ward, S. A., 'Will women soon outrun men?', *Nature*, **355** (1992), 25

Wilson, G. and Nias, D., *Love's Mysteries* (London, Open Books, 1976)

Chapter 3　*Creatures of emotion*

Abplanalp, J. M., Donnelly, A. F. and Rose, R. M., 'Psychoendocrinology of the menstrual cycle: 1. Enjoyment of daily activities and moods', *Psychosomatic Medicine*, **41** (1979), 587–604

Abplanalp, J. M., Rose, R. M., Donnelly, A. F. and Livingston-Vaughan, B. S., 'Psychoendocrinology of the menstrual cycle: 2. The relationship between enjoyment of activities, moods and reproductive hormones', *Psychosomatic Medicine*, **41** (1979), 605–15

Bem, S. L., 'The measurement of psychological androgyny', *Journal of Consulting and Clinical Psychology*, **42** (1974), 155–62

Benedek, T. and Rubenstein, B. B., 'The correlations between ovarian activity and psychodynamic processes: 2. The menstrual phase', *Psychosomatic Medicine*, **1** (1939), 461–85

Broverman, I. K., Broverman, D. M., Clarkson, F. E., Rosenkrantz, P. S. and Vogel, S. R., 'Sex role stereotypes and clinical judgment of mental health', *Journal of Consulting and Clinical Psychology*, **34** (1970), 1–7

Brush, M. G., *Premenstrual Syndrome and Period Pains* (London, Women's Health Concern, 1981)

Byrne, D., 'Sex differences in the reporting of symptoms of depression in the general population', *British Journal of Clinical Psychology*, **20** (1981), 83–92

Cayleff, S. E., '"Prisoners of their own feebleness": women, nerves and Western medicine—a historical overview', *Social Science and Medicine*, **26** (1988), 1199–208

Cochrane, R. and Stopes-Roe, M., 'Women, marriage, employment and mental health', *British Journal of Psychiatry*, **139** (1982), 373–81

Cooper, C. and Davidson, M., 'The pressures on working women: what can be done?', *Bulletin of the British Psychological Society*, **34** (1981), 357–60

Dalton, K., *Once a Month* (London, Fontana Paperbacks, 1978)

Dimitriou, E. C. and Didangelous, P. A., 'Premenstrual tension and personality', *Personality and Individual Differences*, **1** (1980), 300–3

Doering, C. H., Brodie, H. K. H., Kraemer, H. C., Moos, R. H., Becker, H. B. and Hamburg, D. A., 'Negative affect and plasma testosterone: a longitudinal human study', *Psychosomatic Medicine*, **37** (1975), 484–91

Gordon, R. A., *Anorexia and Bulimia* (Oxford, Blackwell, 1990).

Goudsmit, E., 'A study of anxiety and depression in the premenstrual syndrome', unpublished paper, St Thomas's Hospital, London, 1978

Grove, W. R., 'Sex differences in mental illness among adult men and women: an evaluation of four questions raised regarding the evidence on the higher rates in women', *Social Science and Medicine*, **12** (1978), 187–98

Nicholson, J. N. and Barltrop, K., 'Do women go mad every month?', *New Society*, 11 February 1982, 226–8

Nolen-Hoeksema, S., 'Sex differences in unipolar depression: evidence and theory', *Psychological Bulletin*, **101** (1987), 259–82

Rolls, B. J., Fedoroff, I. C., and Guthrie, J. F., 'Gender differences in eating behaviour and body weight regulation', *Health Psychology*, **10** (1991), 133–42

Roy, A., 'Vulnerability factors and depression in men', *British Journal of Psychiatry*, **138** (1981), 75–7

Simon, A. and Ward, L. O., 'Sex-related patterns of worry in secondary school pupils', *British Journal of Clinical Psychology*, **21** (1982), 69–70

Walsh, R. N., Budtz-Olsen, I., Leader, C. and Cummins, R. A., 'The menstrual cycle, personality, and academic performance', *Archives of General Psychiatry*, **38** (1981), 219–21

Chapter 4 Brain and intellect

Allen, L. S., Hines, M., Shryne, J. E. and Gorski, R. A., 'The sexually dimorphic cell groups in the human brain', *Journal of Neuroscience*, **9** (1989), 497–506

Archer, J., 'Gender stereotyping of school subjects', *The Psychologist*, **5** (1992), 66–9

Bales, D., 'X-linkage of spatial ability: a critical review', *Child Development*, **51** (1980), 625–35

Barinaga M., 'Is homosexuality biological?', *Science*, **253** (1991), 956–7

Benbow, O. P., 'Sex differences in mathematical reasoning ability in intellectually talented preadolescents: their nature, effects, and possible causes', *Behavioural and Brain Sciences*, **11** (1988), 169–232

Benbow, O. P., 'Gender differences: searching for facts', *American Psychologist*, **45** (1990), 988

Buffery, A. W. H. and Gray, J. A., 'Sex differences in the development of spatial and linguistic skills', in C. Ounsted and D. C. Taylor (eds.), *Gender Differences: Their Ontogeny and Significance* (London, Churchill, 1972)

Coltheart, M., 'Sex and learning differences', *New Behaviour*, 1 May 1975, 54–7

de Lacoste, M. C., Adesanya, T. and Woodward, D. J., 'Measures of gender differences in the human brain and their relationship to brain weight', *Biological Psychiatry*, **28** (1990), 931–42

Eynard, R. and Walkerdine, V., *The Practice of Reason. Investigations into the Teaching and Learning of Mathematics in the Early Years of Schooling* (London, Thomas Coram Research Unit, University of London Institute of Education, 1982)

Fairweather, H., 'Sex differences in cognition', *Cognition*, **4** (1976), 231–80

Genetta-Wadley, A. and Swirsky-Sacchetti, T., 'Sex differences and handedness in hemispheric lateralization of tactile-spatial functions', *Perceptual and Motor Skills*, **70** (1990), 579–90

Gibbons, A., 'The brain as "sexual organ"', *Science*, **253** (1991), 957–9

Gould, S. J., *The Mismeasure of Man* (New York, Norton, 1981)

Halpern, D. F., 'The disappearance of cognitive gender differences: what you see depends on where you look', *American Psychologist*, **44** (1989), 1156–8

Hampson, E. and Kimura, D., 'Reciprocal effects of hormonal fluctuations on human motor and perceptuo-spatial skills', *Behavioral Neuroscience*, **102** (1988), 456–9

Heister, G., Landis, T., Regard, M. and Schroeder-Heister, P., 'Shift of functional cerebral asymmetry during the menstrual cycle', *Neuropsychologia*, **27** (1989), 871–80

Hyde J. S., Fennema, E. and Lamon, S. J., 'Gender differences in mathematics performance: a meta-analysis', *Psychological Bulletin*, **107** (1990), 139–55

Hyde, J. S. and Linn, M. C., 'Gender differences in verbal ability: a meta-analysis', *Psychological Bulletin*, **104** (1988), 53–69

Janowsky J. S., 'Sexual dimorphism in the human brain: dispelling the myths', *Developmental Medicine and Child Neurology*, **31** (1989), 257–63

Kelly, A., *Girls and Science* (Stockholm, Almqvist & Wiksell, 1978)

Levay, S., 'A difference in hypothalamic structure between heterosexual and homosexual men', *Science*, **253** (1991), 1034–7

Lewis, R. S. and Christiansen, L., 'Intrahemispheric sex differences in the functional representation of language and praxic functions in normal individuals', *Brain and Cognition*, **9** (1989), 238–43

Maccoby, E. E. and Jacklin, C. N., *The Psychology of Sex Differences* (London, Oxford University Press, 1975), chapter 3

McGlone, J., 'Sex differences in human brain asymmetry: a critical survey', *Behavioural and Brain Sciences*, **3** (1980), 215–63

St John Brooks, C., 'Must girls always be girls?', *New Society*, 1 April 1982, 9–11

Singleton, C. H., 'Sex differences', in B. M. Foss (ed.), *Psychology Survey No. 1* (London, George Allen & Unwin, 1978)

Spender, D., *Invisible Women: The Schooling Scandal* (London, Writers and Readers, 1982)

Stamp, P., 'Girls and mathematics: parental variables', *British Journal of Educational Psychology*, **49** (1979), 39–50

Stanworth, M., *Gender and Schooling* (London, Hutchinson, 1983)

Starr, B., 'Sex differences among personality correlates of mathematical ability in high school seniors', *Psychology of Women Quarterly*, **4** (1979), 212–20

Waber, D. P., 'Sex differences in mental abilities, hemispheric lateralization, and rate of physical growth at adolescence', *Developmental Psychology*, **13** (1977), 29–38

Chapter 5   Who wants what?

Ekehammar, B. and Sidanius, J., 'Sex differences in sociopolitical attitudes', *British Journal of Social Psychology*, **21** (1982), 33–41

The Facts about Accidents (Birmingham, Royal Society for the Prevention of Accidents Safety Education Publications, 1981)

Feild, H. S. and Caldwell, B. E., 'Sex of supervisor, sex of subordinate, and subordinate job satisfaction', *Psychology of Women Quarterly*, **3** (1979), 391–9

Heilman, M. E. and Saruwartari, L. R., 'When beauty is beastly: the effect of appearance and sex on evaluation of job applicants for managerial and non-managerial jobs', *Organizational Behaviour and Human Performance*, **23** (1979), 360–72

Horner, M. S., 'Fail: bright women', *Psychology Today*, November 1969, 36–9

Jabes, J., 'Causal attributions and sex-role stereotypes in the perceptions of women managers', *Canadian Journal of Behavioural Science*, **12** (1980), 52–63

Kaufman, D. and Fetters, M., 'Work motivation and job values among professional men and women', *Journal of Vocational Behaviour*, **17** (1980), 251–62

Liddell, A. and Morgan, G., 'Superstitious compulsions', *British Journal of Medical Psychology*, **51** (1978), 365–74

Maccoby, E. E. and Jacklin, C. N., *The Psychology of Sex Differences* (London, Oxford University Press, 1975), chapter 4

Miner, J. B., 'Motivational potential for upgrading among minority and female managers', *Journal of Applied Psychology*, **62** (1977), 691–7

Place, H., 'A biographical profile of women in management', *Journal of Occupational Psychology*, **52** (1979), 267–76

Rapoport, R. B., 'Sex differences in attitude expression: a generational explanation', *Public Opinion Quarterly*, **46** (1982), 86–96

Sandler, B. R., 'Women faculty at work in the classroom: or why it still hurts to be a woman in labor', *Communication Education*, **40** (1991), 6–15

Siegfried, W. D., 'A reexamination of sex differences in job preferences', *Journal of Vocational Behaviour*, **18** (1981), 30–42

Slovic, P., 'Risk-taking in children: age and sex differences', *Child Development*, **37** (1966), 169–76

Vallance, E., 'Women in the House of Commons', *Political Studies*, **29** (1981), 407–14

Yogev, S., 'Are professional women overworked? Objective versus subjective perception of role loads', *Journal of Occupational Psychology*, **55** (1982), 165–70

Zuckerman, M. and Wheeler, L., 'To dispel fantasies about the fantasy-based measure of fear of success', *Psychological Bulletin*, **82** (1975), 932–46

Chapter 6   Dual careers

Allen, I., Fogarty, M. and Walters, P., 'Stuck on the way to the top', *New Society*, 9 July 1981, 56–8

Beail, N., 'The role of the father in childcare', paper read at British Psychological Society Social Section Annual Conference, University of Edinburgh, September 1982

Beail, N. and McGuire, J., *Fathers: A Psychological Perspective* (London, Junction Books, 1982)

Bowlby, J., *Maternal Care and Mental Health* (Geneva, World Health Organization, 1951)

Brannen, J. and Moss, P., *Managing Mothers: Dual Career Households after Maternity Leave* (London, Unwin Hyman, 1991)

Brown, G. W. and Harris, T., *Social Origins of Depression* (London, Tavistock, 1978)

Clarke, A. M. and Clarke, A. D. B. (eds.), *Early Experience: Myth and Evidence* (London, Open Books, 1976)

Clarke-Stewart, A., *Day Care* (London, Fontana Paperbacks, 1982)

Defronzo, J., 'Female labour force participation and fertility in 48 states: cross-sectional and change analyses for the 1960–1970 decade', *Sociology and Social Research*, **64** (1979/80), 263–78

The Fact about Women is . . . (Manchester, Equal Opportunities Statistics Unit, 1982)

Frodi, A. M. and Lamb, M., 'Sex differences in responsiveness to infants', *Child Development*, **49** (1978), 1182–8

Fry, P. S. and Thiessen, I., 'Single mothers and single fathers and their children: perceptions of their children's needs, their own needs and career needs', *British Journal of Social Psychology*, **20** (1981), 97–100

Halsey, A. H. (ed.), *Trends in British Society since 1900* (London, Macmillan, 1972)

Jones, L. M. and McBride, J. L., 'Sex-role stereotyping in children as a function of maternal employment', *Journal of Social Psychology*, **111** (1980), 219–23

Juneja, R. A., 'A comparative study of working and non-working mothers with regard to practices and problems of rearing children', *Indian Psychology Review*, **18** (1979), 20–4

Klaus, M. H. and Kennell, J. K., *Maternal-Infant Bonding* (St Louis, Mosby, 1976)

Kotelchuk, M., 'The infant's relationship to the father: experimental evidence', in M. Lamb (ed.), *The Role of the Father in Child Development* (New York, Wiley, 1976)

Lewis, S., 'Dual career families in the UK: an update', *Women in Management Review and Abstracts*, **6**(4) (1991), 3–8

Martin, J. and Monk, J., *Infant Feeding 1980* (London, Office of Population Censuses and Surveys, 1982)

Mitchell, G., Redican, W. K. and Gomber, J., 'Lesson from a primate: males can raise babies', *Psychology Today*, April 1974

Parke, R. D., *Fathering* (London, Fontana Paperbacks, 1981)

Robson, K. and Kumar, R., 'Delayed onset of maternal affection after childbirth', *British Journal of Psychiatry*, **136** (1980), 347–53

Rubenstein, J., Howes, C. and Boyle, P., 'A two-year follow-up of infants in community-based day care', *Journal of Child Psychology and Psychiatry*, **22** (1981), 209–18

Scott, H., *Sweden's Right to be Human: Sex Role Equality: The Goal and the Reality* (London, Allison & Busby, 1982)

Veenhoven, R., 'Is there an innate need for children?', *European Journal of Social Psychology*, **4** (1974), 485–91

Wilsher, P., 'A woman's place', *Sunday Times*, 2 May 1982, p. 33

Working Women's Uneven Progress (London, Lloyds Bank Economic Bulletin No. 42, 1982)

Chapter 7 Sexual behaviour

Bancroft, J., 'The relationship between hormones and sexual behaviour in humans', in J. Hutchison (ed.), *Biological Determinants of Sexual Behaviour* (London, Wiley, 1978)

Beck, S. B., Ward-Hull, C. I. and McLear, P. M., 'Variables related to women's somatic preferences of the male and female body', *Journal of Personality and Social Psychology*, **34** (1976), 1200–10

Crowe, L. C. and George, W. H., 'Alcohol and human sexuality: review and integration', *Psychological Bulletin*, **105** (1989), 374–86

Farrell, C., *My Mother Said* (London, Routledge & Kegan Paul, 1978)

Feingold, A., 'Gender differences in effects of physical attractiveness on romantic attraction: a comparison across five research paradigms', *Journal of Personality and Social Psychology*, **59** (1990), 981–93

Fisher, W. A. and Byrne, D., 'Sex differences in response to erotica? Love versus lust', *Journal of Personality and Social Psychology*, **36** (1978), 117–25

Hunt, M., *Sexual Behaviour in the 1970s* (Chicago, Playboy Press, 1974)

Jay, T. B., 'Sex roles and dirty word usage: a review of the literature and a reply to Haas', *Psychological Bulletin*, **88** (1980), 614–21

Kinsey, A. C., Pomeroy, W. B. and Martin, C. E., *Sexual Behaviour in the Human Male* (Philadelphia, Saunders, 1948)

Kinsey, A. C., Pomeroy, W. B., Martin, C. E. and Gebhard, P. H., *Sexual Behaviour in the Human Female* (Philadelphia, Saunders, 1953)

McCauley, C. and Swann, C. P., 'Male–female differences in sexual fantasy', *Journal of Research in Personality*, **12** (1978), 76–86

Madsen, T., Shine, R., Loman, J. and Håkansson, T., 'Why do female adders copulate so frequently?', *Nature*, **355** (1992), 440–1

Masters, W. H. and Johnson, V. E., *Human Sexual Response* (Boston, Little, Brown & Co., 1966)

Mosher, D. L. and Abramson, P. R., 'Subjective sexual arousal to films of masturbation', *Journal of Consulting and Clinical Psychology*, **45** (1977), 796–807

Peplau, L. A., 'Power in dating relationships', in J. Freeman (ed.), *Women: A Feminist Perspective* (Palo Alto, Mayfield, 1978)

Peplau, L. A., Rubin, Z. and Hill, C. T., 'Sexual intimacy in dating relationships', *Journal of Social Issues*, **33** (1977), 86–109

Short R. V., 'Sexual selection and its component parts, somatic and genital, as illustrated by Man and the Great Apes', in J. S. Rosenblatt, R. A. Hinde, C. Beer and M.-C. Busnel (eds.), *Advances in the Study of Behaviour* (London, Academic Press, 1979), vol. 9

Talbot, R., Beech, H. and Vaughan, M., 'A normative appraisal of erotic fantasies in women', *British Journal of Social and Clinical Psychology*, **19** (1980), 81–3

Tavris, C. and Offir, C., *The Longest War: Sex Differences in Perspective* (New York, Harcourt Brace Jovanovich, 1977), chapter 3

Traupmann, J., Hatfield, E. and Wexler, P., 'Equity and sexual satisfaction in dating couples', *British Journal of Social Psychology*, **21** (1982), 33–40

Wales, E. and Brewer, B., 'Graffiti in the 1970s', *Journal of Social Psychology*, **99** (1976), 115–23

Wilson, G., 'The sociobiology of sex differences', *Bulletin of the British Psychological Society*, **32** (1979), 350–3

Chapter 8   Aggression and the balance of power

Alban Metcalfe, B., 'Male and female managers—an analysis of biographical and self-concept data', *Work and Stress*, **1** (1987), 207–19

Bourantas, D. and Papalexandris, N., 'Sex differences in leadership', *Journal of Management Psychology (UK)*, **5**(5) (1990), 7–10

Cacioppo, J. T. and Petty, R. E., 'Sex differences in influenceability: towards specifying the underlying processes', *Personality and Social Psychology Bulletin*, **6** (1980), 651–6

Campbell, A., *Female Delinquency in Social Context* (Oxford, Blackwell, 1980)

Cohn, L. D., 'Sex differences in the course of personality development: a meta-analysis', *Psychological Bulletin*, **109** (1991), 252–66

Duncan, P. and Hobson, G. N., 'Towards a definition of aggression', *Psychological Record*, **27** (1977), 545–55

Eagly, A. H. and Crowley, M., 'Gender and helping behaviour—a meta-analytic review of the social psychological literature', *Psychological Bulletin*, **100** (1986), 283–308

Eagly, A. H. and Johnson, B. T., 'Gender and leadership style: a meta-analysis', *Psychological Bulletin*, **108** (1990), 233–56

Eagly, A. H. and Karau, S. J., 'Gender and the emergence of leaders: a meta-analysis', *Journal of Personality and Social Psychology*, **60** (1991), 685–710

Eagly, A. H. and Staffen, V. J., 'Gender and aggressive behaviour—a meta-analytic review of the social psychological literature', *Psychological Bulletin*, **100** (1986), 309–30

Esposito, A., 'Sex differences in children's conversations', *Language and Speech*, **22** (1979), 213–20

Flora, C., 'Changes in women's status in women's magazine fiction: differences by social class', *Social Problems*, **26** (1979), 558–69

Frodi, A., Macaulay, J. and Thome, P. R., 'Are women always less aggressive than men? A review of the experimental literature', *Psychological Bulletin*, **84** (1977), 634–60

Furnham, A. and Henderson, M., 'Sex differences in reported assertiveness in Britain', *British Journal of Clinical Psychology*, **20** (1981), 227–38

Gilligan, C., *In a Different Voice* (Cambridge, Mass., Harvard University Press, 1982)

Griffiths, A., 'Some battered women in Wales: an interactionist view of their legal problems', *Family Law*, **11** (1981), 25–9

Hyde, J. S., 'How large are gender differences in aggression? a developmental meta-analysis', *Developmental Psychology*, **20** (1984), 722–36

Jason, L. A., Reichler, A. and Rucker, W., 'Territorial behaviour on beaches', *Journal of Social Psychology*, **114** (1981), 43–50

Jennings-Walstedt, J., Feis, F. L. and Brown, V., 'Influence of TV commercials on women's self-confidence and independent judgement', *Journal of Personality and Social Psychology*, **38** (1980), 203–10

Leventhal, G., 'Female criminality: is "Women's Lib" to blame?', *Psychological Reports*, **41** (1977), 1179–82

Lorenz, K., *On Aggression* (London, Methuen, 1966)

Maccoby, E. E., Doering, C. H., Jacklin, C. N. and Kraemer, H., 'Concentration of sex hormones in umbilical-cord blood: their relations to sex and birth order of infants', *Child Development*, **50** (1979), 632–42

Maccoby, E. E. and Jacklin, C. N., *The Psychology of Sex Differences* (London, Oxford University Press, 1975), chapter 7

Maccoby, E. E. and Jacklin, C. N., 'Sex differences in aggression: a rejoinder and a reprise', *Child Development*, **51** (1980), 964–80

Marsh, P., *Aggro: The Illusion of Violence* (London, Dent, 1978)

Martocchio, J. J. and O'Leary, A. M., 'Sex differences in occupational stress: a meta-analytic review', *Journal of Applied Psychology*, **74** (1989), 495–501

Morris, D., *The Naked Ape* (London, Cape, 1967)

Olweus, D., Mattson, A., Schalling, D. and Löw, H., 'Testosterone, aggression, physical, and personality dimensions in normal adolescent males', *Psychosomatic Medicine*, **42** (1980) 253–69

Plomin, R., Foch, T. and Rowe, D., 'Bobo clown aggression in childhood: environment, not genes', *Journal of Research in Personality*, **15** (1981), 331–42

Rada, R. T., Laws, D. R. and Kellner, R., 'Plasma testosterone levels in the rapist', *Psychosomatic Medicine*, **38** (1976), 257–68

Saville, H., Wilkinson, P., O'Donnell, C. and Colley, I., 'Sex role inequality and spouse abuse', *Australian and New Zealand Journal of Sociology*, **17** (1981), 83–8

Scaramella, T. J. and Brown, W. A., 'Serum testosterone and aggression in hockey players', *Psychosomatic Medicine*, **40** (1978), 262–5

Spender, D., *Invisible Women: The Schooling Scandal* (London, Writers and Readers, 1982)

Steffensmeier, D. J. and Cobb, M. J., 'Sex differences in urban arrest patterns, 1934–1979', *Social Problems*, **29** (1981), 37–50

Susman, E. J., Inoff-Germain, G. *et al.*, 'Hormones, emotional dispositions and aggressive attributes in young adolescents', *Child Development*, **58** (1987), 1114–34

Tieger, T., 'On the biological basis of sex differences in aggression', *Child Development*, **51** (1980), 943–63

Walden, T. A., Nelson, P. A. and Smith, D. E., 'Crowding, privacy and coping', *Environment and Behaviour*, **13** (1981), 205–24

Index

Freud, S. 29, 167

games 101; aggression and 188–9, 199, 200; luck and skill 130–1
gender 1, 6, 16; children's awareness of 25–33; parents and 20–4, 28; roles and culture 20–30; *see also* femininity; masculinity; stereotypes
genes 11, 56, 99, 146–7; genetic instructions 12, 14
genital tubercle 14, 174
genitals 1, 14, 29, 167; ambiguity 15, 16
geometry, *see* mathematical ability; visual-spatial ability
gibbons 49
goal-setting 133
gonads 14
graffiti 178
group violence 194
growth 34–40

haemophilia 57
head size 39, 86
health 52–8
heart 41, 42, 48
heart attacks 53, 58
heart disease 53, 54, 57
height 34, 35, 37; advantages of 50–1; IQ and 38; mate selection and 49–50
helplessness 69, 110, 131
hips 39, 40
homosexuality 28, 88–9, 178
hormonal diseases 53
hormone replacement therapy 68, 79
hormones: emotions and changes in 63, 67; environmental influence on 77; influence on brain mechanisms 87–8; male 79–85; menstrual cycle 72–9; *see also* sex hormones
Horner, M. 122
housework 136, 138
hunter-gatherer societies 18
hypothalamus 88, 195–6
hyperthyroidism 56

idiopathic hypogonadotropic hypo-gonadism 104
illness, *see* disease and illness
immunoglobin deficiency 56
impotence 177
impulsiveness 93, 126
industrialized societies 20
infant mortality 141
infanticide 53, 147
infection 56, 57

inherited diseases 56
intellect: lateralization 102–6; scientific achievement 107–14; types of intelligence and gender difference 90–101
internal locus of control 130, 135
interpersonal skills 101, 137
interruptions 199
interviews 3
IQ 89–90, 95; early maturity and 38; male and female average scores 90–2
irritability 75

Jacklin, C., *see* Maccoby, E.
jobs: ambition and achievement 118–22; biological need to work 142; child-rearing 118–20; confidence and self-esteem 126–32; equal opportunity 115–18; factors holding women back 132–8; fathers' role in child-rearing 153–5; fear of success 122–6; female managers 133–6; low-paid 143; marriage and 138; men in prestige posts 6, 115, 116–17, 139; new professions 140; number of working women 140, 143, 209; part-time 140; pressure on women to abandon 161; scientific achievement and 112–13; women's earnings 143–4; women's mental health and 68, 83, 141; working wives and mothers 150–3
Johnson, Samuel (Dr) 92, 208
Johnson, V. E., *see* Masters, W. H.
journals 5

Kinsey, A. 4, 166, 168, 169, 173, 177, 178, 179

labia 14
laboratory experiments 2–3, 51, 82, 189–90, 191–4
lactic acid 46
language development 93
lateralization 102–6
leadership 201–6
learned helplessness 110
leg to body-length ratio 46
legs 39
libido 170, 171–2
life expectancy 53, 54, 55–6
locus of control 130, 131–2, 135
Loesser, F. 61, 79
Lorenz, K. 6, 17, 187
love, falling in 181
low-paid work 143